Designing Digital Space

AN ARCHITECT'S GUIDE
TO VIRTUAL REALITY

Daniela Bertol
with David Foell, R.A.

John Wiley & Sons, Inc.

New York ▪ Chichester ▪ Brisbane ▪ Toronto ▪ Singapore ▪ Weinheim

Library of Congress Cataloging in Publication Data:

Bertol, Daniela, 1958–
    Designing digital space : an architect's guide to Virtual reality
/ by Daniela Bertol with David Foell.
      p.   cm.
    Includes bibliographical references and index.
    ISBN 0-471-14662-5 (pbk. : alk. paper)
    1. Architectural design—Data processing. 2. Virtual reality.
I. Foell, David. II. Title.
NA2728.B47   1996
720'.285'6—dc20   96-26224
                                           CIP

Printed in the United States of America

10 9 8 7 6 5 4 3 2 1

Designing Digital Space

008

To Daphne

CONTENTS

Part II—The Present

tual reality affect design? Will the impact of the latest technology bring a redefinition of the architectural profession? Several proposals for virtual environments based on visionary architecture will be presented and illustrated. The discussion of these and similar issues provides the reader with food for thought, going beyond the excitation and infatuation which accompanies the latest technological marvels and instead focusing on the effects these have on the quality of our lives and the spaces in which we live.

WHAT DOES FILIPPO BRUNELLESCHI AND BAROQUE ARCHITECTURE HAVE TO DO WITH WIRED BODY SUITS AND LCD DISPLAYS?

This is the question you may have asked yourself in reading the table of contents of this book. At first sight it seems that there is no link between what is considered part of our past inheritance and what, for the majority of us, is a future vision. The architecture of the past, based on pen-and-ink representation, and the computer-generated world of the present, made of brilliant colored pixels, are centuries apart and seem to represent two completely different universes, both valuable in their own times, but with nothing in common. This is not true; the history of architectural representation is a gradual step-by-step development in thinking and technology starting with perspective and arriving most recently at virtual reality (VR).

Virtual reality is the ultimate representation, with the aim of simulating reality in such a way that our perceptions of the *virtual* environment replace the perception of our *real* environment. The development of perspective in the fifteenth century was indeed the first milestone in the path which leads to the simulation of three-dimensional forms through two-dimensional media. Paper, which up to only a few decades ago was the only two-dimensional medium offered to architects and designers for the representation of a three-dimensional world, has been replaced by the computer screen where the computer-generated visualization is displayed. In the last decade, computer-generated visualizations are increasingly presented through virtual reality interfaces. One of the objectives of this book is to retrace this historical path in the development of visualization means, finding continuity between processes which are apparently of such a different nature.

DEMATERIALIZATION OF ARCHITECTURE IN THE INFORMATION AGE

The history of representation leading to a discussion of virtual reality cannot be separated from the more general theme of the transformation of architecture in the information age. At the end of the millennium, architecture faces diverse challenges. The complexity of information space, which often takes over physical space in our daily lives, broadens the task of architecture—once well-defined in the shaping of the physical environment. Social functions once performed in physically defined spaces, such as banks, libraries, museums, and trading floors, have moved to the electronic space defined by networked computers. With the advent of cyberspace, many meeting places do not need spaces built of physical materials any longer. The coincidence of physical space with existential space, once the realm of architecture, must be translated into cyberspace, whose informational content is delivered not as a permanent solid artifact but in the form of images and dynamic representations.

The other phenomenon contributing to the transformation of traditional architecture is the reduction of architectural and urban space to a series of images. City streets, buildings, and homes are something more than a collection of sidewalks, walls, floors, and roofs—that is, the physical three-dimensional elements they are made of. The visual communications giving life to our cities and homes happen through light and images. Lights, billboards, LCD, Liquid Crystal Displays and neon signs in the urban space and TV and computer screens in domestic architecture, are legible expressions of the fragmentation of the three-dimensional solidity of our living environment. *Mediascape,* a word used in recent literature, aptly expresses this transformation of the urban environment. Images take over physical space in the perception of our urban and domestic environment, creating a dichotomy between the solidity of built architecture and the fluidity of information space. This challenges the quality of permanence which historically bestows one of the main attributes of architecture.

The control that telecommunications and digitally delivered information is taking over our social life as well as the overwhelming presence of images in the built environment are two main causes responsible for the dematerialization of traditional architecture. Virtual reality, as the ultimate dynamic generation of spatial representations, can be purposefully integrated in the

VIRTUAL REALITY AS THE ULTIMATE REPRESENTATION (AND BEYOND)

CAD (computer-aided design) has already revolutionized architectural representations and, in some instances, design too. Virtual reality (VR) seems to be the next logical step in the path laid by CAD, but it will have a more extensive impact, since it not only transforms the way architects design and visualize, but can also be integrated into the final product of architecture itself: buildings.

Virtual reality is the ultimate computer-generated representation in which people are not only passive viewers, but also players in real-time interaction; this interaction is the generator of the representations of the virtual world. Mathematical models, planets and stars, human body organs, virtual cities resurrected from archeological sites, and financial data become three-dimensional worlds that can be accessed, inhabited, walked through, and manipulated. While the content of the virtual world could also be provided in different computer simulations and visualizations—animations, graphics charts, and rendered images—only in virtual reality applications can interaction between the perceiving subject and the object of perception be possible, often following natural actions such as moving the head and hands or walking. It is because of this "natural" interaction between the computer-generated world and the user that VR is defined as the ultimate interface between man and machine. Architectural design in a VR environment provides for the expression of ideas and the exploration of alternatives in a way which is both comprehensive and revolutionary.

But the impact of VR in architecture goes further. Virtual-world representations can involve not only our sense of sight, but also the other senses; images, sounds, and tactile sensations surround us in a rich virtual environment which is interposed between ourselves and our "real" physical environment. In this relation, between the virtual and the built environment, VR becomes of great interest to architects. If the traditional task of architecture is that of shaping physical environments, the integration of virtual worlds within the actual built space becomes a design issue.

In this context, we can see the motivation behind a book dealing with virtual reality in architecture, not only from a technological standpoint but also from a more critical approach discussing virtual reality systems as related to the design of built architecture. The grasp of cyberspace, as well as the shaping of dynamic "virtual" environments, is the next (or present?) task awaiting architects. At this time in history, only in the integration of virtual space with actual space can architecture go beyond the role of physical container of information-based worlds, creating better places for human interaction.

The contents and organization of this book revolve around space and time. While space is the entity permeating the essence of architecture and its representations, time provides the structure which organizes the different contents. The book is arranged according to past (Part I), present (Parts II and III), and future (Part IV)—which reflect the continuity of the history of representation. The reader who is interested only in the discussion of virtual reality environments can skip Part I.

Part II offers a discussion of current virtual reality technologies of interest to architects. Devices such as Head-mounted Display, BOOM, CAVE, retinal display, and a variety of technical terms are simply explained and illustrated. The current uses of virtual reality architectural applications such as simulations, interactive walk-throughs, or networked environments are discussed in great detail. A brief discussion of virtual reality applications in other fields such as medicine, physics, astronomy, and art is also presented, pointing at possible developments for interdisciplinary research involving architecture. In an effort to offer a thorough depiction of the present architectural applications in virtual reality, Part III includes a collection of essays by researchers from all over the world who are pioneers in this emerging field. Each essay is also extensively illustrated, showing graphs and sequential imagery necessary for a more complete understanding of the operations involved.

The last two chapters, which comprise Part IV, revolve around a series of questions asked and tentatively answered: What is the future of architecture in a digital world? How will architectural language be affected? How does vir-

metamorphosis of permanent solid architecture into dynamic representations. This process is not new but has historical foundation in the tradition of trompe l'oeil representation and illusionary spaces explored in Baroque architecture. Several chapters will be devoted to the history of representation and its integration with the built environment, investigating the transformation of architecture into images, from its origins in Renaissance and Baroque architecture to the projected images of artificial worlds.

PART

I

The Past

The Quest for Three-dimensionality

We are about to start our journey, departing in 1435, from the first written discussion of perspective and arriving in 1996, at state-of-the-art VR. The journey will trace the origins of the expression of a three-dimensional world in two-dimensional images, from art to architecture. You will be surprised to discover how many similarities can be found in this continuous quest for three-dimensionality, between what was sought and achieved six centuries ago and what is pursued in contemporary times. Artists, architects, scientists, and mathematicians several centuries apart tried to achieve the same results using completely different technologies.

The first theoreticians and practitioners of perspective reduced our visual perceptions to geometric entities such as points and lines, making them coincident with images of real scenes. The development of perspective brought about an identity relation between vision, nature, and geometry. All the first theories and demonstrations on perspective expressed the idea that the man-made world of buildings and monuments as well as people, animals, and landscapes could be simplified, decomposed, and described through geometric entities such as lines and points. Or, to express it more concisely, perspective representations established a mapping between the physical world and the geometric universe. In the seventeenth century there was another major leap in the history of mathematics and knowledge: The French philosopher and mathematician René Descartes, also known as Cartesius, surmised that a point, line, or surface can be coincident to numbers. The reduction of images to points, then of points to numbers—that is, mapping—will lead us in the computer age to virtual reality. The history of representations can be summarized in the history of mapping, realized with different processes and media: from graphite, ink, and color pigments to the phosphorus or liquid crystals of the computer screen.

THE DEVELOPMENT OF PERSPECTIVE

The purpose of perspective is to represent in a two-dimensional medium a three-dimensional scene as it would appear to our eyes. For simplicity's sake the word perspective is used to denote linear perspective. This is based on the distance cue of retinal size according to which objects of equivalent size are perceived as of different size according to their distance from the observer (Shepard 1990); the further the object, the smaller its perceived size. The other type of perspective, defined as **aerial,** reflects the perceptual phenomenon that makes distant objects appear of a lighter color, tending to blue, similar to the color of the sky; this phenomenon is due to the short wavelength of sunlight which is reflected back to the eye, coming not from the object itself but from the atmosphere.

The three-dimensional world is perceived as a projection on the two-dimensional surface of our retina. The stereoscopic effect, which causes the perception of **depth,** is given by our binocular vision. Several common phenomena (Figure 1.1) occur in our most basic visual perceptions: The size of an object decreases with the distance from the observer, rectangles are perceived as trapezoid, angles change amplitude, parallel lines meet in a point called the **vanishing point,** and parallel planes meet in a line—the **horizon**—which we know from our everyday experience as the place where the sky meets the earth. Only the relations of objects parallel to the **picture plane**—the plane in which the two-dimensional representation is formed—are conserved. Any visual representation takes form in a two-dimensional image. There is immediate mapping between a two-dimensional image and the three-dimensional form the image is representing. Similar to what happens in our visual perception, the **perspective** rendering of a three-dimensional object is a projection of the object from a viewpoint (coincident with our eye) on the plane of the representation. The medium of the plane can be paper, canvas, or the computer screen.

The construction of a perspective rendering requires systematic graphic constructions which can be codified in axioms and rules. The three parties involved are vision, the physical world, and its representation; the development of perspective, as theory and practice, revolves around the relations

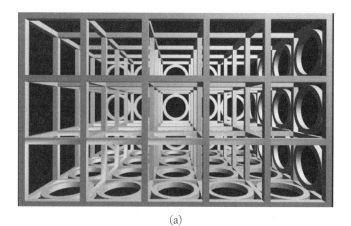

(a)

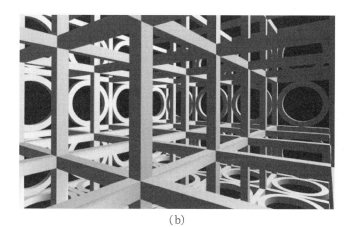

(b)

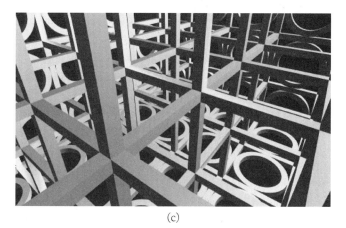

(c)

Figure 1.1 (a) *One-point perspective,* (b) *two-point perspective, and* (c) *three-point perspective. Copyright © Daniela Bertol*

among these parties. The physical three-dimensional world can be described through **Euclidean** geometry, the high school geometry that responds to our intuition and is concerned with the measurable properties of objects. Surprisingly enough, the geometry which explains perspective rules is not Euclidean. However, this is not so surprising if we rely on common observations; parallel lines do not converge in the physical world, but they do in our perception of it. Railroad tracks, even if parallel in reality, are seen as converging. The geometry which better explains perspective principles as the geometrical properties of vision is **projective** geometry. Late in the eighteenth century, **descriptive** geometry was formulated as a systematic demonstration of perspective providing an elaborated system of rules to construct exact representations and unambiguous relations between what is seen and what is represented.

The development of perspective theories covers several centuries (Figure 1.2). From the first written exposition, found in Leon Battista Alberti's *Della Pittura,* the number of treatises on perspective has grown at an exponential rate. The basic rules of geometric construction are still used in computer visualization of three-dimensional scenes and, therefore, in VR representations. The graphic constructions used in the traditional hand perspective construction may be obsolete in a computer elaboration, but the matrix principle of transformation of three-dimensional coordinates into two-dimensional perspective projection still provides the foundations for any realistic computer visualization of three-dimensional objects.

Leon Battista Alberti's First Treatise on Perspective

In 1435 the first written exposition of rules for perspective drawing construction made its appearance in Leon Battista Alberti's treatise *Della Pittura* (On Painting). It was not the first time that perspective constructions were used: Earlier painting experiments such as Giotto's famous triptychs of the early fourteenth century already showed an attempt to simulate the three-dimensionality of architectural environments on two-dimensional media such as the canvas or the wall. But it was in Alberti's treatise that perspective for the first time finds a systematic and clear discussion, offering demonstrations and empirical examples. Perspective laws were discussed in a systematic order, deriving authority and credibility from geometric principles. Beyond its widespread use in art, perspective had also become a science, where the geometric rules were related to optics, borrowing principles from Euclid's theory of vision. This synergy between scientific theories and art experiments is another perfect example of the general spirit of

Figure 1.2 *Vredeman de Vries: perspective renderings.*

the Renaissance, where any type of knowledge was a product of cross-disciplinary efforts.

In Alberti's treatise terms such as "pyramid of sight," "centric point," and "plane of the picture" denote fundamental concepts for graphic constructions. The purpose of perspective in Alberti's definition was "to treat the two-dimensional picture plane (the wall, or panel, or canvas) as if it were a window in which a three-dimensional scene appears" (Gadol). Each three-dimensional object was considered as bounded by surfaces, each of them broken up or simplified to planar polygons, reproducible according to the perspective projections. Each surface can be measured by **visual rays** connecting the eye with each point defining the perimeter of the surface. The "pyramid of sight" has a base imaginarily defined by the intersection of the visual rays with the picture plane. The eye is the apex of the pyramid. All of these graphics and visual aids were used and illustrated also in later treatises and iconography, such as in those by Albrecht Dürer and Jacopo Barrozi da Vignola.

Another theme of Alberti's treatise, which was also seen in later iconography, is the graphic construction noted as "costruzione legittima" (legitimate construction), illustrated in Figure 1.3. This consists of a series of drawings of a checkerboard floor, showing the several steps leading to its perspective representation. In the description of the costruzione legittima the measurable relations between the eye, the picture plane, and object of representation must be precisely calculated as they provide the foundations for the construction of perspective renderings. The key axiom states that the size of a represented object decreases proportionally with the orthogonal distance of the actual object from the observer. Determining parameters for the representation are the height of the viewpoint, which provides the vanishing point, and its distance from the picture plane. The elements to be represented are scaled to fit into the picture. The concept of scaling, which is now part of our most basic knowledge of design, was quite new at that time, especially when applied in a context different from that of plan and elevation views. In a perspective construction where the size and shape of objects is transformed according to the projection center, the establishment of a scaling factor between the real object and its representation becomes particularly crucial for the final rendering.

The use of "perspectival instruments" was also discussed in *Della Pittura*. The Velo (veil) and quadratura (square frame) were used as construction aid for perspective representations. The veil, used by several Renaissance and later painters was a reticulated net framed by a rectangular or square structure, located between the objects to be represented and the viewer. The object is seen inscribed in the frame and intersected by the grid of the reticulated net. A grid proportional to that of the veil can be drawn in paper or in canvas, providing an aid to represent the object as seen intersecting the grid. A visual identity was therefore established between the perceived geometry of the object and the representation. A description and illustration of the process was also shown later in Leonardo Da Vinci's notebooks. Probably Albrecht Dürer's drawings are the best known and offer an accurate visual illustration of the process (Figure 1.4).

With the formalization of perspective laws, a relationship was established between geometry and visual perception. This led to the search for an identity between representation and vision, which, as we will learn from Brunelleschi's demonstrations, began to be investigated by Alberti's contemporaries. The investigations on vision were not new; in the third century B.C. Euclid wrote *Optics,* based on intuitive observations on visual perception. The topic was also reapproached in the Middle Ages, complemented by a discussion of instruments for astronomy and surveying. Many of the per-

Figure 1.3 *Perspective as a graphic construction: An interpretation of Leon Battista Alberti's "costruzione legittima." Copyright © Daniela Bertol.*

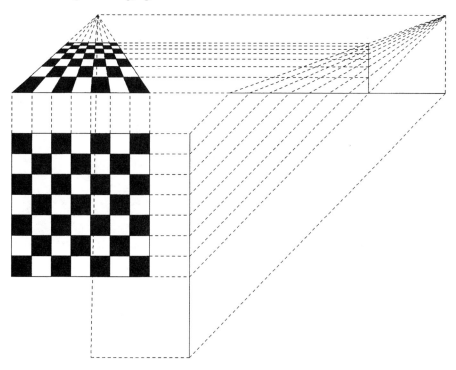

Figure 1.4   Albrecht Dürer's interpretations of the veil and grid.

spective laws were derived from these previous theories and demonstrations on optics. What was relevant and new in the development of perspective was the focus in the identity relation laid between vision and representation; from this stated identity all the axioms and graphic constructions were derived.

Use of Perspective in Paintings and Architectural Representations

Starting from its very first development in the fifteenth century, perspective construction was immediately applied to the iconography of various disciplines, from art to architecture, from geometry to science. The quest was for the realism of representations. Due to the three-dimensionality of the world of our experiences, artists and architects have for centuries used perspective representations to create the illusion of three-dimensionality.

Art, and painting in particular, was probably the first human activity to seek and be greatly influenced by the development of perspective. Until the last two centuries, the imitation of nature had been present in the majority of artistic expressions, from painting to sculpture. Prior to the development of perspective, the most realistic representations were those of subjects such as human figures and animals that could be well expressed using the width and height of the canvas, without a considerable involvement of depth in the pictorial compositions. With no realistic way to express depth, problems arose in the attempt to represent landscapes or architectural scenes. The contradiction between the three-dimensionality of the physical world and the two-dimensionality of the media of representation, such as paper and canvas, provokes the need for finding a way to capture the missing third dimension. Several painters tried to express three-dimensional scenes by using axonometric projections. Often spatial confusion was generated in the representation; in spite of the great attention to detail, the paintings were lacking in realism because of the missing or erroneous representation of depth.

In the early fourteenth century—one century ahead of the discovery of perspective—Giotto's paintings of the Arena Chapel in Padua and the frescos in Assisi are credited as two of the first credible attempts to reproduce a three-dimensional space in painting. The representation of an architectural background suggests the presence of depth. Adding to the perceived three-dimensionality of the paintings is the representation of the people in the scenes: The relation and tension between the human bodies as much as the expressiveness of the look in their faces create an emotional tension which compliments the spatial rendition.

Perspective greatly added to the realism of art and became widely used in paintings from the fifteenth century onward. Among Alberti's contemporaries, Piero della Francesca, Masaccio, Francesco di Giorgio Martini, Paolo Uccello and Donatello offered some of the most outstanding examples of how the science of perspective became art.

The geometric construction of perspective in painting was often combined with the use of color to create realistic representations of three-dimensionality, since light was the necessary complement for the achievement of the illusion of the missing dimension. The masterly use of color and chiaroscuro together with aerial perspective succeeded in defining volumes, masses, and voids as well as the curvature of surfaces. In the contemporary computer age, a geometric construction may be perfectly expressed in a line drawing, yet the addition of color is essential to the creation of a realistic environment.

Perspective had no less an influence on architecture than on art. Until the development of perspective, the main representations used in architecture, known since the time of Vitruvius, were plan and elevation. These views present a diagrammatic representation of a three-dimensional scene, without offering any visual simulation of how the represented scene appears to the eye. Perspective representations offer a means to explore architectural space providing its most complete visual simulation, allowing the appearance of a designed work of architecture before its actual construction. Perspective is the means by which architecture becomes integrated with art, not only as a backdrop, but often as the subject of the representation. In this school of painting the architecture occupies the foreground of the composition in a dynamic interplay with the portrayed human figures: The painting often becomes a design exploration, expressive of the architectural concepts of the era.

The influence of perspective in architecture was not limited only to the representation of urban and interior spaces, but became incorporated in the building design itself. Perspective acts as a visual frame as well as conceptual structure: The inside of architectural spaces become framed by the ceiling, walls, and floors. The spatial organization in Renaissance architecture clearly reflects the centric one-point perspective; the spatial hierarchy and the linear or centric arrangement of architectural elements strengthen the central view determining the visual convergences of planes in the horizon.

Beyond the Wall

In the late fifteenth century a new trend developed from the use of perspective in paintings and frescos, generated by the continuous quest for realism and illusion of depth. In this new form of representation, the wall where the perspective scene is painted became a window, apparently breaking the wall surface. A relation is created between the *actual* space of the wall and the *virtual* space of the representation. The actuality of the physical wall is transformed into the virtuality of the painting. An integration between real architecture and virtual architecture, between physical and represented world, is achieved in the most harmonious visual composition. Each element of the painted image is represented in such a way as to serve as complement to the actual space of the wall. These paintings can hold a lesson for the virtual reality environments of today in the way they try to relate virtual elements to the physical built environment.

Raphael's School of Athens (Figure 1.5), which can be seen at the Vatican Museum in Rome, represents one of the best examples of the window-

Figure 1.5   *Raphael: La Scuola di Atene, Rome. Copyright © Vatican Museum.*

painting artwork. A painted archway illusionarily introduces the viewer to the arched spaces where the Greek philosophers stand facing the viewer. In spite of the fact that the vanishing point and horizon line in the perspective rendering are much higher than the viewer's eye, a very powerful and realistic effect is achieved where the viewer feels completely transported into the assembly of philosophers in the represented space. Chapter II will present many other examples of window-painting which are part of the trompe l'oeil tradition.

BRUNELLESCHI'S DEMONSTRATIONS

While Leon Battista Alberti can be credited as the very first theoretician of perspective, his contemporary architect Filippo Brunelleschi was the first who, with scientific methodology, tried to give an experimental proof by creating two painted panels to demonstrate the validity of perspective in representing architectural scenes.

The most famous of the two panels is the one representing the Baptistery, located next to the Cathedral of Florence (Figure 1.6). The pure geometry expressed by the simple architecture of the Baptistery as well the urban location and juxtaposition with the Cathedral, probably inspired Brunelleschi to choose it as the subject of the experiment. According to his biographer's writings, he painted the Baptistery as seen from the middle door of the church of Santa Maria del Fiore, at a position about three braccia (arm lengths) inside the door. The black-and-white marble pattern of the Baptistery was carefully reproduced; the same attention was paid in painting the surrounding buildings. Instead of painting the sky in the background he used burnished silver, so that the surrounding real sky and moving clouds could be reflected in real-time. A hole was made in the panel, coincident with the vanishing point. According to Brunelleschi's instructions, the viewer was supposed to hold the panel very close to one eye (with the painted side facing away) and look through the hole. In the other hand the viewer held a mirror in a position directly opposite the painted panel. The distance between the viewer and the mirror was proportional to the distance between the perspective viewpoint and the Baptistery. The aim of this experiment was the creation of an illusion: the viewer was not looking at a painted representation of the Baptistery, but at the building itself.

A first reaction to the description of this demonstration is that its success was due not only to the accuracy of the rendering and use of colors, but also to the particular conditions of the experiment. The observer had to stand still in his position and monocular observation—the hole in the painting—was required. The mirrored background, reflecting sky and moving clouds, was another remarkable aid in the achievement of realism.

The two demonstrations represent a sort of *Renaissance virtual reality*. As in contemporary virtual reality environments, the aim was to create the illusion of coincidence between a representation and the subject of the representation. The presence of real elements, such as the moving clouds, can find parallel in the use in VR of photographic imagery for backgrounds and texture maps. Brunelleschi's quest for realism and the use of gadgets to improve the sense of illusion reflects the trend of VR to integrate the various technologies of the computer-generated world to achieve the most realistic sense of "immersion" in the artificial world.

Perceptual Identity between Space and Its Representation

The Brunelleschi apparatus was a perfect demonstration of the identity between what is seen and what is represented. The geometric rules used to paint the two architectural scenes were the most accurate, at least according to principles established in his time. The demonstrations proved the effectiveness of two-dimensional representations in creating an illusion of three-

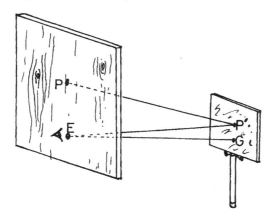

Figure 1.6 *Brunelleschi's demonstration on perspective (from* The Science of Art, *Yale University Press). Copyright © Martin Kemp.*

dimensional space. These experiments had a great impact in the historical and ideological context of the fifteenth century, where the discovery and development of perspective theories established an identity relation between perspective laws, geometric axioms, and visual perception. Perspective was not only a graphics technique, but also stirred many philosophical discussions which are representative of Renaissance thought.

One of the major achievements of perspective was its capacity to make an intellectual process tangible. Perspective renderings on one side provided a realistic visual reproduction of reality and on the other side were a means of expression of the ideal world. The bridge between representation and reality was connected to the bridge between reality and ideas, becoming one of the most powerful means of design. Creative processes in science, as well as art and architecture, could finally find a realistic representation and be visualized on tangible media such as paper and canvas: Ideas could be pictorially communicated in an accurate and understandable means.

Another issue brought by perspective—better understood when considered in the light of contemporary theories—was the validity of geometric interpretations of nature. The physical world was—and still is, at the scale of everyday human reality—interpreted through Euclidean geometry. In the Euclidean world parallel lines do not meet; that is what is validated in our experience. We know that railroad tracks keep their distance, but we still perceive them as converging. What was the most basic characteristic of vision seemed to contradict the most simple geometric explanation of the world. Measuring and seeing represent different approaches to empirical knowledge; while seeing is regulated by laws similar to those underlying perspective, the act of measuring respects Euclidean geometry laws, at least at the perceptual level of everyday life. The perspective axioms laid out the foundations for projective geometry which were fully developed at the end of the eighteenth century by the French mathematician J. V. Poncelet. The introduction of perspective and its geometric value demonstrated that Euclidean geometry, considered one of the most perfect creations of human kind, was not sufficient for the complete understanding of reality.

One of the main objectives in perspective construction, the imitation of reality, still holds true today. At the time of the discovery of perspective, artists, architects, and scientists were interested in investigating and representing scenes and objects from the naked eye, in the form of landscapes, urban scenes, geometric shapes, or anatomic views. The interpretation and representation of reality is still the main focus of investigation in the contemporary world, even if "real" goes beyond our ordinary perceptions, extending to the microscopic world of atomic particles or to the macroscopic scale of stars and galaxies. In this different type of realism, virtual reality becomes a means of visualizing and interacting with the microscopic or macroscopic world.

REFERENCES

Gadol, Joan. 1969. *Leon Battista Alberti*. Chicago: The University of Chicago Press.

Shepard, Roger. 1990. *Mind Sights*. New York: W. H. Freeman and Company.

Photo by Andrea Jemolo.

From Images of Architecture to Architecture of Images

The representation of architectural spaces reached full bloom in the Renaissance. In paintings by Masaccio, Piero della Francesca, Francesco di Giorgio, and Leonardo da Vinci, perspective was the necessary instrument to translate ideated spaces and architectural compositions into perceivable artifacts. The next step was in transforming the two-dimensional representation itself—making it part of the built architecture. From the late fifteenth century the use of perspective shifted from the representation of architecture to the creation of architectural spaces defined by images. The coming centuries saw the development of perspective in paintings and frescos which transformed architectural space, pretending to extend the walls to the outside landscape: The images of architecture created an architecture of images.

PERCEPTION AND ARCHITECTURE

The relativism of the physical world is not by any means a new interpretation. The knowledge we have of three-dimensional space is filtered by our perceptions of it. This applies to both the natural and man-made world. The perception we have of a landscape, let's say a mountain, is completely different depending on if we fly over it, drive around it, or climb on it. Similar observations can be made about the man-made world and architecture in particular: A series of different perceptions arise when we drive and walk around a building or if we are inside.

The visual perception of architecture, as with any other visual perception, is a two-dimensional image mapped on the surface on our retina. The medium of architecture is three-dimensional space; the coincidence between architecture and space is often emphasized, as described by Bruno Zevi who writes about architecture (Zevi 1957) as the "art of space." Creations of architecture are three-dimensional solid artifacts generated by the molding of space. Nevertheless, the final perception is a sequence of two-dimensional images which generate the identity of a certain architectural space. In the act of seeing we not only create an objective image of the external world, but also bring our subjective background, coming as cultural and psychological impressions.

This discrepancy between objective dimensionality and perceptual dimensionality has been the source of inspiration for works of architecture which integrate two-dimensional painted representations with three-dimensional spaces. These two-dimensional representations in our perception are as important as the three-dimensional elements which make solid architecture. This chapter will focus on the representations which simulate or are at least suggest three-dimensionality; these two-dimensional components can be deceptively perceived as derived from three-dimensional elements, modifying greatly our spatial perceptions. Once again we will begin by looking back at the past: What was done in the sixteenth and seventeenth centuries in Renaissance and Baroque architecture may still hold lessons and bring insights in the design of contemporary virtual environments.

TROMPE L'OEIL

The expression trompe l'oeil comes from the French language and literally means "fool the eye." It denotes the painted representation of a three-dimensional scene, rendered in such a way that, from a particular viewpoint the monocular perception of it would be the same as that of the three-dimensional objects represented in the trompe l'oeil. The actual three-dimensional space becomes extended in the plane of the pictorial space of the representation. Trompe l'oeil has often been used to create the illusion of impossible three-dimensional constructions.

Early examples of trompe l'oeil are found in the late fifteenth century, when Donato Bramante designed the choir of San Satiro in Milan. The reason for this illusionary space was completely aesthetic: There was no room for a chancel; therefore, one was simulated by a trompe l'oeil combined with bas-relief. This early example revealed that Bramante, like other artists of this period, had not yet fully developed an effective painting technique for this type of illusionary scene: The effect of this trompe l'oeil is quite obvious and exaggerated, even if seen from the right observation point.

Palazzo Farnese in Caprarola

Palazzo Farnese was built in the second half of the sixteenth century in Caprarola, Italy, from an initial design by Antonio da Sangallo, and later developed by Jacopo Barozzi da Vignola. This palazzo, which was designed with a unique pentagonal floor plan, featured mural paintings which are perfectly integrated with the architecture of the palace, often creating spatial effects that expand the room or give the illusion of curvature. The majority of paintings were executed by Vignola and Taddeo Zuccari.

The fresco in the room Sala di Giove (Figure 2.1a), attributed to Vignola, presents a different approach in trompe l'oeil representations. The painting depicts an expansion of the architecture of the room into a vaulted space ending with a baluster, facing a garden with views of the surrounding landscape. This type of scene, which expands the interior space into the outdoor garden, is quite common in pictorial representations. What is quite surprising is that the vanishing point of the perspective is outside of the painting, probably coincident with the direction of the observer's eye upon entering the room. This creates an innovative perspective representation very different from most contemporary examples which are based mainly on a view point central to the scene. The illusion is quite striking from the observation point according to which the perspective was created, but decreases dramatically as the observer moves away.

Another unique representation is found in the Anticamera del Concilio (Figure 2.1b). The four corners of the room are painted with perspective representations of columns. Each column is painted with its longitudinal axis coincident with the corner of the room, which appears to be open and expanding beyond the painted column. The focus on the corner creates a different spatial conception: Usually the perceptual focal point is coincident with the center of a wall. This off-center spatial concept, already found in the Sala di Giove, seems to imply an exploratory search for new perceptions, quite different from the Renaissance central point visual world. The elimination of the corners also alludes to the opening of the room to other spaces, going beyond the concept of the room as box which was typical of previous Renaissance iconography.

The other outstanding trompe l'oeil of this palace is the painted, vaulted ceiling of the Camera dell'Aurora (Figure 2.1c). This time the representation

Figure 2.1a *Palazzo Farnese: Sala di Giove. Copyright © 1975 by Bonechi, Edizioni "Il Turismo."*

Figure 2.1b *Palazzo Farnese: Anticamera del Concilio. Copyright © 1975 by Bonechi, Edizioni "Il Turismo."*

Figure 2.1c *Palazzo Farnese: Camera dell'Aurora. Copyright © 1975 by Bonechi, Edizioni "Il Turismo."*

follows a traditional approach. The focal point is that of an observer standing in the middle of the room looking up straight at the center of the ceiling. Painted columns and niches expand the height of the ceiling. The open view this time is not a natural landscape, but the allegory of the sky with flying angels, horses, and mythological characters. The communion of realistic and symbolic imagery, given by the perceptual illusion combined with a realistically painted image, goes beyond the concept of trompe l'oeil as a tool of architectural expansion and could become the subject of exploration with today's virtual reality technology.

Sant'Ignazio in Rome

The church of Sant'Ignazio in Rome was built in the first half of the seventeenth century, from the design of P. Orazio Grassi. The "dome" and the vaulted ceiling present outstanding examples of trompe l'oeil, both painted by Andrea Pozzo. The dome (Figure 2.2a) was painted in 1685 on a flat canvas with a diameter of 17 meters, stretched across the aperture of a circular drum. The motivation for commissioning a painted representation of a dome instead of building the real structure was financial; since there was not enough money left for building a three-dimensional structure, a trompe l'oeil representation was considered the right solution for achieving the same aesthetic results at a little cost. The complete illusion of three-dimensionality is best perceived from a specific position at the center of the aisle through which parishioners pass upon entry to the nave.

The painted ceiling (Figure 2.2b), as at the Aurora room in Palazzo Farnese, simulates the opening of the church to the sky, extending the existing walls to painted perspectives of arches. Angels and other symbolic figures populate the painted sky. Once again a fusion between realistic representation and allegory is presented, marrying the real world with the imaginary.

More Trompe l'oeil Examples from the Past

Beyond the examples discussed earlier, many other artists and architects have used trompe l'oeil representation to render illusionary spaces, frequently as stage design. Often the trompe l'oeil was used in residential and religious architecture with the intention of adding a theatrical dimension, to surprise and amaze the spectator. Sometimes painted characters at human scale became integrated into the representation, such as the trompe l'oeil of Villa Paveri Fontana (Figure 2.3) in Collecchio di Parma (Italy), realized by Francesco Galli Bibiena in the years between 1695 and 1703.

(a)   (b)

Figure 2.2   *Sant'Ignazio:* (a) *Trompe l'oeil dome.* (b) *Trompe l'oeil ceiling.*

In other examples the detail of the architecture represented in the trompe l'oeil is accurately designed as in the Sacrestia of the Cremona Cathedral (eighteenth century) by Antonio Bibiena (Figure 2.4) or the church of Santa Maria del Serraglio (Figure 2.5) in San Secondo (Parma, Italy) by Ferdinando Bibiena (eighteenth century). Another outstanding example of early trompe l'oeil (sixteenth century) in domestic architecture is offered by the Sala delle Prospettive (Figure 2.6) di Villa Farnesina in Rome, by Baldassare Peruzzi.

Contemporary Trompe l'oeil

Probably some of the most outstanding contemporary examples of trompe l'oeil are offered by the artist Richard Haas. His fresco paintings cover exte-

Figure 2.3 *Francesco Galli Bibiena: Villa Paveri Fontana, Collecchio di Parma. Photo by Andrea Jemolo.*

rior as well as interior walls; the theme of these trompe l'oeil representations is predominantly of an architectural nature. The exterior trompe l'oeil murals are site-specific: The painted wall is completely integrated with the urban environment of which it is a part. Often the mural defines a facade on a blank wall, architecturally mimicking an existing adjacent facade (Figure 2.7a). In other situations the mural breaks with the preexisting architecture, recalling a historical style within the twentieth century urban landscape. A good example of this approach is the Boston Architectural Center building (Figure 2.7b): In this case, the mural does not represent a facade but a section, portraying a coffered dome, balustrade, and ionic columns. From afar, the

Figure 2.4 *Antonio Galli Bibiena: Duomo, Cremona.*
Photo by Andrea Jemolo.

observer sees what appears to be a half-demolished neoclassical temple, its figural interior spaces illuminated by direct sunlight.

Haas' interior murals often portray an expansion or opening of the interior space toward an outside world. The mural can conceptually take two approaches; it either breaks open the wall, revealing an imaginary scene of nature, or expands the interior space (Figure 2.7c), creating an imaginary depth and continuation of the existing architecture.

Many other contemporary artists have been intrigued by trompe l'oeil, this author included. In my computer-generated trompe l'oeil images, visionary architectures are integrated with visual illusions. Mathematical space is a source of inspiration for my work based on walls as solid-void compositions.

Figure 2.5 *Ferdinando Galli Bibiena: Santa Maria del serraglio, San Secondo (Parma). Photo by Andrea Jemolo.*

Figure 2.6 *Baldassare Peruzzi: Sala delle Prospettive, Villa Farnesina, Rome. Photo by Andrea Jemolo.*

Figure 2.7a *Richard Haas: 112 Prince Street Facade, New York. Copyright © Richard Haas.*

Figure 2.7b *Richard Haas: West Facade, Boston Architectural Center. Copyright © Richard Haas.*

Figure 2.7c *Richard Haas: Atrium, Meredith Communication Headquarters, Des Moines. Copyright © Richard Haas.*

There are two different types of wall: the actual wall and the wall represented in the artwork with its realistic shading and accurate perspective construction. The two walls interrelate and become integrated with each other. The actual wall seems to lose its rigidity, becoming a bending and twisting fabric (Figure 2.8a). Unusual geometries and visual ambiguity are generated, where surfaces turn inside out and a background plane seems to belong to the foreground. Often the composition is designed to be integrated with actual corners of rooms (Figure 2.8b): A visionary grid opens the corners to the outside suggesting the expansion of the actual interior space to an imaginary space. My goal as artist is to reaffirm the validity of themes already investigated in Renaissance and Baroque concepts of space using a contemporary vocabulary.

FALSE PERSPECTIVE

Another type of illusionary architectural space is created by false perspective. As opposed to the previous examples, the illusion is not created by the juxta-

Figure 2.8 *Daniela Bertol,* (a) Knotted Surfaces. (b) Corners. *Copyright © Daniela Bertol.*

(a)   (b)

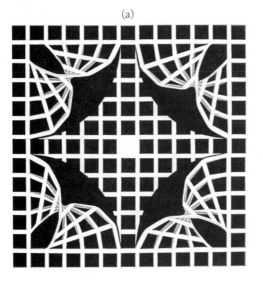
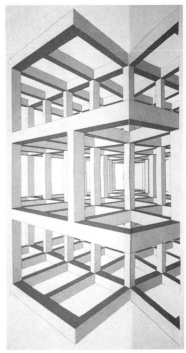

position and integration of two-dimensional images with the "solid" three-dimensional architecture. Instead, it is created by an arrangement of relatively flat three-dimensional elements designed in such a way that their visual perception is the same of that generated by a fully three-dimensional composition. As with trompe l'oeil, false perspective was often used to expand views where the construction of a designed three-dimensional space was impractical or uneconomical.

A false perspective is constructed in such a way that lines orthogonal to the picture plane which appear to be parallel are actually converging to a vanishing point; this is achieved for all the planes orthogonal to the picture plane. A false perspective works best in a box parallelepiped "room" type of spatial configuration where there are four walls perpendicular to the observer; what is essential is a linear composition with a view that is centered and directed parallel to the linearity.

The advantage of false perspective versus a trompe l'oeil representation is in the achievement of real, though distorted, three-dimensionality of the objects of perception. The architectural elements are not two-dimensional representations, but actual three-dimensional objects. The effect of aerial perspective complements the designed geometric perspective of the distorted environment, creating the illusion of a space in reality different from that which is perceived.

The effectiveness of trompe l'oeil and false perspective was limited, however, by the condition that the observer view the work from a particular viewpoint. In his book *Mind Sight* (1990), psychologist Roger Shepard states six conditions for viewing these works which can be summarized as follows. The observer's position and looking direction must be coincident with that from which the perspective was constructed, distant enough that the texture of the painted surface is not recognized and also that binocular vision does not interfere with the perception of the painted images. The observer must be stationary, so that motion parallax does not intervene. The representation must be located behind an opening, such as window, doorway, arch, so that its surface is uniformly illuminated and its edges are hidden from direct observation; shadows and highlight must be consistent with the ambient illumination of the architectural space of which it is part. The satisfaction of all these conditions, seldom accomplished, can be achieved only with the complete integration of two-dimensional rendering and built architectural space.

Palazzo Spada in Rome

The gallery of Palazzo Spada (seventeenth century) in Rome is one of the best known examples of false perspective. The gallery (Figure 2.9), designed by

Francesco Borromini, transformed a blind alley into a theatrical space, providing surprise and amusement in a composition which offers the spatial richness typical of Baroque architecture. The gallery measures 8.60 meters in depth, but is perceived as 37 meters deep—as seen from the designated viewpoint (Portoghesi 1968). The effect is achieved by raising the floor and decreasing the height and size of the columns and arches which define the progression of arcades. The plan view shows a trapezoidal space which is instead perceived as rectangular. The shape of the floor pattern—trapezoidal in reality but perceived as square—also aids in the distorted perception of depth. The parallelepiped shape of the volume which we perceive is, in reality, a truncated pyramid. This shape can be clearly read in the plan and section views of the gallery.

Figure 2.9 *Francesco Borromini; Palazzo Spada, galleria. Photo by Andrea Jemolo.*

The focal point of the composition is defined by a statue located just beyond the gallery at the end opposite from the observation point; the statue completes the sense of surprise generated by the false perspective, since it defines a fixed reference scale. I have memories of visiting the gallery as a child during school trips and being amazed (and I still am, as you can see from the photo in Figure 2.9!) when my schoolmates were transformed into giants when posed next to the statue—a statue which is initially perceived as being of superhuman scale, but discovered to be smaller than a child!

The Room of the Four Elements

The site-specific art installation *Room of the Four Elements* offers a contemporary interpretation of false perspective. This installation (Figure 2.10), created in collaboration with architect David Foell and presented at First Night '89 in Boston, dealt with the correspondence between physical objects and their visual representation. Light, the primary representational medium, was used to alter the viewer's perceptions in order to achieve several different spatial illusions. Video images and black (ultraviolet) light shaped the installation more than did the solid materials comprising the set. A small room was constructed in a false perspective; in its interior was a trompe l'oeil represen-

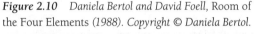

Figure 2.10   *Daniela Bertol and David Foell,* Room of the Four Elements *(1988). Copyright © Daniela Bertol.*

tation of a three-dimensional grid, generated from a perspective view from a three-dimensional computer model.

The whole environment was painted black and white: Black light makes the phosphorescent white glow and the black disappear, creating an environment where the ephemeral elements become stronger than their permanent properties in the viewer's perception. The trompe l'oeil grid framed four monitors showing videos of the four elements of nature—earth, water, fire, and air. The monitors' housings were hidden with only the images visible. The use of video images alluded to Brunelleschi's demonstrations on perspective—especially his use of mirrors to reflect the moving clouds in the sky. The *Room of the Four Elements* was but one of a series of experimental installations which I created in collaboration with other artists, in my continuing exploration of the theme of visual illusion.

BINOCULAR VISION

Illusions such as trompe l'oeil ignore the sense of depth achieved by binocular vision. As already seen in Brunelleschi's demonstrations, the determining factors in achieving a complete illusionary effect were that the observer be standing in a fixed position, coincident with the viewpoint from which the perspective was painted, and that the painting be observed from a peephole. The monocular observation was a requirement to compensate for the perceived lack of depth due to binocular vision which is typical of human vision.

The dimension of depth can be considered the most subjective of the dimensions of the three-dimensional space of our experiences, strictly connected to the process of human visual perception. The philosopher Maurice Merleau-Ponty writes about depth as "the most existential of all dimensions . . . not impressed upon the object itself, quite clearly belongs to the perspective and not to things."

Binocular vision supplies depth cues through eye convergence and stereopsis. When you view an object normally with both eyes, two different views are generated, one for each retina. The two images are seen from observation points which are separated by a distance of about 6.5 centimeters (average distance between the two eyes). The images converge in the final perception, generating the impression of depth. Depth can also be monocularly perceived thanks to motion parallax and perspective. Motion parallax happens if there is a movement between the observer and the object of observation. Perspective, as explored in the previous chapter, provides depth cues through the size of the perceived image, projected on the retina—a size which decreases proportional to the distance between the observer and the object.

Stereoscopic images—those which create the effect of stereopsis—are one of the main characteristics of virtual reality, differentiating it from other types of computer visualization in the achievement of greater perceptual realism. But virtual reality applications are but the latest in a series of devices which were developed to create and aid in the perception of stereoscopic images.

Stereoscope

A stereoscope (Figure 2.11a) is an instrument which reproduces the perception process provided by binocular vision combining two images—usually photographs (Figure 2.11b)—taken from two different positions, separated by a distance equal to that between the two eyes. Optical instruments, such as mirrors and lenses, are used to converge the two images in such a way that they can be seen as one, analogously to the convergence which happens in binocular vision. The use of lenses serves also to enlarge the images, to fill the field of vision. The stereoscope was developed in 1833 by Charles Wheatstone, before the invention of photography. Wheatstone initially used pairs of perspective renderings of the same scene, drawn from two different viewpoints at the usual eye distance. The device was refined a decade later by David Brewster; this led to a format that, a century later, was used for the popular mass-produced stereoscope known as the Viewmaster. The time of the development of the stereoscope was coincident with the popularization of photography; the combination of the two representation media became very popular in the Victorian era, allowing for the first time an achievement of great realism, previously explored only through pictorial representations.

The stereoscope is the first device developed from the investigation of the process of binocular vision, which manipulated visual representations in such a way as to recreate the binocular perception conditions. It can be considered the precursor of VR head-mounted display: A single apparatus containing the images as well as the devices to achieve the illusionary perception.

SENSORAMA

The Sensorama was quite an unusual device, developed in the 1950s by Morton Heilig. He envisioned an expansion of the experience offered by television and cinema—which are limited to our visual and auditory perception of recorded images and sound—to include touch and smell. Heilig thought that the future of cinema was in the increase of realism offered to the audiences; his focus was in the achievement of the most complete realism of the representation. To achieve it he carried out a thorough research on human perception, trying to isolate the factors which separate the perception of a

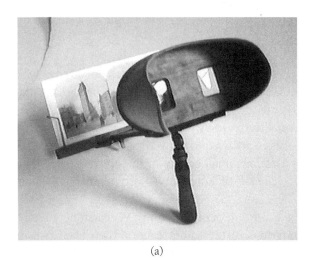

(a)

1925, A. C. CO.   33 Flat Iron Building, New York City.

(b)

Figure 2.11   (a) *Stereoscope (1988).* (b) *Stereo pair of images. (From the collection of Mr. and Ms. Whittemore.)*

representation from the perception of reality. A complete multimedia experience was envisioned, similar to Morel's invention. Unfortunately the film industry—the main commercial target of his research and prototype—was not very receptive to his vision and, because of financial limits, he could not realize a complete concrete example of the "experience theater."

His ideas were nevertheless concretized in the "Sensorama" which he built in 1960 as a prototype for individually experiencing what was supposed to be a collective experience. The Sensorama resembled a contemporary arcade machine. A motorcycle ride through Brooklyn provided content for the represented "experience." The sensorama was equipped with devices not just to view and hear, but also to produce wind and odors—such as those we would feel and smell riding a motorcycle through city streets. A vibrating seat, reproducing the vibrations felt in the motorcycle ride provided the most complete and realistic representations ever constructed. But the experience, though more complete than other media, was not yet at a level reached by contemporary virtual reality environments: What was missing was interaction. The participant was restricted to passively viewing, hearing, feeling, and smelling prepackaged representations, without the possibility of interacting with the represented model of reality to generate other representations.

TOWARD VIRTUAL REALITY

The works of art, devices, experiments, and demonstrations discussed in this chapter provide the background for virtual reality. All the examples tried to generate three-dimensionality and integrate two-dimensional rendering with built architectural space by using the available technology of the particular period. The reciprocal influence between them generates what is defined as an architecture of images. What truly differentiates virtual reality applications from their historical antecedents is the dynamism of the medium and the interaction between viewer and representation. In a comparison between contemporary VR environments and earlier representational methods we find that only the integration with built architecture is missing. The achievement of this goal is the task awaiting us as architects.

REFERENCES

Portoghesi, Paolo. 1968. *The Rome of Borromini*. New York: George Braziller.

Shepard, Roger. 1990. *Mind Sights*. New York: W. H. Freeman and Company.

Zevi, Bruno. 1957. *Architecture as Space*. New York: Horizon.

The Present

The Electronic Revolution in Architecture

The historic journey through visual representations—with particular emphasis on their integration with architecture—is at the arrival point: virtual reality. Before getting into the heart of our discussion, we should focus on another factor crucial to the development of virtual reality: The change in the architectural profession brought by the computer revolution. The last 10 years have witnessed a major transformation in the media used by architecture as discipline and as practice, from representations to design. This shift is most evident in the use of computer-related technology for drafting and visualization purposes. In addition, the design process, which up to a few years ago appeared to be untouched by the introduction of electronic media, now seems to be open to a redefinition of its methodology to integrate the computer. The introduction of the architectural profession to virtual reality can be seen under these auspices. The present chapter does not presume to explore in depth the quite complex and articulated influences of the computer on the architectural profession; it can be read as a brief summary to taste the environment from which virtual reality applications will evolve.

COMPUTER-AIDED DESIGN (CAD)

Ten years ago in a visit to an architectural office, we would have observed a series of drawing boards, pencils, paper, erasers, stencils, and other drawing tools. A lone computer was more than likely used for administrative and accounting purposes. The scene today is quite different; in the architect's workspace the drawing board is accompanied, if not completely replaced, by a computer. Drawing boards and drafting equipment are no longer the tools of choice for the architect. Computer monitors and keyboards, diskettes, plotters, and printers are the work tools for the majority of architectural offices.

All this transformation can be summarized in the word **CAD (Computer-aided Design)**. But does the replacement of the drawing board with the computer monitor or the holding of the mouse instead of the pencil really mean a different way of designing? What is the outcome of this change of media, from tangible materials into bits of information? How will this affect the actual design or the actual built architecture?

These are legitimate questions, considering that architecture is going through a major transformation: Not only is cyberspace invading the territory which was once the property of architecture, but also the use of the computer is revolutionizing how architects design and draw.

SIGNS AND PIXELS

Traditionally in architectural design, the communication of knowledge and information has been communicated through **signs** made of ink on paper. The signs are two-dimensional representations of a three-dimensional artifact such as a building. **Sketches** on paper—the paper napkin—are often the very first communication of an idea. The hand-drawn line, which is bold to emphasize and thin to maintain ambiguity, allows a perfect continuity between hand and imagination in the conception of forms and design alternatives.

The power of sketches to immediately record ideas must be translated into an automated environment such as CAD. At a computer workstation, the hand does not immediately impress signs on paper to signify ideas; the action is mediated by the keyboard or the mouse. When we substitute CAD for pencil and paper, we create a computer database, organized by the CAD application, which is, in computer terminology, a **database management system (DBMS)**. **Pull-down menus** often guide the user, displaying the universe of allowed actions to create electronic drawings. The results of our action appear in the screen as an array of color **pixels.** The color can automatically change, bringing different values to the pixel-signs, analogous to soft-bold reading in hand-drawn lines. The impact is completely different from that of the hand-drawn sketch which has a unique and definite output.

The manipulative operations of CAD appear abstract when compared with the immediacy of the sketch on paper. This difference often scares architects—especially those from older generations who see the automated drafting environment as a threat to the fresh creative act of drawing. Architects have always been infatuated with their own drawings, which are often a direct expression of their ideated world. The precision of the CAD drawing, where lines must be explicitly defined in an exact mathematical input, can often be seen as a denial of the spontaneous and direct impact given by hand-drawn renderings. In this context, the efficiency of electronic drawing is seen as counterpart to the loss of spontaneity of the hand-drawn sketch.

The Electronic Pencil

CAD has different meanings for different professions. In architectural firms, CAD is mainly used for drafting construction documents, operating primarily in a **two-dimensional** environment. The primitive entities which are used to create a CAD drawing are part of a two-dimensional geometry and are basic elements such as **circles**, segments of **lines**—straight or curved—and **text**. More complex drafting symbols and dimension strings can be created out of these simple primitives. Lines can assume a different thickness, can be dashed or dotted, or follow whatever electronic template is defined by the user. The choice of text from the CAD menus is extremely rich, offering several font styles and justification methods, together with an almost unlimited selection of sizes.

A more complex utilization of CAD involves the use of a **surface** or **solid modeling** system, dealing with **three-dimensional** shapes. The so-called primitive elements are represented by solid shapes such as cubes, spheres, pyramids, wedges, torus, and so on. The geometry used to manipulate these shapes is called **constructive solid geometry.** The **Boolean** operations of union, intersection, and subtraction allow the generation of an unlimited number of shapes by combining and modifying two primitives, similar to the physical sculpting of forms obtained through gluing and carving of materials. This type of modeling is also applicable to production use in a **CAD/CAM** (Computer-aided Manufacture) environment.

A common characteristic in the use of CAD by these different fields is its employment as an **electronic pencil,** where the task of representing three-dimensional objects—either architectural or industrial—becomes extremely efficient: The traditional drafting media are challenged and overcome by the accuracy and velocity of CAD capabilities. While the only editing feature of manual drafting is the eraser, CAD menus include very powerful capabilities for manipulating an initial set of graphic entities: These **editing operations** are usually applicable to both two-dimensional and three-dimensional environments. New elements can be automatically generated by using geometric transformations such as **translation, rotation, scaling,** and **stretching. Chamfer** and **fillet** capabilities can be powerfully used to manipulate surfaces and solids—in a three-dimensional environment—as well as two-dimensional lines. Built-in geometric constraints allow the designer to easily construct lines and surfaces according to the relations of **perpendicularity, intersection, tangentiality,** and **bisection.** Lines, circles, surfaces, and solids can also be electronically **extend**ed, **trimmed,** and **divide**d into equal parts. **Text** can be easily manipulated and **dimensioning** is automatically generated from the entered graphic entities. These CAD editing features facilitate drafting and make it extremely accurate.

Another great advantage in the use of CAD is the fact that architectural representations, such as plans, elevation, and section are entered in **full scale.** Contrary to traditional drafting, where the choice of scale limits the use of a certain representation, electronic drafting allows the use of the entered data for drawings at different scales. A plan designed at urban scale can be developed at detail level, using the same base elements.

The organization of the CAD data structure also allows a correlation between drawings and their use by the various disciplines involved in building design and construction. One characteristic of the data structure of CAD is the use of **layers** as an organizing element. Analogous to acetate sheets, these create different sets of information to be overlaid or separated according to the task. The use of a standard set of layers allows different design professionals, such as mechanical and structural engineers, architects and interior designers, to share the same document. In a similar fashion the geometry of CAD entities can have associated **attributes** which define, for example, materials, cost, and energy specifications: If this information is linked to other **database** programs, project schedules can be automatically generated. These operations, typical of a CAD environment, are united in the transformation of architectural representations from drawings to **models.**

Electronic Models

Long before the advent of computers, physical **models** served as the tools to visualize and interpret abstract data. Architects often use scale models of buildings as presentation tools to show what the designed building will look like after construction. Three-dimensional models offer a more powerful visual simulation than two-dimensional drawings, and facilitate communication of ideas to the layman. Physical models are limited in their ability to express an interior space or series of spaces because the human viewer cannot fit inside. This feature has been historically achieved by perspective renderings. This type of representation offers realistic visual simulation, but is time-consuming to draw and can visualize a design only for the viewpoint from which each perspective is constructed.

CAD brings a complete revolution in the construction of models. CAD models are not made of wood and cardboard but—similarly to CAD drafting—are electronic (Figure 3.1). Therefore, it becomes possible to build **visual** models of three-dimensional forms defined by a data structure in the computer memory containing information about the geometric primitives constituting each form. The first step in constructing a CAD model is in defining a database which describes a three-dimensional model for the envisioned design; this consists of sets of three numbers representing the coordinates for each solid or boundary surface which defines the composition. The CAD operations and editing features described in the previous section are fully utilized to facilitate the construction of the electronic model. The translation of an ideated architectural composition into a three-dimensional model defines the **geometry** of the composition. The models not only create a visualization tool, but also serve as design aid. Simple methodologies to generate several design alternatives from a CAD model will be explored in the following chapters.

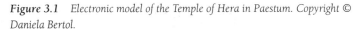

Figure 3.1 *Electronic model of the Temple of Hera in Paestum. Copyright ©
Daniela Bertol.*

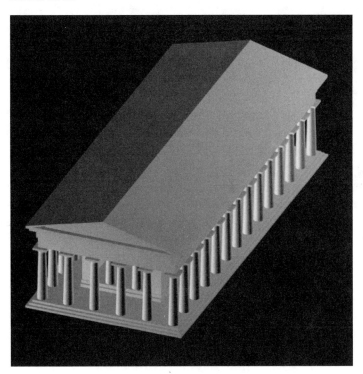

VISUALIZATION

Visualization of designs is another motive for the use of CAD applications by the architectural profession. The construction of a three-dimensional CAD model is the starting point for visualization. The database which comprises the three-dimensional electronic model can be visualized in **two-dimensional representations** such as **plan, elevations, sections, axonometric,** and **perspective** views (Figure 3.2). The CAD built-in capabilities allow an unlimited number of different perspective and axonometric views according to parameters, such as point of view and rotation of axis, defined by the user. The departure point for visualization of a three-dimensional model is a simple wireframe representation: This can evolve into either a hidden line or a shaded representation, which provides a better visual sim-

Figure 3.2 *Different two-dimensional representations from a three-dimensional model. Copyright © Daniela Bertol.*

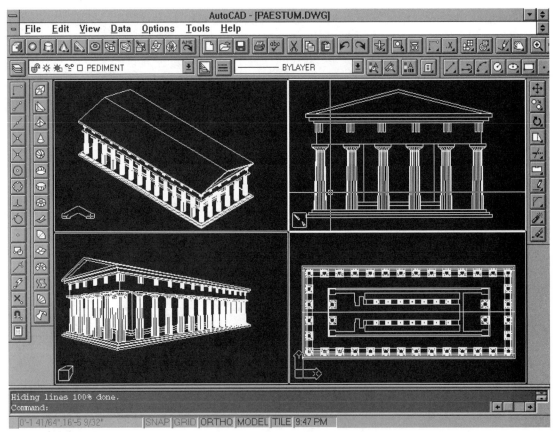

ulation of the geometry of the model. The model can be imported into a rendering program; with further steps, it can lead toward more realist images when more visual characteristics are assigned to the basic geometry of the design. **Materials characteristics** and **textures** can be associated to the geometric surfaces. Textures are often created from photographs of real materials. The model becomes part of a scene when **lighting** conditions are added (Figure 3.3). The behavior of materials with light, including properties such as **transparency** and **reflectivity** as well as **radiosity** can be successfully simulated in the computer-generated rendering. Views of CAD models can also have a background provided by digital images of photographs of real elements, such as sky, clouds, mountains, or landscapes. **Photomontages** can be electronically created, superimposing the designed CAD model on photographs of a real site.

Figure 3.3   *Visualization in CAD. Copyright © David Foell.*

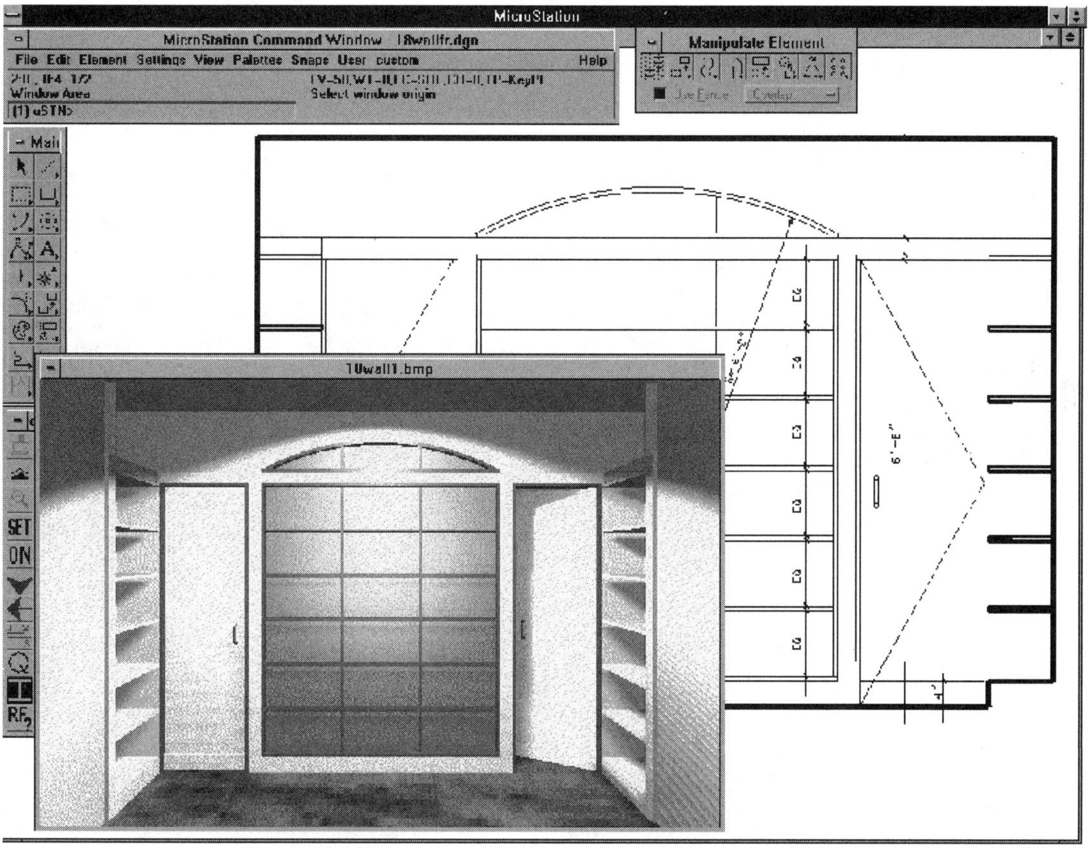

Computer visualization of architecture must be approached from an aesthetic viewpoint different from that typical of architectural imagery. The flavor of traditional pen-and-ink renderings, so much celebrated in architectural history, is replaced with the eye-catching aesthetics of brilliant colors and textures. The realism of computer-generated renderings allows the comparative evaluation of design alternatives based on the aesthetics of the visual simulation.

2-D versus 3-D

The use of CAD as a drafting tool versus its employment as a modeling aid can be synthesized in two buzzwords: 2-D and 3-D. This is seen in the differentiation between images that serve as representation of three-dimensional compositions, such as perspective and axonometric views, and two-dimensional drawings—**plans, sections, and elevations**—used as **construction documents** (Figure 3.4). This separation, often emphasized in the traditional practice, can be overcome by a correct and well-coordinated use of CAD. In fact, the most popular CAD applications are capable of operating

Figure 3.4 *Construction documents.*

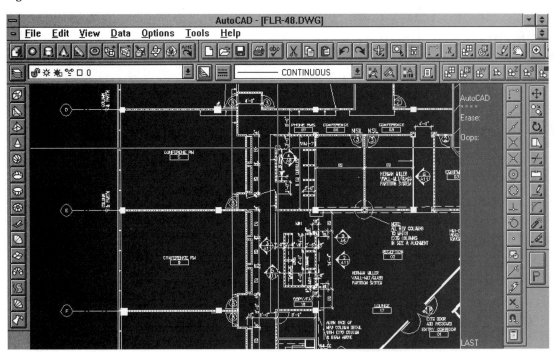

in both worlds. The same database which, according to the complexity of the projects, represents the whole building or just one floor, can be the source for construction drawings as well as presentation renderings. The organization of the same database into different layers of information can assign different semantic values to different graphics entities. A wall can be represented by textured surfaces in a model or by projected lines and other graphic symbols in a floor plan: Even if the visual representation looks different, the geometric characteristics are the same. In traditional drafting and design, each time we go from one graphic representation to a another, we have to start the process all over. The integration between 2-D and 3-D makes CAD once again the tool of choice for efficiency, even if some effort is required for the correct settings of the database.

DESIGN

Despite its name, CAD (computer-aided design) is least used for the activity of design. A more appropriate definition, for which CAD already provides initials, would be computer-aided drafting. While the efficiency of electronic drafting versus traditional drafting is unquestioned, architects are hesitant to design straight from the keyboard. Often design capabilities are misinterpreted as 2-D efficiency or rendering capacity. But the efficiency of electronic drafting by itself does not give a legitimate reason to state that the computer is used in the design process. The reality is that, in the majority of practices, while drafting is highly automated, the hand sketch is still the primary medium in the exploration of design alternatives.

How is the use of the computer going to influence our creativity or problem-solving capability? This is one of the primary questions to be answered for the effective use of the computer as a design partner. Being able to build a three-dimensional, CAD-generated model is already a good start for design exploration. But visualization by itself does not investigate design strategies or alternatives. The method of creating three-dimensional models can be extended to generate automated design. As yet, there are no commercial applications which really focuses on design generation. Customization is required to achieve a computer/architect partnership in the design process.

Interestingly, the drafting and modeling capabilities brought by CAD seem to not have had a great influence on architectural vocabulary. Despite the availability of complex modeling functions which facilitate the creation of forms such as NURBS (non-uniform rational B-spline surfaces), hyperbolic and revolution surfaces, and tessellated volumes, there is little evidence that these new capabilities influence the aesthetic of the building.

From CAD to Other Applications

CAD branches out to grasp all the other major computer graphics applications such as multimedia, desktop publishing, and virtual reality. Both CAD products—two-dimensional drawing as well as three-dimensional models—can be transferred into diverse applications.

We have already mentioned that a CAD three-dimensional model can be easily imported into a rendering application; in a similar fashion, an architectural composition created as a CAD database can be imported into an animation software to create **walk-throughs.** Animations based on walk-throughs provide an effective simulation of a design, understandable to lay people and architects alike. Walk-throughs not only generate a simulation of what we would visually perceive by walking through an unbuilt space, but also can be purposefully utilized to test designs and their efficiency. Clients of architectural firms usually appreciate a dynamic multimedia presentation better than static renderings, even though renderings have the potential for greater aesthetic quality. Virtual Reality represents the ultimate interactive walk-through, where the viewer not only passively looks at a video animation, but can also interact in real-time with the path of motion and direction of sight.

Decentralization

Another change brought by electronic drafting and design can be seen in the **decentralization** of the architectural office. With the use of networks, modems, and faxes, the electronic database which comprises the project can be shared by all participants whether they share an office or work continents away. The typical meeting involving architects, structural and mechanical engineers, interior designers, and clients, is not limited to a central meeting room. A floor plan—or any other electronic drawing—can be seen, discussed, and revised by parties thousands of miles away from each other, using the phone lines as carrier of the electronic files instead of regular mail, converting the delivery time from days to seconds. In the same spirit, an architectural office does not demand the sharing of the same common working place from all its architects, when drawings in electronic format are used. When bytes and pixels are substituted for pencils and paper, the decentralization of the architectural office becomes an effective reality.

The sharing of documents, however, is no substitute for face-to-face contact; for this mode of interaction, video conferencing can integrate voices and images of people with text and drawings. It is not unrealistic to envision a virtual meeting between a client in London and architect in Boston, both "walking through" a building site in California with a computer model of a proposed design; the integration of virtual reality walk-throughs with video conferencing will soon allow the real-time surrogate of reality with images and sounds.

This dematerialization of the architectural office can be seen as part of the more general decentralization of the work space brought by cyberspace, which will be discussed more in depth in the next chapter. The velocity of telecommunications and computer processing is the key factor in making the previous description of a "virtual" meeting a reality. An effective decentralization of the architectural office can be seen as one of the many achievements of the links between computer graphics and global connectivity, in the vision of connecting everybody to everything.

GEOGRAPHIC INFORMATION SYSTEMS

One area still unexplored by the majority of architectural practices is the integration of CAD with Geographic Information Systems (GIS). GIS visualizes and analyzes different types of information according to geographic location, achieving a complete digitalization of the territory. GIS utilizes varied information sources: two-dimensional satellite imagery, computer-generated, three-dimensional models, geophysics information, and socio-economic data. Maps are linked to charts and tables, and relations between different types of data are established to generate visual presentations which provide an intuitive comprehension of the several layers of information contained in the same geographic location. GIS links data analysis tools such as spreadsheet and business charts with geographic maps as well as photographic and video images. A complete spatial analysis of the territory becomes possible integrating physical representations with socio-demographic data. Different scales of representation are enabled, allowing a closer look (zoom) of a chosen area and utilizing spatial and tabular data as well as images. Data is available from government agencies as well as private sources.

GIS is mainly used by urban, social, and financial analysts and planners in a broad range of fields extending from resource and waste management to civil engineering, geology, and the military. An integration with CAD databases and VR applications could provide an efficient tool for design by providing a complete understanding of the territory, combining analytical tools with visualization techniques.

Copyright © Daniela Bertol.

4

Solid and Digital Architecture

At this point of the narrative path we find ourselves at the convergence of two separate trails. The first trail led us through the history of representation in architecture and its relation to actual built forms; the focus was on the realism of the representation. The other trail passed through the world of electronic media in architecture and architectural design. The two trails now merge in cyberspace.

A DEFINITION OF SOLID ARCHITECTURE

Architecture as a **physical space** can be described as a **solid-void** dialectic. The presence (solid)-absence (void) of matter configures the space of our physical experience, giving the most primitive information on the world outside ourselves. Our body itself can be perceived as a solid. Our perception of the outside world consists of an articulation of solids separated by voids. If a solid occupies a position in space, no other solid can have the same position at the same time.

Accordingly, architecture molds space through the articulation of solids and voids. Often in architecture, solid is defined as positive space while void is negative space. Traditionally, architecture has been made of physical three-dimensional materials, such as concrete, stone, glass, and bricks, with an evident three-dimensionality, perceivable through all our senses. The laws of physics such as gravity, collision, friction, and temperature apply equally. Often the laws of physics determine the formal characteristics of a building; gravity as well as materials influence the shape of domes, columns, and vaults.

Architecture creates boundaries articulating solids and voids. A closed solid boundary encloses a void space defining an inside from the outside. In the most basic architectural artifacts the boundaries consist of architectural elements such as floor, ceiling, and walls. The relation between enclosure and boundaries characterizes a given architecture. Bruno Zevi writes (Zevi 1957): "The experience of space, which we have indicated as characteristic of architecture, has its extension in the city, in the streets, squares, alley and parks, in the playgrounds and in the gardens, wherever man has defined or limited a *void* and so has created an enclosed space." The design of voids as well as solids defines the process of architectural thinking.

Being inside or outside is another principle characteristic in our perception of the space created by architecture. We experience it differently according to scale and spatial context: If we are in a street, the buildings become the container of the space between them. Similarly, if we are inside a building, the building itself becomes the container. The inside-outside relation in the built environment is relative to the context and is recursive at several levels. The natural landscape offers a similar dicotomy; the openness of the desert is absolute whereas configurations such as canyons, instead, give the impression of being "inside."

To summarize, the composition of physical three-dimensional elements creates enclosure separating inside from outside with formal and functional characteristics. These are the qualifications which will provide the definition of solid versus digital architecture.

Physical Space and Place

The essence of architecture goes beyond the mere articulation of solids and voids. Both architecture and sculpture build solid forms with physical material; their perception has similar characteristics since they are both discernible not only visually but also through all our senses. However, a major difference in their "use" distinguishes them. While sculpture can be thought of as a pure built form which follows an aesthetic approach, a building must be inhabited. One of the tasks of architecture is the creation of a man-made environment where specific functions are performed and social interaction happens. This task assigns a certain character to a built form transforming an architectural artifact into a place. The hollows created by solids provide us with shelter; the solid articulation which makes up a building protects us from the elements as well as provides a suitable physical container for actions of everyday living.

We can analyze an architectural artifact at several different levels: Architectural elements such as floor, walls, and roof in a geometrical reading can be assimilated to parallelepipeds or other geometric primitives. At a perceptual level the same elements can be recognized as made of materials such as brick, stone, or wood. These elements can also be seen as components of a house, a library, or a school. In a crescendo of perceptions and readings of the geometric construction of architecture we have arrived at its functional characteristics.

An architectural environment is also associated with certain feelings and psychological reactions to its physical shape. Walking through the street after a lover's first kiss can give us joy or perhaps evoke sadness. The complexity of our memories continuously creates associations, allowing us to transcend the properties of a place which define its physical organization. It is this spatial character—not the material input—that extends architecture beyond its solid characteristics. The theatre is one of the most familiar examples of nonmaterial spaces: The place created by the drama happening on stage transforms the physical properties of the actual place of the theatre. In this context digital spaces arise as another example of places whose definition goes beyond the solid architecture they are made of. The realm of the imaginary becomes integrated with physical reality.

A DEFINITION OF DIGITAL ARCHITECTURE

Digital architecture does not exist in physical material, such as stone, glass, bricks, concrete, and so on, but is made of databases—sets of numbers stored in electromagnetic format. These databases will create representations as visual simulations of architecture made of the same physical materials: A perfect correspondence or mapping between a digital model and a built artifact can be established (Figure 4.1).

But digital architecture is not only a series of representations of an ideated physical place; it also serves as a metaphor in the creation of places in cyberspace. Here the use of architecture is meant for the creation of places for human interaction, which does not necessarily resemble traditional physical architectural places. Places in the Internet universe, such as *MUDS* and *MOOS, chats* and *Web sites* (see following sections of this chapter) can be portrayed as examples of digital architecture.

Digital architecture is not solid or physically three-dimensional, even if its representation medium—the computer monitor or projection screen—has solid characteristics. Neither is it permanent: The same computer screen can show images of many different places and buildings as well as words and graphics. Digital architecture does not create enclosure; even in virtual reality, where the sense of "immersion" is fundamental for the complete perceptual experience, the immersion is still only illusionary since the solidity of the

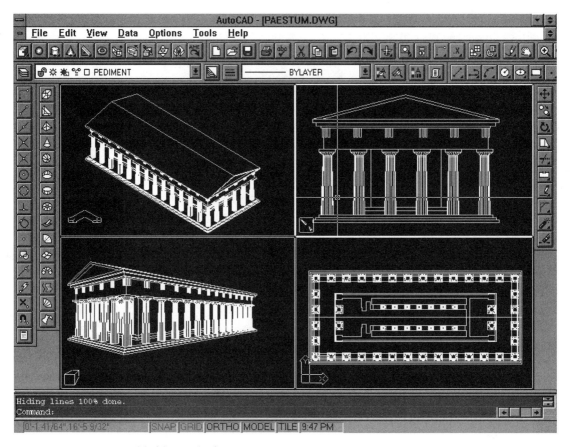

Figure 4.1 *Computer model of the temple of Hera in Paestum.*

enclosure is different from that perceived. However, the virtual reality environment, where the representations completely surround our visual universe, still represents the most sophisticated example of digital architecture.

MAPPING

The process of mapping is fundamental to any type of representation. We have already witnessed how in perspective and other traditional representations using paper, a mapping was established by the description of a three-dimensional shape in terms of geometrically definable elements; the mapping of these three-dimensional elements into lines and filled surfaces of color created representations on paper. In computer-generated models a mapping is established between three-dimensional forms and their geometric description; the geometry is mapped into sets of numbers which make up the database for a given model. The database is interpreted by the appropriate software and creates many different types of representations; they are mapped into images that can be displayed on the computer screen, converted into video signal, or printed on paper. A house, for example, is separated into architectural components, such as floors, walls, and roofs; these are assimilated to the corresponding geometric shapes—as parallelepipeds, triangles, spheres, and so on—and entered in the CAD software. The database comprising the three-dimensional model will again be mapped onto two-dimensional representations to generate plan, elevation, axonometric, or perspective views, represented through wireframe or shaded renderings. The multiple mappings, or correspondences, between elements of a different nature, are at the heart of the process: In the digital universe all our perceptions of reality made of images, sounds, smells, and tactile sensations become identified with numbers (Figure 4.2). The understanding and control of these different types of mappings becomes one of the tasks of digital architecture, as important as the determination of the content of these virtual environments.

CYBERSPACE

Oceans of ink and billions of bits have been used in the discussion of cyberspace, from scholarly publications to magazines and daily newspapers. Cyberspace has become one of the most popular words to be coined in the last two decades. The general definition of cyberspace as "an infinite artificial world where humans navigate in information-based space" (Benedikt 1991) describes its physical existence as a world of computers linked by telecommunication lines.

Cyberspace does not have a physical identity: The networked computers do not follow any specific physical structure. Cyberspace has a life of its own independent from its physical support—wires, cable, and chips. The web of information with billions of interconnected hyperlinked threads is rich with colors, sounds, images, and text; in fractions of a second one image leads to another, stored thousands of miles away. Physical architecture cannot by any means be related to the places of cyberspace. The Cartesian grid, which has always been a reference point in the spatial knowledge of a territory, no longer serves

Figure 4.2 Computer representations and reality. Copyright © Daniela Bertol.

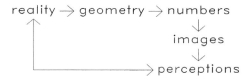

as a bearing for a nonlinear universe, where multidimensional information-based worlds are interconnected in a fashion completely divorced from geographical physical identity.

Where Is the Site?

Cyberspace completely alters traditional concepts and experiences of space and time. The architecture of cyberspace does not exist in any physical geographic location. In cyberspace you can be everywhere at any moment and the same site can be experienced simultaneously by many different people worldwide. From a terminal in Rome I can read my email sent to my computer address in New York and reply—my correspondent will never know where I am replying from. No geographic barrier is interposed between people who want to communicate, operate business transactions, exchange love letters, or make plane or hotel reservations.

In cyberspace there is no local time or date; the same message sent from New York on October 18 at 6 P.M. can be read in London at 11 P.M. and in Bombay at 7:30 A.M. of October 19. This simultaneous communication makes the relative measurement of time and space obsolete. Jet travel has already revolutioned our sense of distance—travelling by Concorde plane from London to New York, one arrives earlier than the departure time. But cyberspace goes further, to the territory where communication travels at the speed of light.

Places in Cyberspace

In cyberspace we can perform many functions that were once assigned to specific architectural typologies: We can learn, read, communicate, exchange documents, make bank transactions, or buy cloths and furniture. William Mitchell in his most recent book *City of Bits* discusses how places in cyberspace are replacing traditional building types: libraries, museums, bookstores, shopping malls, and even schools could eventually become condensed into the computer screen. Even if many of these examples of digital architecture seem to be part of a science fiction vision, numerous examples are present.

One of the most dramatic transfers of functions from physical buildings to cyberspace is witnessed in the field of banking. The classical Greek temple was the preferred architectural image for traditional bank buildings, conveying an image of solidity and permanence. With the introduction of ATM machines in the early 1970s, most banking functions became decentralized and depersonalized. In the competitive rush to bring these new services to convenient neighborhood locations, banks leased small vacant storefronts, filling them with ATM machines. As a result of this shift, the sense of "place" began to erode as the identity of the institution was no longer associated with a large architectural monument, but instead was replaced by the anonymity of commercial storefronts. In the early 1990s this metamorphosis continued with the introduction of on-line banking services and the accelerated expansion of credit card use. With the move toward a cashless society, there is no longer any need to physically visit the bank facility; the bank has become an invisible entity, no different than a mail-order business.

Another building which is on the path to dematerialization in cyberspace is the museum. As Mitchell has pointed out:

> In a virtual museum digital images of paintings, videos of living organisms, or three-dimensional simulations of sculptures and works of architecture (perhaps destroyed or unbuilt ones) stand in for physical objects, and a temporal sequence on the display plays the role of a spatial sequence along a circulation path. This yields tremendous spatial compression; a huge collection can be viewed, exhibit by exhibit, on a personal computer or in a small video theater. Sprawling gallery spaces become unnecessary. Arrangement and sequencing of material remain crucial issues, of course, but the solutions to the problem are implemented in software instead of being built inflexibly and irrevocably into bricks-and-mortar constructions. Each item in the collection can have hyperlinks to other items that are related in some interesting way, so that the virtual museum visitor can construct a particular path through the collection according to personal interest. A virtual museum can offer far more choices for exploration than even the Pinakothek. As virtual museums develop, the role of actual museums will shift; they will increasingly be seen as places for going back to the originals. The diagram is clear in the new Sainsbury wing of London's National Gallery. Near the entrance there is a room called the Micro Gallery, containing computer workstations from which visitors can explore the entire collection in hypermedia form. As they do so, visitors note items they will want to see in the original. At the conclusion of the virtual tour, they get a printed plan for a correspondingly personalized tour of the actual museum. An overlay of virtual space thus changes the use of the actual space.

Email, Chats, MUDs, and MOOs

Social interaction in cyberspace can happen in many different ways. The most simple type of digital communication is electronic mail (Figure 4.3). The content and processes involved in email are no different from those of ordinary mail. In both cases the communication happens through written words. However, email does not involve the transfer of any physical medium from one party to the other as ordinary mail does. Email does not use paper or ink, only digital media. The transfer of bits to the message recipient happens anonymously: The message appears on the computer screen without any personal sign left by the sender other than a name. Besides the content of the communication itself there is no sensorial sign which could refer to the sender of the message; communication happens at its purest state, without any physical "contamination."

Besides email, cyberspace offers many other social communication means. The electronic Internet-based *chats* establish interactive communications among networked participants. As the word denotes, all the different parties communicate through words, but the words instead of being spoken are typed on the computer keyboard. Initially started as text-based, chats have recently developed into more elaborate environments, integrating graphics and sounds (Figure 4.4). In the most sophisticated version the participants can be represented by an "avatar," a term taken from Sanskrit denoting "the descent of a deity to the earth in an incarnate form or some manifest shape."

Special places in cyberspace for social interactions are MUDS and MOOS. MUDS stands for MultiUser Dungeons (some would say "Domains"). A MUD is a sort of networked game accessed by multiple players which share a common database. Each player is located in a series of virtual rooms where he can interact with objects and other players. The initial versions of MUDS were only text-

Figure 4.3 *Email.*

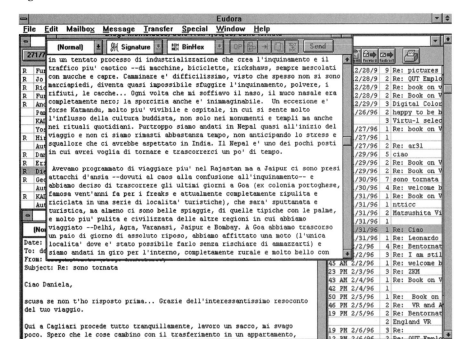

based and appeared in the early age of the Internet: The first MUD appeared in 1979, developed by Roy Trubshaw, a student at Essex University, in UK.

MUDS have many different forms; one of the most interesting is the MOO—MultiObject-Oriented. A MOO is a more elaborate version of a MUD based on object-oriented programming, developed in 1990. The user is allowed to build objects linking prewritten modules. The first MOO was called LambaMOO. Both MUDS and MOOs are usually developed and maintained by university students and are available as public domain software. Interaction is

Figure 4.4 Worlds Chat: rooms, places and avatars. All contents copyright © 1995 Worlds, Inc.

the main quality which characterizes MUDS and MOOs from the other computer games. Players located thousands of miles away can interact with each other. Different dynamics of human interaction take place in the MUDS; competition and disagreement often become transformed into cooperation.

In the world of cyberspace the imagination takes over reality. In MUDS, MOOS, and chats the participants/avatars, though separated by thousands of miles, share an imaginary world. The famous joke, "On the Internet no one knows you are a dog" exemplifies the question of identity in cyberspace; personas are created and destroyed, changed at leisure as you wander from site to site. You can assume a completely different identity in your cyberspace existence, changing sex, age, name; your cyberspace citizenship can be transformed at any moment to interact with other millions of fictitious personas.

The Architectural Metaphors

Often architectural terms have been used in the computer vocabulary: sites, windows, platforms, screens, and the word architecture itself, expressing the system configuration. Architectural metaphors are appropriate for computer hardware whose complexity of parts assembled to realize the whole system

Figure 4.5 *Architecture as a metaphor for information space. Copyright © Daniela Bertol.*

can well resemble the different architectural components comprising the whole building. The architectural metaphor is not limited to denote physical parts of the computer hardware, but becomes visually endorsed by the software in the interface design and contents as well. Games, virtual museums, shopping malls, and other places in cyberspace often visually repropose buildings, with representations of doors, windows, arcades, and furniture. We are accustomed to traditional architectural forms in daily life, since they comprise the majority of our spatial perceptions; their use in computer interfaces and visual simulations serves the purpose of providing the computer user with a familiar environment. By using the mouse or arrow keys on the keyboard we are able to orient ourselves in virtual rooms, zooming in or out, or pretending to walk through or fly over the simulated building: The architectural metaphors become the access tools to the information world (Figure 4.5).

From the Chicago Window to the Computer Screen

The introduction of the glass curtain wall in buildings typified by the Chicago skyscrapers of the last century represented a breakthrough in architecture; the building started to open to the world outside. Walls, which previously were a solid barrier interposed between the life of the city and the interior of the building, became a transparent diaphragm allowing the integration of space and life happening at its inside and outside—a huge window open into the world.

As with the curtain wall, computer and television screens bring the outside world inside our living rooms and offices. But while the view allowed by the curtain wall is limited to the visibly accessible surroundings, computer and television screens bring us images and sounds of places far away. In cyberspace we go beyond the physical separation of inside-outside established by traditional architecture; the inside of buildings and rooms, which still provide us with shelter from the physical elements, are completely open to interact with the world outside, providing information, communication, or entertainment.

REFERENCES

Benedikt, Michael, ed. 1991. *Cyberspace.* Cambridge: MIT Press.
Zevi, Bruno. 1957. *Architecture as Space.* New York: Horizon.

Composite image courtesy of Fakespace, Inc.

5

Virtual Reality

Several different types of computer simulations are labeled as virtual reality (VR). The sensors and head-mounted display, which are so often identified with VR systems by the layman, are not always present: In some instances, the only display device is the computer screen and such interactive devices as the mouse or the keyboard. Hardware, software, interfaces, display systems, and sensorial devices vary widely, according to the type of application for which VR is used. If the hardware, software, and peripherals of a VR environment are not strictly defined, what differentiates VR from the multitude of computer-generated simulation and visualization applications?

WHAT IS VIRTUAL REALITY?

From the many definitions of virtual reality, there is one which is concordant to the logical thread of this narration: **Virtual reality** is a computer-generated world involving one or more human senses and generated in real-time by the participant's actions. The *real-time* responsiveness of the computer to the participant's action distinguishes VR from other kinds of computer-generated simulations. The participant in a VR environment is perceiver and creator at the same time, in a world where the object of perception is created by actions.

The other essential factor in a virtual world is the sense of *immersion:* The user is surrounded by a three-dimensional environment. The computer-generated world is visualized from its inside as well as its outside as in other types of simulation. An immersive VR environment acts as a surrogate for the actual physical environment. The sense of immersion is often the defining factor in a VR experience. The success of the VR system, hardware, and peripherals is often dependent on the sense of "presence"; the perception that the user is actually present in the virtual environment.

In contrast to a multimedia application or an animated walk-through where the viewer is passive, the participant in a virtual reality world is active. The term "participant" versus "user" or "viewer" is used intentionally to denote the complete integration and interaction between perceiving subject and perceived world. The position and orientation of the participant's body determines the output which is perceived as a three-dimensional world made of images and sounds. The participant is always present in VR, either actively engaged in the creation of the virtual world or simply navigating the virtual environment, without changing its geometry, behavior, or lighting source. With the use of interactive devices the participant's body movements actively create the images and sounds he sees and hears as real-time response in the virtual world.

The way we view the virtual world is also essential for achieving a sense of immersion. Virtual reality visual representations are provided by stereoscopic perspective views. Images based on perspective, often presented as shaded renderings, are used not only in virtual reality but also in many other three-dimensional computer applications, such as animation and multimedia. The introduction of depth simulation, obtained by stereoscopic viewing, which reproduces the process of binocular vision, is an essential factor in virtual reality environments. Stereoscopic viewing, achieved by displaying left and right perspective views to be viewed by the left and right eye, marks a real breakthrough for VR, differentiating it from other types of computer visualizations.

Virtual Reality and Illusion

Often, virtual reality is defined as illusionary: This definition is quite misleading. Illusion refers to the perception of an actual object which is mistaken for something else. For instance, in Ames' distorted room, a space of trapezoidal shape is perceived as being rectangular. In common optical illusions involving two-dimensional graphics, nonexisting dots are perceived at the intersection of a square grid, or two parallel segments are seen to converge and diverge according to certain viewing conditions. Common to all these types of illusions is the perception of nonexisting objects or situations.

Virtual reality does not utilize illusion as a means to trick the perception of the viewer; instead it creates a complete world as substitute for the outside actual world in our perceptions. The images from the virtual world are not to be mistaken for something else, but constitute an alternate reality on their own.

Virtual Reality Is an Oxymoron

The term virtual reality was coined by Jaron Lanier, the founder of VPL Research, one of the pioneer companies dedicated to the development of hardware and software for VR systems. The designation is, from any viewpoint, a contradiction in terms. Notwithstanding the philosophical acceptance of different views about the ontological meaning of reality, from a day-to-day experience, reality is defined as a collection of objective experiences which surround our life in contrast to dreams, fantasy, hallucinations, or any other type of subjective creation. As defined in the dictionary, "virtual" is "being so in effect or essence, although not in actual fact or name."

The contradiction between the two words is evident; reality cannot be defined as virtual from an existential perspective because virtuality denotes the opposite. Nevertheless, the term expresses the fact that "virtual reality" is not about illusion but rather is about the creation and physical expression of an imaginary world, created and controlled by the participant. The expression virtual environment has a more semantically correct meaning. In the course of this book the expression virtual reality denotes the technology involved, while the creative contents and specific applications utilize the terms virtual worlds or environments. In spite of the semantic contradiction, the term has become immediately accepted by both the computer community and the general public.

A BRIEF HISTORY OF VR

It is difficult to pinpoint the very first virtual reality application. Some publications point at Ivan Sutherland's *Sketchpad* system (1962) as one of the prototypes; the program allowed the drawing of vector lines on a computer screen using a light pen. Surely we can identify this system as the first computer graphics system which attempted to create an intuitive interface through which the man-machine interaction could happen.

The development of computerized flight simulators has had an important impact on VR. Since the early days of flying, simulators have been used for pilot training. The most rudimentary examples consisted of a mock-up of a cockpit on a motion platform. The advent of computer graphics made the inclusion of visual feedback possible in the simulator. Computer-generated models of landscapes and cityscapes were included in the simulator; the scenes, initially displayed on projection screens, were generated by the actions of trained pilots. In the late 1970s, head-mounted displays replaced projection screens, facilitating the realization of a simulator of reduced cost and size. Another technological advance which contributed to the interactivity of VR was the tracker: a sensor mounted on the body which fed information on body movements to the computer simulator.

Flight simulators can be considered the first examples of virtual reality systems, trackers, and stereoscopic vision. The funding for the research and development of flight simulators came from the military, which in an effort to improve war training, contributed greatly to the state of this fledgling technology.

Pioneering Work: Artificial Reality

Contemporary to the military research, but with completely different purposes, Myron Krueger worked on environments named *Artificial Realities* in the mid-1970s. These large-scale environments combined video projections with computer-generated images to create installations at the borderline between art and technology (Figure 5.1). The participant's image taken by a video camera was shown in a video projection manipulated by a computer program interacting with other computer-generated imagery. The abstract nature of the generated images lacked the sense of realism which often pervades a virtual environment. Nevertheless, the use of projections and the creation of an *artificial* environment transforming the *actual* place makes Krueger's environment of interest for architects.

INSIDE THE DATA SPACE

Virtual reality finds applications in a myriad of fields and disciplines. The very visual nature of VR leads to an appreciation of its value primarily in disciplines which require visual feedback and where the presence of three-dimensional models is implied. Architecture, mechanical and structural engineering, geometry, molecular biology, and fluid dynamics represent such fields where visualization based on three-dimensionality takes full advantage of the virtual reality technology. Nevertheless, many other different types of applications can be developed and can offer a better problem-solving approach in an immersive environment. Any type of information, usually provided as sets of numbers and charts or displayed in a two-dimensional environment, can be better analyzed using a three-dimensional interface, which allows natural gesture and manipulation of three-dimensional objects as metaphors for information containers. Instead of looking at a problem from its outside, better insights are provided by walking through its three-dimensional embodiment, often using architectural metaphors.

Figure 5.1 *Myron Krueger's Artificial Realities. Copyright © Myron Krueger.*

AUGMENTED REALITY

Augmented reality merges the virtual reality world with the real, actual environment; the participant can see the actual surrounding environment combined with computer-generated imagery. Instead of creating representations whose perception replaces that of the real world, an augmented reality application complements the real world perception with information not ordinarily discernible by human senses. The actual and virtual world coexist in the participant's perceptions as a tool to improve the participant's understanding of his environment.

One of the best known applications of augmented reality was developed at Boeing for the manufacturing of jet airplanes. Augmented reality is used in the manufacturing process, where models of a piece of machinery are superimposed onto the image of the actual machine in the operator's display device. Other examples of augmented reality include the medical applications at the University of North Carolina (discussed later in this chapter) and the "architectural anatomy" environment developed at Columbia University (presented in Part III).

DATA REPRESENTATION AND INFORMATION MANAGEMENT

Any type of data can be displayed in a multidimensional environment. Please note that in this context dimensions denote not only the spatial dimensions defined by the x, y, and z coordinates, but also other nonspatial attributes, such as shape, color, texture, and sound that could be used as additional "dimensions" to augment visualized information.

Three-dimensional objects can purposefully be used for the display of statistical data. What is usually provided as abstract sets of numbers gains better understanding and manipulation if graphically visualized. Just think of the facility of a bar graph in the representation of population growth. When information-based models are investigated using a three-dimensional environment instead of a two-dimensional graph, the complexity of the information is better handled. The final visualization will be based not only on spatial dimensions; the time variable often needs to be incorporated in the graphic representation. In a virtual reality immersive environment, the time variable is by default part of the visualization, allowing an easier intuitive interpretation of the visualized data; the gesture control often integrated in a VR environment can also provide better navigation than typical interaction devices such as a mouse or keyboard.

Kim Michael Fairchild, of the Institute of System Science (ISS) at the National University of Singapore, has extensively researched the use of virtual reality technology in information management systems. His projects cover theoretical solutions as well as working prototypes: Several models establish the mapping of information space—of a semantic nature—to the sensorial space of visualizations using multimedia and VR-based environments. According to Fairchild:

> If objects are placed into a three-dimensional display as opposed to a two-dimensional display, the perceived complexity of the information is reduced. This can be further reduced by the use of a head-mounted-display to create a virtual space. This spatial metaphor allows users to see part of the information within a restricted viewing angle when looking in a particular direction from the viewpoint. The user is able to concentrate on the subset of objects within this viewing angle. Moreover, the perspective view makes objects nearer the viewpoint appear larger, helping the user to examine local neighborhoods more effectively. These local neighborhoods will be understandable only if related elements are within the same neighborhood. In other words, proximity in semantic space should correspond to proximity in the Euclidean space.

In socio-economic analysis two-dimensional graphs are usually inadequate to portray complex economic data. Scenarios, such as those provided by financial markets and stock trading, require fast and intuitive interpretations which are also accurate; scenarios can be visualized as three-dimensional surfaces where the polygons of the surface represent stock values. Access to real-time databases such as virtual reality environments can also improve the performance of other models based on databases which change with time, such as air traffic controllers.

TELEPRESENCE

Telepresence denotes the process through which a participant is allowed to view and interact with a remote location thanks to the use of cameras and other communication devices. Telepresence may involve different types of environments and tasks, from robotic control to simple video conferencing. Telepresence is often used for human control of activities in inaccessible or dangerous places, such as the monitoring of toxic and radioactive substances or the observation of a volcanic eruption.

The Graphics and Imaging Group at the University of North Carolina in Chapel Hill, is developing a telepresence application where several stationary cameras are utilized to acquire both photometric and depth information of a remote environment. The reconstruction and visualization of a virtual environment is then achieved by tracking the local participant's head position and orientation. Several users from different remote locations wearing head-mounted displays are able to walk around this virtual environment and interact with others as if they were sharing the same actual space [http://www.cs.unc.edu/stc/teleconsult_html/telep.html]. The main application of this telepresence project to date is in remote medical consultations.

Videoconferencing

Videoconferencing is a simpler type of telepresence where the participant is not actually performing remote tasks, but is only sharing his image and words with other remote participants. Two or more participants attend the meeting, which takes place neither here nor there, but in cyberspace. Videoconferencing brings together many different technologies, including audio/video, capture, compression and playback technology, telephony and network communications. The success of the output depends on the performance and integration of these different technologies. Videoconferencing can eliminate travel and bring a surrogate to the face-to-face meeting, where the attendant of the meeting, though not physically present, can see and hear the other meeting attendants in real-time.

The idea of integrating images with the telephone goes back to the very early days of telephone. The first public demonstration of a "picturephone" took place at the 1964 New York World's Fair, where it was envisioned that the picturephone would replace the traditional voice phone within a decade (Egidio 1988). Only the more recent technology of computers and digital transmission have made teleconferencing a reality. Teleconferencing is of interest not only for technological aspects, but also for factors of an economical, sociological, and psychological nature. Research studies incorporating these approaches, including but extending beyond the technological factors, are carried out at the Ontario Telepresence Project at the University of Toronto [http://www.dgp.utoronto.ca/tp/papers/papers.html].

MEDICINE

Medicine is one field where VR applications have proliferated. Computer-generated representations and simulations are applied in many medical fields, from surgery simulation to microsurgery and medical training on computer. Other medical applications involve the exploration, manipulation, and visualization of computer models for biological and pharmaceutical research. The use of the computer-aided technologies goes beyond the static representation of the human body and reaches out to VR simulations of the functions of various organs. The heart is one of the main subjects of ongoing research in this field. By utilizing models of fluid dynamics, researchers have gained an understanding of the functioning of organs. The 3-D hydrodynamic model of the heart, realized at the Pittsburgh Supercomputing Center represents one of the most outstanding simulations of the heart. The image shown in Figure 5.2 is part of an animation showing muscle fibers of the heart wall, the mitral valve, and the aortic valve.

Senses Extension

Certain medical procedures, though not immediately recognizable as typical VR applications, in reality operate according to the basic principles of virtual reality. The technology of X-rays was the starting point for the development of a series of technology-aided diagnostic tools based on views of the inside of patients' bodies, tools which developed decades later as computer imaging such as ecography, MRI (magnetic resonance imaging), and CAT (computer-aided

Figure 5.2 *3-D hydrodynamic model of the heart at the Pittsburgh Supercomputing Center. Image by Gregory Foss. Pittsburgh Supercomputing Center.*

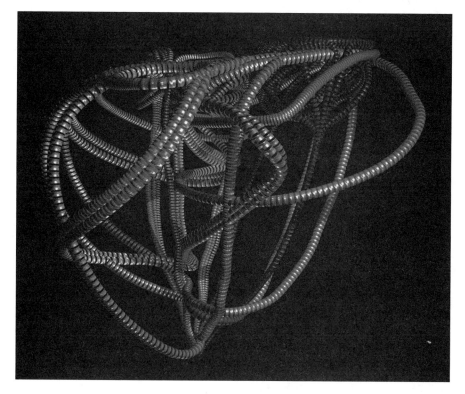

tomography) scans. The scanning techniques of these technologies provide a detailed view of the inside of the body of the patient, without performing any surgery. Life-threatening illnesses as well as simple tissue and ligament fractures can be detected, thanks to the use of this highly developed type of imaging.

The journey inside the human body is not limited to the viewing of images provided by procedures such as CAT scans and MRIs, but gets to the actual interaction between the body's inside and outside. Laparoscopy and endoscopy are procedures which allow viewing and interacting with the inside of the patient's body, thanks to the use of devices based on fiber optics and miniature cameras. Images of inaccessible parts of the body are displayed on a video monitor. This procedure can be seen as a type of telepresence and becomes particularly valuable in microsurgery, which operates on sites of the body which are inaccessible or so small that they cannot be seen and manipulated with normal tools. The doctor is able not only to view organs from his remote location outside the patient's body, but also to perform surgical procedures using tools inserted in a small hole cut on the surface of the body. The contact and impact of the tools on the interior tissues and organs is monitored and controlled through the images appearing on the video monitor.

An interesting application of endoscopic tools was developed at the University of North Carolina at Chapel Hill; the project called "Augmented-reality Ultrasound Visualization Research" combines virtual reality technology with ultrasound imaging. In this application, a head-mounted display (HMD) unit is connected to an ultrasound scanner. The screens of the HMD are transparent and allow the viewing of images provided by ultrasound machines; these images are then superimposed on the image of the actual body. This procedure can be identified as augmented reality. The overlaying of the real and simulated views provides a unique diagnostic tool, displaying ultrasound data in a three-dimensional virtual environment. In the words of Andrei State, researcher for the project:

> The goal of this project is to develop and operate a system that allows a physician to see directly inside a patient. The project explores the application of augmented reality for this purpose. Augmented reality combines computer graphics and virtual-reality displays with images of the real world. The ultrasound project uses ultrasound ecography imaging, a video see-through head-mounted display (HMD), and a high-performance graphics computer to create live images that combine the computer-generated ultrasound imagery with the live video image of a patient—we are also using the term "computer-augmented vision." A computer-augmented vision system displaying live ultrasound data in real-time and

properly registered to the part of the patient that is being scanned could be a powerful and intuitive tool and could be used in obstetrics (Figure 5.3a), diagnostic procedures such as needle-guided biopsies, cardiology, etc.

In recent years, ultrasound-guided biopsy of breast lesions has been used for diagnostic purposes, partially replacing open surgical intervention. Ultrasound guidance is also often used for needle localization of some lesions prior to biopsy, as well as for cyst aspiration. Ultrasound guidance for such interventions, however, is difficult to learn and perform. One needs good hand-eye coordination and three-dimensional visualization skills to guide the biopsy needle to the target tissue area with the aid of ultrasound imagery (Figure 5.3b, c). We believe that the use of computer-augmented vision technology can significantly simplify both learning and performing ultrasound-guided interventions. We are, therefore, targeting our current and near-term future research efforts toward building a system that will aid a physician in performing an ultrasound-guided needle biopsy.

The researchers recently designed and built a prototype real-time computer-augmented vision system based on a Silicon Graphics, Inc.

Figure 5.3a Artist's impression of obstetrics examination using computer-augmented vision. The physicians wears a tracked head-mounted display and uses a tracked handheld ultrasound probe as a "flashlight" into the patient. Illustration by Andrei State. Courtesy of University of North Carolina at Chapel Hill, Dept. of Computer Science.

Figure 5.3b Artist's impression of ultrasound-guided needle biopsy of the breast using computer-augmented vision. The physician uses a mechanically tracked ultrasound transducer (left hand) and a biopsy needle (right hand). The system displays a synthetic opening into the patient's breast, inside which the ultrasound image is displayed, correctly registered to the patient. The synthetic opening is visible only inside the head-mounted display). Illustration by Andrei State. Courtesy of University of North Carolina at Chapel Hill, Dept. of Computer Science.

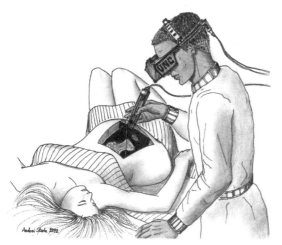

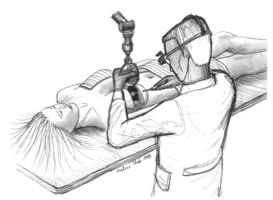

Figure 5.3c *View inside the head-mounted display of experimental UNC computer-augmented vision system. Note synthetic opening into the breast (a training phantom is used here) and the ultrasound image attached to the handheld probe. A biopsy needle has been inserted into the cyst and is visible both in the real world image and in the ultrasound image. Courtesy of University of North Carolina at Chapel Hill, Dept. of Computer Science.*

Onyx with RealityEngine2 (RE2) high-performance graphics workstation equipped with a Sirius Video real-time frame grabber unit. This system makes heavy use of the high-speed, image-based texturing capability available in the RE2. The frame grabber captures both HMD camera video and ultrasound video. The camera video is displayed in the background; the ultrasound video images are transferred into texture memory and displayed on polygons emitted by the ultrasound probe inside a synthetic opening within the scanned patient. First phantom and human subject experiments with this new system have yielded encouraging results. The system is far from reaching its inherent limits, however, and the development of many algorithms to improve the system's performance remains to be done. For example, it is expected that the system can be enhanced to present an image that is almost completely free of spatial misregistration and perceived lag.

With future developments, medical telepresence could expand from an interaction with the patient's body to the examination of patients located in remote geographic locations. Video connections could eliminate the office visit and lead to a decentralization of medicine. A further evolution might involve remote examination followed by remote surgery or other types of interventions. Science fiction scenarios, such as a doctor from San Francisco performing surgery on a patient in a remote African village may become a feasible procedure thanks to the use of telepresence and telecommunications.

Virtual Body

The different representations provided by computer-aided imaging can generate a complete computer model of the human body in a simulation which covers its inside as well as its outside. A "virtual" body has been constructed combining all the different types of photography and computer-aided imaging, allowing an analytical tool as valuable as any cadaver dissection.

A multimedia software company in Georgia has produced ADAM (Animated Dissection of Anatomy for Medicine), an electronic atlas of the human body. ADAM is comprised of computer databases covering every part of the human body, from muscular and vascular systems to organs and skeletons. The software offers exploration and dissection of approximately 1,000 layers as well as a study of the body anatomy from four different views. It also allows access to radiologies, histologies, cross-sections, and MRIs. This computer simulation or virtual body can be used in several kinds of applications. In medical training, students can learn in a visual and interactive way about all the interior organs of the human body—research formerly carried out by autopsy or dissection. Virtual surgery can be utilized not only for student training purposes, but also as sort of a "rehearsal" for the actual intervention on the patient's body.

Removing Barriers for the Disabled

As previously presented, human senses can be extended by using virtual sensory devices in diagnosis and microsurgery. This virtual "senses extension" can also be a major aid to overcoming disabilities, where VR tracking systems and applications become sophisticated prostheses to replace missing or nonfunctional human components. Good examples are tracking devices such as the DataGlove and DataSuit that can translate hand and body gestures into words. Augmented reality for people with disabilities can overcome visual and other sensorial impairment through virtual simulations.

You are probably familiar with the story of the world renowned astrophysicist Stephen Hawking. One of the greatest minds of this century, he was struck over 30 years ago by ALS (amyotrophic lateral sclerosis) disease, which caused almost total loss of body control. His speech inability is overcome by the use of a speech synthesizer activated by selecting words on a computer screen using one finger. The speech synthesis device is Stephen Hawking's only communication with the outside world and has allowed him to write, teach, and lecture in spite of his major handicaps.

Virtual reality can simulate buildings and how they are accessible to disabled people. Wheelchair navigation through virtual environments can provide designers with evaluation tools about the accessibility of buildings, furniture, and other products. At the same time, VR can be purposefully used to train nurses and staff to assist people with disabilities or to rehabilitate injured people.

MOLECULAR BIOLOGY

Molecular biology was one of the first applications of VR; in the early 1970s Frederick Brooks of the University of North Carolina developed the GROPE-II system, which evolved into GROPE-III years later. The initial system was based on a device called ARM (Argonne remote manipulator). The objective of the project was molecular docking; given the three-dimensional complexity of molecular configurations, an interactive visual environment became an indispensable aid to the process.

Another groundbreaking project currently being developed also at UNC is the Nanomanipulator, merging VR technology with scanning probe microscopes. In the description of the project, the researcher stated:

> The Nanomanipulator provides an intuitive interface to scanning probe microscopes (SPM), allowing scientists to examine and manipulate nanometer-scale structures. The Nanomanipulator presents a rendered 3D color surface image of the surface in real time. Using a force-feedback stylus, a scientist can view and feel the surface to enhance his or her understanding of its properties. The scientist may also use the stylus to directly modify the rendered surface; the tip of the SPM follows on the real surface. Experience has shown that the Nanomanipulator greatly increases productivity by acting as a translator between the scientist and the instrument being controlled. The scientist can concentrate on interacting with the surface rather than with the interface. Data, whether live from a microscope or saved from a previous experiment, is rendered as a 3D surface that looks somewhat like plastic. Surfaces can be shown monoscopically or in stereo on a variety of displays. The rendering is done on either UNC's Pixel-Planes 5 graphics engine or a Silicon Graphics Onyx. The PHANToM force-feedback device allows the operator to feel the surface. An i486- or Pentium-based PC controls the microscope during the experiments. The user may interact with the surface in several ways. Surface orientation, scale, and lighting are controlled by naturally "picking up" the surface. Lighting control allows adjustment of shading effects to improve surface feature visibility.

More information on the project is available via WWW [http://www.cs.unc.edu/nano/etc/www/nanopage.html].

Virtual environments are often used in the pharmaceutical industry for drug design. In virtual environments not only the three-dimensional forms of atoms and molecules are simulated, but also their behavior according to the electronic force acting upon it. The feedback offered by the virtual environment greatly enhances the research process leading to the discovery of new drugs.

ASTRONOMY

Virtual reality technology is most appreciated where it enables us to experience places and objects which would be beyond our reach in the real world. Astronomy is one of those fields where the virtual experience can compensate for impossible actual experiences. Direct human exploration is not possible in many instances, because of the great distances and harsh conditions of space travel.

Astronomy takes advantage of the VR technology not only for simulation and access to inaccessible places, but also for simulating physical behavior in nonterrestrial physics. NASA is currently engaged in the Virtual Environment Generator (VEG) project, supported also by the European, Canadian, German, and Japanese space agencies. VEG is based on space life science experiments, which could have some interesting implications for architecture. According to the NASA description:

> Among these are several experiments which explore human sensory-motor adaptation to weightlessness. The Neurolab VEG consists of a 3D graphics workstation, wide field of view helmet mounted display, head tracker, and joystick. It is designed to provide a controlled, interactive virtual environment to support these experiments. The subject wears a harness which permits testing both with free-floating and with "downward" tactile restraint cues. For example, one of the Neurolab experiments investigates human visual orientation in weightlessness. The goal is to better understand how astronauts maintain their spatial orientation without the "down arrow" usually provided by gravity and how perceived orientation influences their ability to recognize visual objects. Three different tests are used. In the first, the astronaut subject views a three-dimensional room interior in a variety of different orientations and indicates the direction of "down." Room architectural symmetry and tactile cues are varied between trials. In the second test, the subject views a moving star field display and signals the onset and strength of illusory self-motion, with and without downward restraint. The third test quantifies the subject's ability to recognize random two-dimensional figures in several different

body orientations. The effect of perceived orientation on interpretation of shading gradients is also measured. The objective is to improve our understanding of visual reorientation and inversion illusions, which have been frequently reported by astronauts on previous shuttle missions and which are known to trigger the onset of space sickness. [http://192.52.89.174/IPDL/VEGhome.html]

Virtual Planetary Exploration

The Virtual Planetary Exploration (VPE) project was developed by the Ames Research Institute for Advanced Computer Science at NASA and directed by Michael McGreevy. The purpose of the project (Figure 5.4) is the development and evaluation of the design of a workstation for planetary exploration. The planetary images are real satellite photographs of the planet terrain and provide the visual data for the simulation of the planet in a virtual environment. In the words of Michael McGreevy:

> The Virtual Planetary Exploration (VPE) project at NASA Ames Research Center included studies of the behavior of field geologists and development of virtual reality systems based on kilometer-scale and human-scale terrain data (McGreevy 1991, 1992a, 1992b, 1993, 1994, 1995; Hitchner and McGreevy 1993). The images shown in Figure 5.4 illustrate the inspection of rock samples in the field and in the VPE "walkabout" VR system. Other capabilities of the VPE walkabout VR system include physical and virtual walking among the boulders; virtual gravity and terrain interaction so that rocks can be thrown and then bounce and roll on landing; a finger-guided "laser" pointer which causes rocks to speak, telling their distance and rock-type; virtual mode control panel; and complexity management to concentrate terrain detail in the center of the field of view.

ENTERTAINMENT

From its very early days, virtual reality has found a hungry audience in the entertainment field. From movies to games, from rides to the arcades, VR represents the perfect technology for facilitating explorations of a fantasy-generated world.

The movie industry, in its craving for special effects, has always interacted with the computer graphics industry, not only as a user but also as a promoter. Computer-generated animations and effects are often cost-effective compared to traditional cinematic methods. Recently VR has gone beyond its role as a tool of film production; it now is frequently used as the subject of the film script. Movies such as *Lawnmower Man*, *Total Recall*, or

(a) (b)

(c) (d)

Figure 5.4 (a) *Field geologist, wearing a video vision system, inspects a rock sample at the Amboy lava field during a field study of exploration behavior (McGreevy 1992a). (b) The geologist's view of the rock sample, recorded by the video vision system. (c) Field geologist flexes his virtual hand and forearm in a computer-generated terrain created from laser range finder measurements of Mars Hill in Death Valley, California. (d) Field geologist flexes his computer-generated hand and rotates his forearm. (e) Field geologist reaches to pick up a rock sample in the virtual terrain of Mars Hill. (f) The geologist's view as he reaches to pick up the rock sample. (g) Field geologist inspects the rock sample in the virtual terrain of Mars Hill. (h) The geologist's view of the rock sample. All photos M. McGreevy NASA ARC.*

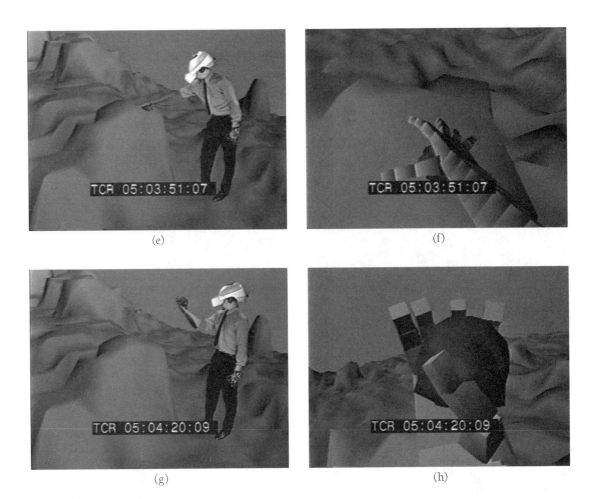

(e)

(f)

TCR 05:03:51:07

TCR 05:03:51:07

(g)

(h)

TCR 05:04:20:09

TCR 05:04:20:09

Figure 5.4 *(Continued)*

Johnny Mnemonic are based on stories which directly involve virtual reality from a more philosophical standpoint. The virtual reality experience is often rendered at its maximum potential when the main movie characters travel through computer-generated imaginary worlds.

Virtual reality and games are the perfect match. The fantasy world of games is portrayed with great realism, augmented by a sensory immersion. Several players can share the same virtual world, which becomes a battlefield, a racing track, or a space shuttle (Figure 5.5). The image of the player is sometimes displayed as part of the virtual world with which she interacts, as in Turbo Kourier by the Vivid Group (Figure 5.6). VR-based games can also be used for educational purposes: in the Logic Quest™ software (Figure 5.7)

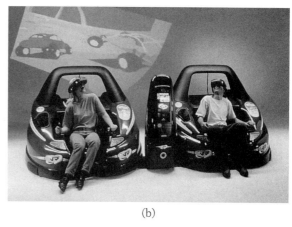

(a)

(b)

Figure 5.5 (a) *Virtuality series 2000. Stand-up.* (b) *Virtuality series 2000. Sit-down.* Copyright © *Virtuality Inc.*

employing the 3D Interactive Technology by Sense8™, children can construct or modify three-dimensional worlds based on medieval history.

Numerous VR theme parks are planned for the near future. In the Hawaii-based park "Atlantis," state-of-the-art VR technology will transport guests to different worlds. A variety of platforms, from waterbeds to gyroscopes and hydraulic units, will provide a new kind of travel into cyberspace. These will feature VR environments where one can swim with the dolphins and experience intense sensory stimulation or, for more adventure or shoot-em-up type of experiences, two or more players can interact with each other in challenging play/reality situations.

SPORT

In several sports, especially ball-based games, VR offers quite diverse and innovative types of applications. A complete interaction between the participant and the virtual environment is vital to the successful outcome of the simulation. In this type of VR application the interaction is not limited to simple arm or head motions, but extends to a full range of body movements necessary to play the simulated sport—golf, tennis, volleyball, and basketball are the most common applications. In a typical setting, the participant performs a movement related to the sport he is playing in response to a virtual computer-generated ball displayed on a projection screen (Figure 5.8). The participant must perform in front of a background—of the proper color for the chroma key effect—and his image is captured by a video camera and displayed in real-

Figure 5.6 *Turbo Kourier. Courtesy of The Vivid Group.*

Figure 5.7 *Logic Quest. Courtesy of Sense8 Corp. and The Learning Company.*

(a)

(b)

(c)

Figure 5.8   *Virtual sports, (a) Golf, (b) Volleyball,*
(c) Basketball. Courtesy of The Vivid Group.

time on a projection screen. The participant's image is completely integrated with the virtual environment; the virtual ball moves according to the participant's efforts. Often a virtual adversary is displayed as well. Virtual reality applications become particularly worthwhile for sports requiring large amounts of space and landscape usually not available in urban settings.

ART

The use of VR technology in individual artistic expressions is not as widespread as in the other fields since the economics implied in the development of a virtual environment, require not only powerful computing hardware and a series of peripherals, but also programming expertise. Usually, the most outstanding examples of virtual environments in art are developed with the partnership of major computer software and hardware companies or as efforts of museum or major art and cultural centers.

In the period between 1992 and 1995 the Banff Centre for the Arts, in Canada, sponsored several virtual reality environments designed by artists. These were some of the first occasions in which the creative use of VR was explored without any functional purpose other than the aesthetic appreciation and communication of the employment of a technological medium for artistic expressions. *Dancing with the Virtual Dervish* (Figure 5.9a-b), by Marcos Novak, Diane Gromala, and Jacov Sharir, integrates immersive VR (experienced with a head-mounted display) with dance performance and projected images; spatial experience is provided by navigating through interconnected chambers. In *Archeology of a Mother Tongue* (Figure 5.9c-d) by Toni Dove and Michael Mackenzie, VR is combined with multimedia theatrical experience to explore worlds based on the etchings of Piranesi and the human skeleton.

VIRTUAL REALITY AND THE WORLD WIDE WEB: THE VIRTUAL REALITY MODELING LANGUAGE (VRML)

According to Mark Pesce, one of the creators of VRML, it brings "architecture, space and place" to the World Wide Web (WWW). VRML is currently one of the greatest areas of interest for the World Wide Web with major attention focused on its technological developments and business potentials.

VRML is a computer language, used as a standard for creating three-dimensional scenes. The three-dimensional world implemented in VRML offers linking capabilities to other Web sites or other VRML worlds available on the World Wide Web. The integration of three-dimensional computer-generated environments adds the third dimension to the two-dimensional

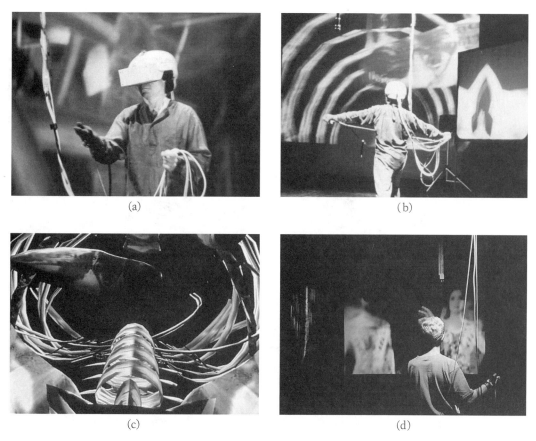

Figure 5.9 *Virtual environments at the Banff Centre for the Arts. (a, b) Dancing with the Virtual Dervish. (c, d) Archeology of a Mother Tongue. (a, b, d) Photography by Donald Lee © 1993. (c) © The Banff Center.*

navigation of the various sites of the Web. The VRML file format is platform-independent, allowing the universality of access to VRML files. Web navigators are enabled not only to walk through the model of a VRML file, but also to follow hyperlinks to other sites of the Web—to text and graphics sites as well as to sound and video formats. The architectural metaphor is usually present, from the modeling stage to the navigation of the model itself, providing actions such as the virtual opening of a door to follow a hyperlink. As Dave Ragget, one of VRML's first developers, affirms:

> The starting point is to specify the outlines of the rooms. Architects' drawings describe each building as a set of floors, each of which is described as a set of interconnected rooms. The plan shows the position of windows, doors and staircases. Annotations define whether a door opens inwards or outwards, and whether a staircase goes up or down. VRML directly reflects

Figure 5.10 VRML worlds by Construct. Copyright © by Construct.

this hierarchical decomposition with separate markup elements for buildings, floors, rooms, doors and staircases, etc. Each element can be given a unique identifier. The markup for adjoining rooms uses this identifier to name interconnecting doors. Rooms are made up from floors, walls and ceilings. Additional attributes define the appearance, e.g. the color of the walls and ceiling, the kind of plaster coving used to join walls to the ceiling, and the style of windows. [http://vrml.wired.com/concepts/raggett.html]

The technology initially available in computer games has been extended to the world of cyberspace, making its navigation more intuitive and easier to handle, thanks to the spatial metaphor used for VRML. The number of VRML worlds which can be accessed on the WWW grows at an exponential rate. Although the use of three-dimensional architectural forms is predominant, VRML cannot be considered a pure VR experience since the immersive environment is missing. Nevertheless the three-dimensionality of the VRML worlds renders the idea of how access of information can be better managed by using an interface which resembles physical three-dimensional space (Figure 5.10).

Courtesy of NCSA/University of Illinois at Urbana-Champaign.

6

The Stuff VR Is Made Of

This chapter discusses the nuts and bolts of a VR environment, focusing on the software, the hardware, and all the various peripherals (often called effectors or sensors) which make a virtual world possible. Different types of VR environments may require completely different configurations: A molecular biology application needs different software and sensors than an architectural application for the walk-through of a building.

In contrast to the majority of CAD applications which are typically self-contained in the computer workstation, a VR system utilizes a physical setup which usually varies from one application to the other. In some VR systems the input and output are distinct components using different software and hardware. In generic terms, a VR system consists of a computer-generated model, a stereoscopic display, a device to interact with the computer-generated world, and the software which orchestrates all the different components. The layman equates virtual reality with head-mounted display and data gloves: This is only one of the many possible configurations of a VR system.

Low-end VR systems display a monoscopic perspective view of the simulated world and provide a very basic means of movement through the environment. The most rudimentary interaction is provided by the cursor keys which allow movement forward and backward or left and right; other keyboard keys allow movement up or down and give the participant the opportunity to manipulate objects. In the next level of sophistication, the use of mice and joysticks allows a better interaction. In high-end systems, tracking devices detect the participant's head and limb movements; the display device provides stereoscopic images in an immersive environment. The transition from a lower- to a higher-end system is often marked by the use of devices which make the interaction and perception more natural and realistic according to human perception parameters.

THE VIRTUAL UNIVERSE

The term **virtual universe** denotes the database defining a static three-dimensional model and the other components needed to simulate and generate the interactions which take place in a virtual environment. The data sets can describe a physical model based on the real world as well as more abstract phenomena. Geographical terrains, data from satellite photographs, or multidimensional databases describing financial transactions can be simulated in a virtual universe. The universe is comprised of many different elements, containing not only the models to be simulated, but also the conditions under which these models are perceived. Variables such as lighting, material textures, and relative viewing position can be manipulated in the VR database.

Static Worlds

In a virtual world some elements are stationary, while others are involved in the interaction processes. If the virtual environment is limited to the walkthrough of a building or an urban space, only static three-dimensional models will be present. The static world will be comprised of the model of buildings or other architectural elements. Complex models require subdivision into a linked collection of submodels. For example, exterior walls and roofs might comprise one submodel while interior rooms and connecting elements such as stairs and elevators might comprise a different set of submodels. The relation and definition of these sets of submodels must be clearly identified and designed for the correct performance of the simulations. When the virtual environment is based only on static objects, the only interaction available is movement of the viewing position.

Dynamic Worlds

A dynamic world starts with all the elements inherent to a static world and adds the attribute of interactivity. Individual components of the model can be moved, rotated, scaled, mirrored, and stretched. Almost any standard geometric transformation can be applied to these objects, according to the application used. In the typical example of a virtual model comprised of a building, movable objects such as doors can be swung open. Often the interaction with an object triggers the loading of a different static model. Hence, the opening of a door could actuate the unloading of the exterior model of a building and the loading of the model of a lobby.

Geometry

Both static worlds and dynamic objects are comprised of databases of three-dimensional models which define the geometry of the elements to be simulated in the virtual environment. These data sets can be generated using many CAD softwares as well as 3D modeling applications: AutoCAD, Intergraph, 3D Studio, Alias, and Multigen are some of the most popular modeling softwares for the generation of geometry for a virtual world.

There are several different approaches to model creation. A three-dimensional object or environment can be defined as a set of solids or as bounded by polygonal shapes. Accordingly, three-dimensional models can be generated using polygon-based modeling or Constructive Solid Geometry, the two available types of computer graphics modeling techniques for the construction of the geometric representation of an object. For visual purposes, a polygon-based model is equivalent to a solid model in defining the geometry of static and dynamic objects; this kind of modeling is also more easily importable into a VR application.

Constructive Solid Geometry (CSG) builds the geometry of complex geometric environments out of simple primitives, such as planes, boxes, cones, and spheres. In this approach, a cube is not considered to be bounded by six polygons—as in polygon-based modeling—but by the intersection of six half-spaces. The Boolean operations of intersection, subtraction, and union can also be used to derive more articulated forms out of the basic primitives. A geometric model generated using CSG must be converted into polygons when used by a VR application.

Physics and Virtual Worlds

Geometry is not the only attribute required for the definition of a model in a VR simulation. In the quest for realism, many other factors are essential for the definition of a model simulating an object in the real world; the links between different objects, the hierarchical organization of the different parts of the same object and their dynamic behavior are only some of the many characteristics of a realistic simulation. A geometric definition suffices to describe the static models used in architectural worlds. Nevertheless, some objects, such as furniture, doors, and windows, can be movable and must be assigned a dynamic behavior.

Models grow in complexity when physical behavior is added. Laws of physics such as those ruling gravity, friction, motion, or fluid dynamics can add realism to a virtual model. Collision detection in a virtual world happens when the geometric models of two different objects—one representing the participant—intersect. The inclusion of collision detection in the simulation of an architectural space makes the interactive navigation more realistic and provides a better design evaluation.

Lights

The virtual universe is defined not only by geometric models; lights are the other essential component for a visual simulation. The same geometry will produce completely different images under different lighting conditions. Many different light sources can be simulated: Lights can be directional, spot, or ambient, and can have any location and orientation in the geometric model of the virtual universe.

A perspective scene acquires a much higher degree of realism when shadows are added as determined by the lighting conditions. The shading algorithms can be very complex and require much computational time. Very realistic images are obtained by using the radiosity algorithm requiring even longer computational time. Because of the laborious computations required by radiosity, the algorithm is usually precalculated, then imported into the VR application, making the change of scene in real-time possible.

Texture-mapping

The geometry of models is usually constructed of polygons; the more complex the model, the larger the number of polygons required. The use of large numbers of polygons in the virtual universe can be costly in terms of real-time interactivity. Until computing speed is increased, the most effective means of realistic rendering in real-time is the use of texture-mapping. This can be very effective in saving computing resources, since the texture map is a two-dimensional image stored in memory. A similar visual effect achieved through the use of polygons would require recalculation each time the scene changes. The texture map is a bitmap image, often obtained from digitized photographs of real objects. It can be projected on one or more polygons which define the geometry of the model. Texture maps are not only generated from photographs of real objects, but can also be obtained from computer-generated models. For example, a floor pattern can be created from a grid of polygons which are then saved as a two-dimensional image. If you use that floor pattern in the model of a building, you can simply define the floor with one polygon, then apply a texture map derived from the previously rendered image, dramatically reducing the polygon count of the complete model.

Texture-mapping is used to simulate material textures, such as wood, marble, metal, concrete, stone, glass, and so on. Texture maps also provide backdrops, with images of sky, clouds, mountains, or any other natural or man-made landscape. The model of a building can be superimposed on the photograph of a site, creating a realistic simulation for a design evaluation. The drawback of using texture maps for backdrops is in their static quality; in spite of the different viewpoints generated according to the interactive walk-through, the view of the scene in the texture map remains unchanged, disrupting the illusion.

Textures can also be animated: Running water, flickering fire, and moving clouds are examples of some interesting effects quite easily achieved with the use of digitized video frames used as textures applied to the model surfaces.

Level of Detail

The simulation of a real object can be achieved at different degrees of realism, according to the level of detail (LOD) present. In VR the real-time generation of stereoscopic images at a certain rate per second demands a clear organization of the objects which are present in the field of view of the observer. A realistic representation of a three-dimensional scene would require an extremely high number of polygons, usually too large to be handled at the number of frames per second required in VR simulation. But not all the elements present in the observer's field of view deserve the same level of detail: The further the object from the observer, the less is the amount of detail required. The level of detail of each object can therefore be determined according to the field of view and the apparent size of the object in the visual field. The same object can be represented by different models, with different levels of detail. As the user approaches the object, the model can be replaced. Unfortunately, the model substitution is often not smooth and the features of the object appear distorted. Algorithms to deal with LOD are one of the main areas of interest in the programming of a VR world.

Instances

Computer-generated models can be organized using a specific data structure, characterized by the use of **instances** (Bertol 1994). The use of instances is particularly meaningful when the same type of object is repeated several times in the model—doors, windows, columns, or any element which will be consistently repeated in the model. An instance can comprise any of the geometric entities which can be generated in CAD with associated parameters such as position, scale, and rotational angle. The use of instances can reduce dramatically the size of the file of three-dimensional models and makes the hierarchical organization of the components of the model clearer and easier to manipulate in the VR world.

Interaction

Different types of interaction with a virtual world can be established, from simple navigation to more complex operations, including the manipulation of objects which are part of the world. Navigation is the most basic interaction and probably the most used in architectural simulations, allowing the participant to walk through a city street, go inside a building, wonder through a living room, or climb stairs. Navigation through a design can reveal aesthetic or functional problems present in the design but not readable from traditional or noninteractive architectural representations.

More compact types of interaction can also be programmed. In a fluid dynamics simulation, the participant can manipulate wind tunnels or heat flows. Objects and environments can be scaled, translated, or rotated. In a building simulation, floors can be added or removed and roof lines can change slope angles. In this way the VR experience becomes an integral part of the design process.

TRACKING SYSTEMS

A physical object has six different types of movement or degrees of freedom (DOF): three translations and three rotations along each of the three axes x, y, and z. Any type of movement can result from the combination of these basic translations and rotations. Tracking systems communicate the participant's position and movement as signals to be processed by the computer; they are the heart of the interaction, linking the participant to the computer-generated simulation.

Several issues are involved in the functioning of trackers for an effective interaction: the **accuracy** in the individuation of position and orientation, the **delay** between the participant's movement and the processing of the signal, and the distance or **range** between the subject and the sensor. Three main components are essential for a tracking device: a **source,** creating a signal; a **sensor,** receiving the signal; and a **control** box, processing the signal and transmitting it to the computer. Trackers can be constructed according to the nature of the signal utilized and are accordingly categorized as magnetic, optical, ultrasonic, mechanical, and gyroscopic.

Magnetic trackers, comprising the majority of tracking devices, are based on electromagnetic fields, created with coils of wire. Thanks to their small size, they can easily be integrated with input devices. The participant's change of position and orientation is detected by the reading of alternate magnetic fields. The drawback of this type of tracker is the time lag between the participant's movement and the system response. The most popular manufacturer of electromagnetic trackers is Polhemus, which started the development of tracking systems for military uses.

Optical tracking systems are based on infrared signals and comprised of several infrared LEDs (light-emittent diode), mounted on a ceiling. Although they are very accurate and cover an extensive motion area, they use quite expensive hardware; they are often utilized in flight simulations.

Ultrasonic tracking systems are based on ultrasonic transducers and microphones. Inexpensive to build and subjected to a insignificant time lag, they still do not represent an optimal solution because of their susceptibility to external noises.

CONTROL DEVICES

A key element of the computer process is the input device. It has undergone a dramatic evolution from the early days of computing, when the user fed punch cards to the processing unit; an equivalent contemporary system utilizes human voice commands.

If this is true for computers in general, it becomes even more dramatic in VR. Because of the complexity of the action and the achievement of maximum realism in the simulation of the real world, the input device should ideally be the most natural and closest to human communication. The development of new input systems is directed to the design of devices which best correspond to the complexity of human action. The implementation of thoughts into actions—which is the heart of any communication process—must happen in a smooth sequence. Particular attention is focused on the selection of media which do not interfere with the spontaneity of action. This "mediation" can be seen in normal human communication where, for instance, the action of talking is more immediate than that of writing and handwriting is more immediate than typing. This distinction is applicable to the range of VR systems, where low-end systems use a less immediate input process, such as keyboards and mice, and more sophisticated systems use inputs such as data gloves.

The use of the body in VR as control and a representation device provides a very interesting concept of the man-machine relationship and interaction. VR extends beyond other typical computer applications, where the computer is an object completely separated from the body. In VR, the computer becomes a body accessory as an extension of the human senses. In some devices, such as the HMD and the digital glove, the computer becomes an extension of one's eyes and hands.

Keyboard and Mouse

Keyboards and mice are the most primitive input devices for a virtual world. The arrow keys of a keyboard assume the function of navigation in directing the viewpoint of the participant forward or backward, left or right, and up or down. Keys can also be mapped to functions to provide object control.

The mouse is a simple device also, only slightly more advanced than the keyboard since the movement of the hand can impress directions of navigation. Computer users are already familiar with mice as the most popular device for interaction with the computer. The point-and-click operations, already used for interacting with menus in the majority of software, can be used for object control and transformation in a primitive VR system. The traditional mouse can be an effective interaction device for very simple VR applications such as walk-throughs.

The functionality of mice can be expanded to several control options: 6-DOF mice allow interaction with the virtual world using six degrees of freedom in the participant's hand movement. Several buttons on the mouse can be programmed to perform controls in the virtual world such as picking, rotating, and scaling objects. Tactile feedback, linked to different events as defined by the software, can also be provided.

Wired Glove

Wired gloves allow the participant to communicate with the virtual world with hand gestures. Often the image of the hand and its movements are shown in real-time in the computer-generated representations. The bending and flexing of the fingers can be accurately tracked and measured, as they are translated into electric signals used for tracking positions and input control. Fiber optics cables and LEDs (light-emittent diodes) are used to detect the bending of the fingers while the position and orientation are detected by a magnetic tracking device incorporated in the glove. Transistors convert the light coming from the LED into an electric signal. Programmed accordingly, a movement of the hand can invoke a command to the virtual environment; a sort of sign language can be implemented, where hands and individual finger movements become communication means in the human-machine interaction. Wired gloves represent one of the easiest-to-use interaction devices because of their control through one of the most natural and spontaneous human expressions.

Wired gloves can be used in a large range of applications, including CAD CAM, entertainment, medical training, and military simulation. The Mattel Power Glove is one of the simplest examples, often used in video games. Another popular model with more complex features is the CyberGlove™ by Virtual Technologies (Figure 6.1). Generally, the high cost of wired gloves prevents their use in low-end systems.

Wand

Wands are another simple control device; based on 6-DOF sensors, they are often provided with switches and buttons. Wands allow the selection of a command in the VR environment by pointing in the direction of a selection area. A laser beam is emitted; its intersection with the image of the closest

Figure 6.1 (a) *Virtual Technologies' CyberGlove™ 18-sensor instrumented gloves. Photo courtesy of Virtual Technologies, Inc. Palo Alto, CA.* (b) *Virtual Technologies' CyberGlove™ 18-sensor instrumented gloves and GesturePlus™ gesture recognition system. Photo courtesy of Virtual Technologies, Inc. Palo Alto, CA.*

(a)   (b)

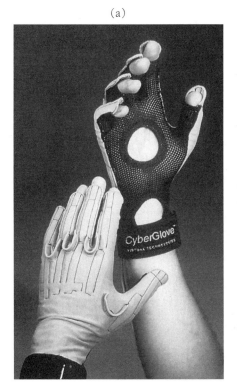

object on the display selects that object. The participant can also navigate the virtual environment by pointing the wand in the intended direction of travel. In a building simulation, pointing to a certain area in the image of the building and clicking on a button will implement the navigation toward that point. For example, pointing at an office door and clicking on the other button will cause the opening of the door; this action usually provokes the loading of the model file for the interior of the office. Navigation and object control are not the only functions performed by wands. In some of the more sophisticated models, vibrations are also generated for tactile feedback.

Treadmill

Treadmills are a natural navigation device, since the movement of walking is a spontaneous action. The treadmill used in VR is a stationary tracker and resembles the typical treadmills found in health clubs, with handlebars added for steering. Treadmills provide the optimal navigation system for architectural environments which are best evaluated by the action of walking. A steerable treadmill, such as that developed at University of North Carolina at Chapel Hill can have control over speed and direction (Figure 6.2), offering a suitable interface device for realistic walk-throughs.

Figure 6.2 *Devices used to navigate through the Sitterson Hall model: head-mounted display and steerable treadmill. Photo by Bo Strain. Photo courtesy of UNC-CH Department of Computer Science.*

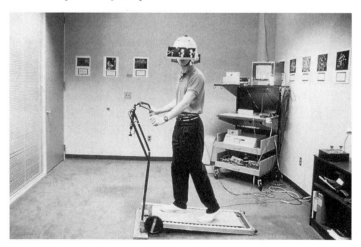

Biological Signals

Some VR applications are based on control devices which make use of biological processes as input. Devices based on myoelectric signals recognize muscular activity. They consist of dermal electrodes which, when applied to a certain part of the body, understand the muscular action of that area of the body. The VR software then transforms this body movement into an action in the virtual environment. BioMuse by Bio Control Systems converts eye movements and muscle tensions into electrical signals. Heartbeat and brainwaves can also be converted into signals for active input. These types of devices based on biological activity are utilized not only in virtual environments, but also in the "real" world, to help people overcome their physical handicaps.

Voice provides another biological input; it is based on speech recognition. However, to date there have not been many VR applications using voice input as control devices. The spontaneity and immediacy of a command communicated through human voice is quite appealing for a virtual environment, where the most natural and realistic input and output are most important. Nevertheless the complexity of the computer speech recognition seems to shade the benefits. Voice recognition is based on continuous or discrete speech. While the latter has been used in several computer applications based on simple commands, the former—which would be of most interest for VR applications—is considerably more complex to implement. Just consider the implementation of a large vocabulary or programming the computer to recognize accents and pauses. Furthermore, navigation is cumbersome to achieve only through voice commands; the actions of walking ahead six feet or moving three feet to the right are more easily implemented through control devices based on bodily movements—mainly hand and arm—such as mice, joysticks, gloves, and wands. Nevertheless, the use of voice in VR provides another example of how computer simulations and interaction move in the direction of the most natural human expressions and communication media. Also, in this case, the more natural the device, the more difficult it is to achieve.

THE FIVE SENSES

The perception of the world outside ourselves is provided by the five senses of sight, sound, touch, smell, and taste. The sense of sight accounts for the most perceptions and knowledge of the surrounding environment while the sense of touch is used for its manipulation and control.

The perception of the surrounding environment is the heart of virtual reality. In contrast to other types of computer visualizations where only the sense of sight is used, virtual reality can potentially involve all five senses, though, to date, only sight, hearing, and touch have been used. Human perception factors, if significant in any type of computer interaction, are fundamental in the design and implementation of a VR system. Often, the success and the cost of a system depends on the realism of the simulation, which is greatly influenced by the effectiveness of the sensors, producing sensations derived from the simulated world. In sensors, as in control devices, the VR simulation increasingly involves the use of the body in a natural perception and interaction; the computer is going through the transition actuated from being a separated object—a piece of furniture—to becoming a clothing accessory, providing body and senses extensions.

The following classification of output devices is based on each of the human senses involved in the perception of the different types of computer-generated representations in the virtual environment. The majority of VR systems tend to isolate the participant from the actual environment she is part of during the VR experience, substituting it with the perceptual simulation of the virtual world. In some instances, the same output device combines two or three different sensorial perceptions, usually visual and audio. The visual and audio systems are by far the most developed and are the focus of attention in the development of a VR system. The sense of touch has been the object of several research projects leading to the development of haptic systems, which are usually not implemented in the more commercial and popular VR systems.

VISUAL DISPLAY SYSTEMS

Sight, more than any other sense, is responsible for our knowledge of the physical world. Consequently, most VR applications focus on visual simulation, even if other types of simulations—mostly audio and sometimes haptic—are often incorporated.

The principle characteristic which defines VR as different from other computer graphics applications is the inclusion of stereoscopic images. As already discussed in Chapters I and II, the perception of depth can be monocularly perceived with motion parallax and linear perspective. Motion parallax occurs when there is movement between the subject observer and the object of observation. Perspective provides depth cues through the size of the image of the observed object—projected on the retina—which decreases in size proportionally to the distance from the observer. Binocular vision instead provides depth cues through eye convergences and stereopsis. The process of stereopsis can be described as follows: when we perceive an object with both eyes, we obtain two different views, one for each retina. The distance between the viewpoints and focal points is the distance between the two eyes, that is about 6.5 cm. These views converge in a final image. In VR display systems this process is recreated providing stereoscopic images to achieve the most realism in the visual perception.

Head-mounted Display

One of the most popular displays associated with VR technology is the head-mounted display (HMD). The use of an HMD (Figure 6.3) provides a complete immersion of the participant in the virtual world, isolating him entirely from the real world environment. Ergonomics as well as technical requirements govern the design of HMDs. The need for adjustability is another

Figure 6.3 *Head-mounted display. Photo courtesy of Virtual Research Systems, Inc., Santa Clara, California.*

design factor, because of mass production of the HMDs and the variety of size and shape of heads each HMD has to fit.

The essential components of an HMD are a display image source and an optical system. (Barfield-Furness 1995). Optical systems focus the image on the display device at a few inches from the eyes and at the same time enlarge the field of view of the image. The field of view of HMD has grown from the 40 degrees of the old models to about 110 degrees, an optimal result considering that the field of view in human vision is 180 degrees horizontally by 120 degrees vertically. LCD (liquid crystal display) or CRT (cathode-ray-tube) devices are used as the display image source. LCD displays are lightweight and flat, therefore optimal from an ergonomics design standpoint. Unfortunately, they have a lower image resolution, usually amounting to 360 × 240 pixels— just consider that a resolution comparable to that of the human eye would be 8,400 × 2,400! CRTs have a much larger resolution but are heavy and bulky; the other main disadvantage is the requirement of high-voltage power supplies.

HMD devices also incorporate a tracking system to detect the position and orientation of the head, therefore the eyes, of the participant. The image to be displayed is generated according to this input coming from the tracking device. The time delay between the head movements and the display of the image is one of the factors to keep in account in the choice of an HMD. If the time delay is considerable, not only the representations of the virtual world lose immediacy and effectiveness, but also a sense of disorientation, nausea, or dizziness can be provoked.

The field of view is another important element, considerably influencing the realism in the perception of the displayed images. An optimal field of view is 180 degrees horizontally by 120 degrees vertically; the older models had a field of view of 40 degrees while the most recent go up to about 110 degrees. The problem with enlarging the field of view is that given the small size (two-three inches) of the display source, the enlarged field of view exaggerates the pixels and makes the image appear pixellated.

The price and performance of HMDs cover a broad range, from low-end systems, such as those used in games, to multimillion dollar military applications.

BOOM

BOOMs (binocular omni-orientation monitor) represent another type of head-worn visual device (Figure 6.4). Since the BOOM uses a counter-weighted boom, the weight problems are eliminated and the device presents a much better ergonomics than the HMD. High-resolution CRT displays can be safely used instead of LCD since the weight limitations are eliminated. An

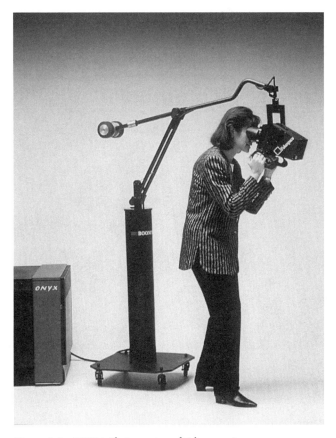

Figure 6.4 BOOM. *Photo courtesy of Fakespace, Inc.*

accurate tracking device is also incorporated, detecting orientation and position of the participant; the time delay between head movement and image generation and display is therefore greatly shortened, making the BOOM an optimal display and tracking device for a broad range of applications.

Projections

Projected displays (Figure 6.5) represent the alternative to the head-worn devices. Even if the display system does not isolate the participant from the "real" world—as an HMD device does—it still can create more perceptually realistic simulation. With projected display a coincidence of actual environment and virtual world happens, where the projection screen becomes a "window" open on the virtual world. If the system has a single projection,

Figure 6.5 VR projections. Courtesy of Calibre Institute.

solid walls can be used as a screen, making the preexisting architecture part of the virtual environment. The scale of representation in the projected images is also close to the human scale of the participant, which creates a better feeling of immersion, without isolation.

CAVE

The CAVE (Figure 6.6), recursive acronym for Cave Automatic Virtual Environment, is one of the most sophisticated displays for VR applications. It was developed in 1992 at the NCSA (National Center for Supercomputing Applications) of the University of Illinois at Urban-Champaign, conceived by Tom DeFanti and implemented by Carolina Cruz-Neira. The CAVE consists of a 10 feet by 10 feet by 9 feet-sided, cube-shaped theater. The faces of the cube are rear-projection screens. The floor serves as a down-projection screen. The participant is inside the projection cube, surrounded by images computed by Silicon Graphics Onyx with three Reality Engines; the participant's movements, providing the interaction with the virtual worlds, are tracked with

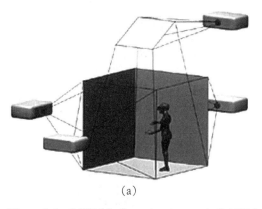 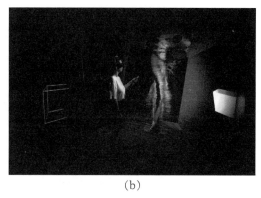

(a) (b)

Figure 6.6 CAVE: (a) *schematic axonometric © 1992 Lewis Siegel and Kathy O'Keefe. Courtesy of NCSA/University of Illinois at Urbana-Champaign.* (b) *Inside the CAVE. Courtesy of NCSA/University of Illinois at Urbana-Champaign.*

electromagnetic sensors. The stenographic projected images are viewed with LCD stereo shutter glasses (see the following section). Differing from other types of immersive environments, such as those provided by HMDs, the VR experience here is not limited to a single participant. Multiple viewers are able to be inside the CAVE experiencing the virtual world, even if the interaction with it is provided only for the single participant controlling the tracking devices.

The high resolution of the projected images and the large scale of the immersive theater provide the optimal environment for scientific visualizations. Another interesting feature is that the CAVE can be coupled to remote data sources, supercomputers, and scientific instruments via high-speed networks [http://www.ncsa.uiuc.edu/EVL/docs/html/CAVE.html]. The CAVE is one of the very few examples where the immersion is due to the perfect integration between the images of the virtual world and the actual environment of the VR system, that is the "projection cube." The stenographic images completely surround the participant, who is free to walk and move in a fairly large space. The CAVE becomes a total theater, where the virtual world of the stage set is generated in real time by the actor's movement.

3D Glasses

Glasses (Figure 6.7) are another popular device for VR displays, adding stereoscopic viewing to the images displayed in the computer monitor or on the projection screen. Typical glasses are comprised of LCD shutters,

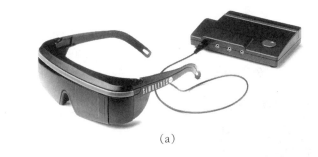

(a)

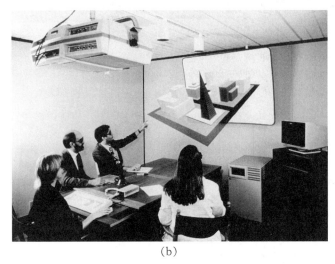

(b)

Figure 6.7 *Stereo glasses:* (a) *SimulEyes.* (b) *CrystalEyes. Courtesy of StereoGraphics®.*

which are controlled by the computer and alternate the images appearing on the screen—left view and right view of a three-dimensional scene. The glasses are synchronized with the display, and open and close the left view and right view lens. Each eye perceives the appropriate image; both left and right images are fused into one, creating a stereoscopic effect. Stereo glasses come with ultrasonic head tracking and need stereo read signals for synchronization.

Retinal Display

The Virtual Retinal Display (VRD) is a unique display technology developed at the Human Interface Technology Laboratory (HITL) at the University of Washington. It projects a computer-generated image on the retina of the participant's eye. According to the HITL:

Using the VRD technology it is possible to build a display with the following characteristics:

Very small and lightweight, glasses mountable
Large field of view, greater than 120 degrees
High resolution, approaching that of human vision
Full color with better color resolution than standard displays
Brightness sufficient for outdoor use
Very low power consumption
True stereo display with depth modulation
Capable of fully inclusive or see-through display modes

In a conventional display a real image is produced. The real image is either viewed directly or projected through an optical system and the resulting virtual image is viewed. With the VRD no real image is ever produced. Instead, an image is formed directly on the retina of the user's eye . . . For 3-D viewing an image will be projected into both of the user's eyes. Each image will be created from a slightly different viewpoint to create a stereo pair. With the VRD, it is also possible to vary the focus of each pixel in the image such that a true 3-D image is created. Thus, the VRD has the ability to generate an inclusive, high resolution 3-D visual environment in a device the size of conventional eyeglasses [http://www.hitl.washington.edu/projects/vrd/project.html].

HAPTIC SYSTEMS

Haptic systems are becoming increasingly present in synthetic environments. A range of applications can benefit from devices which allow you to control and manipulate objects belonging to the virtual world using the sense of touch. The visual feedback can be greatly enhanced if the sensation of pressure or tactile effects are provided when you touch the image of an object or resisting forces are experienced when you try to move it. With the appropriate system, sensations of roughness, smoothness, viscosity, and friction can be experienced. Haptic sensations include the feelings of touch—provided by skin stimulation and experienced by skin and inner tissues—and vibrations, provided by cyclic movements.

In a haptic system electronic signals are converted in the activation of tactile sensations, thanks to the use of inflatable air bladders. The sensation of pressure provoked by "grabbing" an object in the virtual world is generated in this fashion, stimulating a more complete simulation. In a simulation of built architecture, the haptic system could be programmed in such a way so you can feel the surfaces of walls and recognize by touch such texture materials as marble, wood, or carpet.

The simulation of temperature is another haptic factor which would serve a more realistic simulation; when picking an object, a sensation of warmth or cold could be generated. Temperature simulation would be especially useful in telepresence projects, where temperature sensors could be located in remote robotic devices. Thermods can be applied in gloves or other types of digital body suits. However, this type of feedback at the moment is not usually applied, at least in the majority of virtual environments.

Force-feedback

Force-feedback has been used since the very early days of VR, when Frederick Brooks, at the University of North Carolina, developed the GROPE system. In VR applications girded to molecular biology, the integration of force-feedback becomes a great aid; scientists can "grasp" the simulated molecules and study their binding in much better conditions if visual images are supported by tactile sensations and force-feedback.

Force-feedback can be used in several types of applications in the following types of scenarios. When a participant grabs an object, her hands' movement is reflected in the motion of the object in the virtual world. Each object can have assigned weight property, dependent on the form and size of the object as well as on the material properties; if an object collides with static objects such as walls, floors, and ceiling or another object, a perception of pressure would be induced in the participant, restricting her range of motion.

Force-feedback is often incorporated in digital gloves and robotics arms. Exoskeletons, surrounding the arm and hand, make use of hydraulic devices controlled by the computer simulations. Force-feedback is used not only in high-end scientific VR applications, but also in low-end systems for entertainment: several video games are enhanced by vibrations felt through joysticks and digital gloves.

AUDIO SYSTEMS

Sound can be essential to the rendition of a virtual world. The increase in volume as you approach a sound source—for example, a car passing by, a waterfall, or a burning fire—can give more clues in the perception of a scene, complementary to its visual rendering. These clues can be processed by the brain, resulting in a more realistic perception. Sound systems in VR map three-dimensional space of the virtual world to different sound sources which have been assigned specific three-dimensional locations.

VR systems usually provide at least monophonic sound, which can be complementary to the visual rendering but does not provide a realistic simulation of our sound perception. A stereo system, where sounds come from two separated sources, is the next step. The natural evolution of monophonic sound is stereophonic sound where the system differentiates the components of a sound into left and right. In spatial sound the sources of signals do not come only from left and right but from every spatial position. Spatial perceptions can be greatly enhanced if the location of a sound is detectable, especially if associated to the simulation of responses to acoustic signals according to the different materials.

REFERENCES

Barfield-Furness. 1995. *Virtual Environment and Advanced Interface Design*. New York: Oxford University Press.

Bertol, Daniela. 1994. *Visualizing with CAD*. New York: Springer-Verlag.

Courtesy of ENEL spa/INFO BYTE spa, Rome, Italy.

Architectural Design and Virtual Reality

The previous chapters discussed VR applications in various fields and introduced the main concepts and technology available for the realization of a virtual environment. This introduction has prepared a path for an in-depth discussion specific to virtual environments in architecture. The present chapter relates VR to the other electronic media used in architectural design and should be read together with an anthology of research papers which will be presented in Part III.

VR: THE ULTIMATE ELECTRONIC MEDIUM FOR ARCHITECTURE

VR represents the ultimate development in the process of digitalization of design and architecture, which initially started with CAD and expanded into cyberspace. As already witnessed in the VR applications previously discussed, characteristics such as three-dimensionality, interaction, and immersion (the feeling of "being inside" the computer-generated world), are at the heart of Virtual Reality. We can easily observe how these essential VR characteristics find correspondence in architecture. Architectural artifacts are by their own nature three-dimensional and immersive; in contrast to sculptures or other three-dimensional objects which can be perceived and manipulated from their outside, architecture can be inhabited and walked through on its inside. The natural "physical immersion" of architecture can be rendered at its best in immersive virtual environments. While other computer applications related to architecture provide representations in the form of drawings or images displayed on the computer screen, virtual reality environments completely envelope us, providing a surrogate to the real world environment that we occupy.

The perception of architecture is not static—like that of a painting or sculpture—but dynamic; the best enjoyment or aesthetic judgment of an architectural environment is provided by the change of perspectives giving a succession of views. Only the totality of views can provide a fair perception of an architectural space. The act of *dynamic* looking while walking—versus the static viewing of two-dimensional art—gives enough knowledge and analytical tools to judge a work of architecture. In this respect, VR provides the ultimate rendering tool for perception, evaluation, and enjoyment of designed architecture, before its actual construction.

What Differentiates VR from Other Architectural Representations

Traditional hand-rendered representations of architectural scenes have been executed on two-dimensional media, such as pencil, paint, or ink on paper or canvas. These renderings establish a correspondence between the painted or drawn *sign* and the represented three-dimensional element. With the use of computer-related media, this correspondence between a three-dimensional element and its representation is achieved by computer databases, stored as a set of numbers in the computer memory, and transformed by computer software into images and even sounds.

Effective simulations can be achieved by using digital technologies for architectural design and presentations. A unique advantage of computer models over physical models or drawings is that the computer-generated model is a three-dimensional, full-scale mapping of the ideated design and can be viewed from any viewpoint, from its outside as well as its inside. A multitude of renderings, axonometrics, and perspectives can be automatically generated by the machine with minimal human effort. Animations and walk-throughs can also be generated by using the same computer-generated model which is employed for two-dimensional graphic renderings, such as perspective, axonometric, plan, and elevation view.

Realism is one of the major achievements of computer-generated models. Because of the full scale of representation of architectural elements, proportions and relations between different elements of a composition can be visually tested for aesthetic considerations. Materials can also be applied to the surface of the model as texture maps, adding another level of realism to the images. The effect of light is also rendered in representations of computer worlds: Algorithms such as raytracing or radiosity are used to simulate the effects of light on surfaces and volumes.

A common characteristic of all the representations previously described, is the need for preparation prior to presentation. The final rendering or animation can only be seen passively, without any interaction, similar to traditional hand-rendered representations. All the advantages already found in computer simulations of designs can be further enhanced when interaction is added. With the integration of VR technology, computer simulations can be perceived in real-time, offering the advantage of shortened design time and better design evaluation.

VR can be envisioned as an extension of computer-generated three-dimensional models. The database comprising three-dimensional computer-generated models is the base for any further rendering and can be utilized by several different applications such as rendering and animation. Even the most sophisticated and complex VR immersive environments have their beginning in three-dimensional CAD models. CAD models grow into virtual environments in the following progressive order of realism:

- Static perspective renderings, from wireframe models to textured surface renderings
- Animated noninteractive walk-throughs
- Interactive screen-based walk-throughs
- Immersive virtual environments

What Differentiates Architecture from Other Applications of VR

In several of the VR applications described in previous chapters, the simulated world was comprised of both static and dynamic objects. Often the main interest of the VR simulations lies in the dynamic behavior of certain objects—for example, the docking of molecules, where the movement of atoms produces a feedback to the participant. Objects may be subject to the laws of physics as they move about. The static world, which in the majority of VR applications represents only a backdrop, becomes the heart of the simulation for architectural environments made of fixed walls, roofs, and floors.

Navigation is the primary means of exploration for architectural virtual worlds. In this type of environment, navigation must be adapted to the basic action of walking. The viewpoint of the observer must be kept at human height, as opposed to many other applications where the act of flying is often implemented. Another essential factor is the capacity to change the viewpoint position not only in the xy plane, but also in the z coordinate, to simulate the vertical movement of elevators, ramps, and stairs.

In the creation of virtual architectural worlds, a distinction must be made between the use of VR as a design means and its employment as a mere representational tool. The static nature of architectural objects previously described is true only when VR is applied as a representational tool. In a design scenario, the elements which comprise an architectural composition are not static but can change and evolve in the dynamic of the design process; walls are erected and demolished, openings are cut through, and floors change in size and pattern. VR as a design tool requires a different approach in the programming of the software. Although a clear-cut distinction between the use of VR as representational tool and VR as design aid is not possible—there is a lot of overlapping between the two—a separate analysis of these two uses illuminates some of the important issues involved.

VIRTUAL REALITY AS REPRESENTATIONAL TOOL

The use of VR as a representational tool comprises the majority of architectural applications. At its low end, VR is a natural progression of 3D computer-generated models. The sophistication and interactivity of VR tools make them the ultimate rendering interface for unbuilt works of architecture as well as archeological reconstructions. VR representations are also well-suited to the evaluation of alternative designs, since they allow a complete design exploration—viewing a design from any angle and any position. The observer can take imaginary walks through the designed building in a much more intuitive fashion than looking at plan and elevation drawings. From this standpoint VR could become an effective designer-client communication tool.

Terravision

One of the most interesting projects using VR as a representational tool is Terravision (Figure 7.1), created by the German company Art+Com. The project is described by Joachim Sauter, who is partners with Gerd Grueneis, Pavel Mayer, and Axel Schmidt of the Terravision team:

> Terravision is a VR-Earthvisualisation project. It provides a distributed virtual globe as a multimedia interface to visualize any kind of data related to a geographic region. The virtual globe is modeled from high resolution spatial data and textured with high resolution satellite images. A Terravision database and real-time rendering system have been developed to handle this huge amount of data. Terravision specific concept of seamless links between different levels of detail allows the continuous zooming from a global view down to recognizable features of only a few centimeters in size. On the virtual globe any kind of geographically related data can be visually incorporated (e.g. biological, sociological, economical).

Figure 7.1 Terravision. Images courtesy of Art+Com.

Figure 7.1   *Terravision. Images courtesy of Art+Com.*

The Terravision project is based on the concept of a transparent and world-wide broadband networked topography and surface data bank. Because of the impossibility of locally storing and constantly updating all the high resolution data necessary for such visualization application, the system automatically establishes an ATM connection to the Server which provides the most up-to-date and highest resolution data required for the current field of view (and the visualization topic). This data is integrated unobtrusively in the users system on-the-fly. For the navigation on the virtual globe a special Terravision user interface in the form of a large real globe was developed. Thereby the user has full control over which information to view, at what time and at which location.

Terravision was presented on several exhibitions and conferences (*Siggraph '95* Los Angeles, *G7 Konferenz* Bruxells, *Doors of Perception* Amsterdam, *Revue Virtuell Paris, ITU Konference* Kyoto) and was honored with the Impact-Award at the Interactiv Media Festival in Los Angeles.
[http://www.artcom.de/projects/terra]

Interactive Walk-throughs

The architectural walk-through achieves a higher level of realism when the scene we look at is not prepared beforehand but is generated according to our body movements, as in a VR interactive walk-through (Figure 7.2). With many different degrees of complexity and detail the immersive walk-through is probably still the main application of VR. The architectural artifact is visually simulated in computer models according to the level of detail allowed by the computer system used and the complexity of the architectural model. At this stage no emphasis is given to the design/creation aspect; the only impact is on design evaluation. Walk-throughs can become quite sophisticated if the interaction and control devices include voice commands, audio, and a haptic system, allowing not only the ability to see but also to touch walls and furniture. Very realistic simulations can be achieved when photographs of the building sites are combined with the computer-generated design, in an *augmented* reality type of experience.

In a VR walk-through, the virtual world is easily implemented. The majority of objects are static and the only dynamic action is given by the participant's viewpoint movements in space. A navigation can bring to the surface many design problems which would not be detected from static renderings. Only a walk-through can reveal the spatial feeling of a room or a street: the sense of closeness or openness. The perception of proportions of different architectural elements are architectural qualities which are discerned only by dynamic perceptions, such as those achieved by walking and changing the viewpoint and direction of sight.

(a)

(b)

Figure 7.2 *VR walk-throughs: Project Housing corporation* Hertog Hendrik van Lotharingen: (a) *View from parking level apartment building,* (b) *living room. Images courtesy of Calibre Institute.*

Computer-generated walk-throughs of buildings are not a specific VR creation. They have existed since the early stage of computer visualization. The major innovation brought by VR is in the interaction and real-time experience, where the participant's movement determines the path to be followed in the succession of images, generating different perceptions of the building.

The University of North Carolina at Chapel Hill was one of the first to investigate the use of VR technology in walk-throughs. An initial project using this technology was the University's new computer science building, Sitterson Hall (Figure 7.3). The interface device for the walk-through was a steerable treadmill, controlling speed and direction, viewed on a head-mounted display (Figure 7.3c). It is quite impressive to observe the resemblance between the photo of the built lobby and the computer-generated image: In spite of the different lighting conditions, they both give the same spatial feelings.

Matsushita Tokyo Showroom

One of the first publicized architectural applications of VR was the Matsushita kitchens walk-throughs (Figure 7.4) at the Shinjuku showroom in Tokyo. The Virtual Space Decision Support System (VSDSS) allowed customers to design a kitchen by assembling components from the 30,000-item catalogue of Matsushita products. The customer could choose components and assemble them in a computer model, entered by the Matsushita staff. The computer model, which included appliances, cabinets, shelving, and floors was visualized in a VR system. The customer could wear a HMD and a dataglove which gave access to cabinets, appliances, and drawers so that the ergonomics of the design could be verified. Among the main factors in the success of the project were its simplicity and appeal to a mass market; this was in spite of the crude visualization of the kitchen elements and the very simple range of movements offered by the dataglove. The VSDSS team reported on the success of the showroom as a marketing tool:

> The showroom is the point of contact between the customer and the manufacturer. It must contain elements of display, consultation, advisement, and so on. A vast display space and many salespeople are required to display our various products at Matsushita. Since the number of showrooms are limited due to expense, the contact points between the manufacturer and the consumer are reduced. Moreover, it is difficult to display our 30,000 different products in combination with standard parts as well as large scale products such as our system kitchen. The desktop showroom is

(a)

(b)

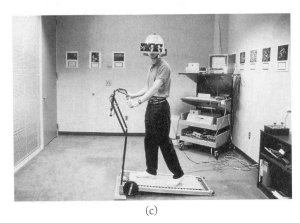

(c)

Figure 7.3 *Walk-throughs at the University of North Carolina: (a) Photographic image of the (built) Sitterson Hall lobby. Photo by Bo Strain. Photo courtesy of UNC-CH Department of Computer Science. (b) Computer-generated view of the Sitterson Hall lobby. Photo by Bo Strain. Photo courtesy of UNC-CH Department of Computer Science. (c) Devices used to navigate through the Sitterson Hall model: head-mounted display and steerable treadmill. Photo by Bo Strain. Photo courtesy of UNC-CH Department of Computer Science.*

an applied with VR, telerobotics, and multi-media technology, and provides a display without display-space or geographic limitations.

The desktop showroom would eliminate space and geographic limitations by immersing the customer in a virtual showroom, where he can see actual product images or hear real salespeople speak. For example, the products displayed in Shinijuku, Tokyo, can be seen by a customer using the desktop showroom at Takamatsu, Kagawa Prefecture as if he was casually walking through the remote showroom. To maintain these situations, VR, telerobotics, and multi-media technology must be applied. Thus, the display space and expense can be kept to a minimum.

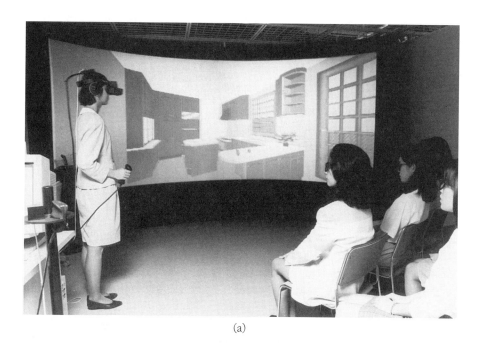

(a)

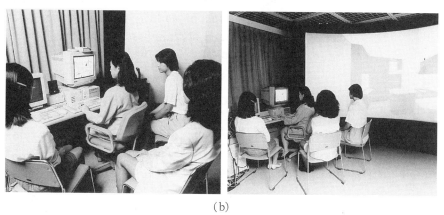

(b)

Figure 7.4 *Matsushita Tokyo Showroom:* (a) *Sharing virtual reality experience,* (b) *KIPS (kitchen planning system) Courtesy of Matsushita Electric Works.*

VIRTUAL REALITY AS SIMULATION AND EVALUATION

VR has been used for some time to evaluate automobile and airplane design. The Ford company, for instance, uses Division's VR software for "human/ vehicle interaction" projects. A proposed car dashboard configuration can be simulated to verify instrument accessibility and driver visibility; in another test, participants determine the functionality of car trunk designs by loading them with virtual luggage.

Simulation using three-dimensional models is a very effective way of testing architectural designs and the impact they will have on the built environment after their construction. Mistakes and problems emerge more clearly from an immersive evaluation than by looking at two-dimensional drawings such as plan and elevation. Evaluation of designs can greatly improve if the simulation reaches a high level of realism.

Representing Elements beyond the Geometry of the Model

The static nature of architectural elements is true only for the geometry of the model. In architectural simulations the main building components, though static by nature (walls, ceiling, columns, and floors do not move!) change visually. The visual perception of a work of architecture is the result not only of the geometry but also of many other factors; light and texture, for instance, greatly affect the visual impact of a certain space. The ability to interactively apply different finishes or lighting on a building during a meeting can help communication with clients in the evaluation and decision-making process. Although these design elements can be explored in traditional 3D computer modeling, it is the immersion and interactivity of a VR system which provides the most accurate and intuitive simulation.

LIGHT

Light has a powerful effect on the perception of a space. The same environment can generate completely different perceptions according to the light conditions. Light often is the main design factor in architectural design. Buildings such as La Tourette and Chandigarh by Le Corbusier or Amiens cathedral are some of the most popular examples of how architectural space becomes greatly influenced by the presence of light.

The effect of lighting can be simulated and manipulated to achieve the desired design effect. If the focus is on optimizing natural lighting, VR simulations can greatly aid in the determination of the size of exterior wall openings in relation to the sun exposure. The change of light color and intensity can be interactively simulated according to different sun angles and seasons.

The behavior of artificial light also can be accurately reproduced to simulate the effect of certain light on the materials and finishes of the designed environment.

ENERGY AND ACOUSTICS

The evaluation of a work of architecture goes beyond its spatial perception. Other valuable building characteristics can be evaluated by VR simulations. Acoustic effects can be digitally reproduced and expressed through the VR audio system, determining the acoustic characteristics as well as appropriate attenuation materials. A VR audio simulation of a concert hall, for instance, would explore the acoustical properties of the designed space according to the participant's location; acoustic problems could be discovered and resolved in the design phase, before going to construction.

Energy use can be a determining factor in the formal characteristics of a building, in its interior spaces and facades as well. Energy efficiency in consideration of heat dispersion and natural ventilation, can greatly influence the design of openings and room proportions. Flow simulation design and analysis provides the tools to optimize the architectural design for energy efficiency. Unfortunately, the computational results are sometimes hard to interpret if they are not properly visualized. In an interactive VR simulation the effect of temperature and wind can be intuitively interpreted and modified.

One of the most interesting softwares in the area of fluid dynamics is the Phoenics VR developed by CHAM (Concentration, Heat and Momentum Ltd.). Phoenics uses state-of-the art VR technology for data input and output along with CFD flow simulation techniques; it can simulate temperature, humidity, and air flows within buildings and other built structures. The external flow around an individual or groups of buildings can also be simulated and visualized.

URBAN DESIGN

Urban design integrates several different disciplines in the effort of planning and designing the best use of spaces in an urban setting. Not only buildings, but also vegetation, circulation patterns, and socio-economic patterns are part of the urban design process. The diverse factors involved in urban design need a dynamic type of simulation showing the evolution of all the elements over time. At the same time, the design product must be communicated in an intuitive manner to all the diverse parties involved—for example, clients, municipal authorities, legislators, lobby groups, the public, and so on. VR can provide the most appropriate presentation, for the accuracy of the simulation as well as the interaction and the possibility of simulating dynamic elements. Clients and planners can virtually walk through urban developments, interactively analyzing the commercial and residential use of different zones, and experiencing, at least at a perceptual level, the changes which would be brought by a proposed zoning regulation.

VR is the most appropriate presentation and evaluation tool to simulate proposed new areas by showing the impact they have on the existing urban spaces; for instance, how a proposed development in a vacant lot would integrate with the urban texture. It could also show how the proposed development would change circulation patterns and the socio-economical configuration of a certain neighborhood by integrating information from a GIS database.

Among the most outstanding examples of city databases used in VR systems are the models of Berlin (Figure 7.5) by Art+Com and Los Angeles (Figure 7.6) by UCLA (University of California at Los Angeles). The Department of Architecture + Urban Design at UCLA integrates different technologies to construct a digital likeness of the city.

> Drawing from technologies developed for military flight simulation and virtual reality, a system for efficiently modeling and simulating urban environments has been implemented at UCLA. This system combines relatively simple 3-dimensional models (from a traditional CAD standpoint) with aerial photographs and street level video to create a realistic (down to plants, signs in the windows and the graffiti on walls) model of an urban neighborhood which can then be used for interactive fly, drive and walk-through demonstrations.
>
> As part of the Virtual Los Angeles and the Virtual World Data Server projects, the UCLA Dept. of Architecture and Urban Design (AUD) is building a real-time simulation model of the entire Los Angeles basin. This model will cover an area well in excess of 10,000 square miles and will elegantly scale from satellite views of the L.A. basin to street level views accurate enough to allow the signs in the windows of the shops and the graffiti on the walls to be legible.
>
> It is estimated that when complete this model will exceed 1 terabyte in size. It will be maintained on a large multi-client server (see Virtual World Data Server) which will allow multiple simulation clients to fly, drive and/or walk through the Virtual LA Model simultaneously.
>
> The Urban Simulator project is more than just the simulation software. It is a methodology which integrates existing systems such as CAD and GIS with real-time visual simulation to facilitate the modeling, display and evaluation of alternative proposed environments. It can be used to visualize neighborhoods as they currently exist or how they might appear after built intervention occurs. [http://www.gsaup.ucla.edu/bill/uSim.html]

Figure 7.5 *Images from the CyberCity Berlin. Courtesy of Art+Com.*

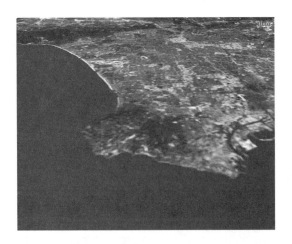

Figure 7.6 *Images from the Los Angeles model (Courtesy of UCLA).*

WALKING THROUGH THE PAST

Another valuable and unique application of VR is in the reconstruction of archeological sites or inaccessible architectural sites. The reconstruction of a demolished historical building is another venue where VR simulations become an optimal solution. The most outstanding presentation of VR reconstruction is offered by the conference *Virtual Heritage,* which took place for the first time in Bath in the UK in November 1995. Figures 7.7 through 7.10 show outstanding examples of digital reconstruction of architectural sites presented at the conference. In the words of Mike Bevan, editor of VR NEWS, and organizer of *Virtual Heritage '95:*

> Virtual Heritage '95, the first event of its kind, was an experiment. It took place in the World Heritage City of Bath, in the West of England, and it brought together the best work being done around the world in the reconstruction of historical sites and objects using virtual reality techniques. It set out to present this work, using audio visual systems comprising graphics supercomputers, 3D-augmented personal computers, multimedia laptops, large screen projection, head mounted displays and stereoscopic shutter glasses, to an audience with widely varying interests in the subject of Virtual Heritage. Delegates included archaeologists, leisure attraction operators, graphics artists, heads of museums, conservation specialists, tourism planners and consultants, historians, educators, property surveyors, leisure marketing executives, civil servants with heritage-related responsibilities, film and animation designers, and VR specialists.
>
> For many in the audience, one of the high points of the day was a presentation by Professor Benjamin Britton, of the University of Cincinnati, of his brilliant reconstruction of the Cave of Lascaux. This combines a meticulously accurate and beautiful recreation of the ancient French cave, and its vast galleries of primitive paintings, with imaginative interpretations of the most striking works. If the viewer pauses for a little while in front of one of these works, the picture dissolves into a filmic animation of the animal portrayed, or of its modern-day equivalent. Of comparable visual quality were the graphical reconstructions carried out by IBM—the Roman Baths in Paris, Cluny Abbey, and the Dresden Frauenkirche.
>
> Another spectacular demonstration was given by Dr. Rejean Baribeau of the Canadian Conservation Institute. He has developed, as part of a team at the National Research Council of Canada, a high-resolution, three-dimensional, full-color laser scanner. This enables museum artifacts to be scanned in microscopic detail, and placed into a computer database in the form of graphical images. These can then be accessed by researchers, and examined in much greater visual detail than would be possible in a conventional museum setting, particularly in the case of rare or fragile objects.

Figure 7.7   Cluny Abbey in France. © IBM Corporation, 1996.

Figure 7.8   *Dresden Frauenkirche in Germany.* © *IBM Corporation, 1996.*

Figure 7.9 *The Roman Baths of Paris. © IBM Corporation, 1996.*

The access can be via networks, such as the Internet, or by using a 3-D viewing station at a museum, or by purchasing a CD-ROM, whose contents can be viewed on any personal computer or graphics workstation.

And there was much to see at the other end of the cost spectrum, too. Professor Tom Maver, at the University of Strathclyde, showed a range of projects using a portable Macintosh computer. These combined 3-D reconstructions—notably a large-scale model of 16th century Edinburgh—and multimedia information displays, to provide highly informative and interactive walkthroughs of historic European sites. The ubiquitous PC was also featured: A range of Egyptian, Nubian and Turkish reconstructions was displayed, carried out by a team led by Donald Sanders, archaeologist at the Getty Institute.

Virtual Heritage '95 was a successful experiment. The enthusiastic response of the audience and speakers, both on the day and subsequently, makes it certain that there will be a Virtual Heritage '96. The media interest was intense, with national and cable TV, radio, and national newspapers providing coverage of the event through into January. Some of the presen-

Figure 7.10 *Edimburgh Old Town. Courtesy of ABACUS, University of Strathclyde.*

ters have reported serious follow-up inquires resulting from the conference, and several substantial new projects and commissions are understood to be under discussion.

The Italian company Infobyte develops VR projects focused on the rendition of monuments and sites, at the borderline between art and architecture. In *The City of Giotto* (Figure 7.11) the participant can walk through the Basilica of St. Francis in Assisi. The nave of the church is texture mapped with frescoes of Giotto. Each fresco can be selected (or entered), initiating a walk-through in imaginary medieval cities inspired by Giotto's pictorial visions. The VR project *St. Peter's Basilicas* (Figure 7.12) combines models of the current church with the Constantinian Basilica and its external clois-

Figure 7.11 *The City of Giotto. Courtesy of ENEL spa/INFOBYTE Spa—Rome, Italy.*

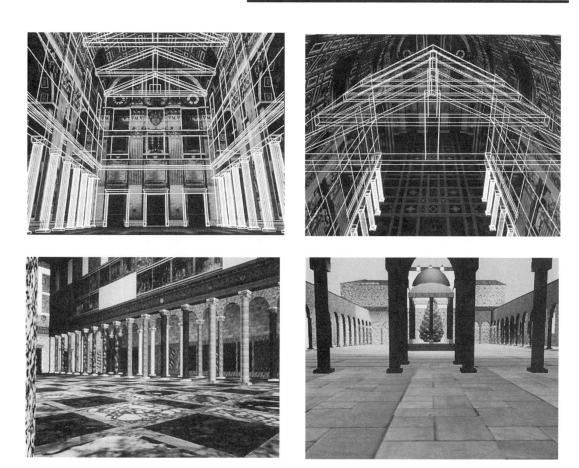

Figure 7.12 *St. Peter's Basilicas. Courtesy of ENEL spa/INFOBYTE spa—Rome, Italy.*

ter, both demolished in the sixteenth century. The project points out the effectiveness of VR in the study of historical layering of sites and monuments.

VR AS DESIGN AID

The potential of virtual reality as design aid is the least explored among the VR applications in architecture. Nevertheless, VR could provide a revolutionary paradigm shift in the design environment. The creative process which is traditionally based on two-dimensional representations or sketches can now be transformed to take advantage of an immersive design environment, visualizing ideas and preliminary sketches in a three-dimensional space, such as that provided by a VR implementation.

Since the early days of architectural VR applications, design issues have been investigated; the three-dimensional modeler 3DM, developed at the University of North Carolina used a HMD system and hand-held pointing device to create three-dimensional models. Features typical of modeling packages—geometric primitives, extrusion, and meshes—can be implemented in the VR session itself. 3DM's transformation and editing capabilities, such as moving, scaling, copying, cutting, and pasting, provide a more intuitive spatial exploration by grabbing and manipulating objects in an immersive mode.

One of the most interesting applications devoted to design is the Conceptual Design Space (CDS) project developed at the Graphics, Visualization, and Usability Center (GVU) at Georgia Institute of Technology (see Chapter 13).

From Diagrams and Sketches to Models

In the design process there are many stages. What differentiates an initial sketch from a construction drawing is the amount and accuracy of information contained in the representation. While a sketch is mostly expressive of an intuitive and unpredictable individual creation, the evolution of the sketch into presentation and working drawings represents a predictable sequence of steps which can be programmed in a series of instructions to be executed by the computer. Computer-aided design provides valuable tools for an automated architectural design. For instance, envisioning a facade as a curved wall with triangular openings is part of the creative process, while the implementation of its model with exact dimensions of the wall and the openings, its curvature angle, and the solid proportion can be accomplished by an automated sequence of steps. Many of the operations which are performed in a repeating fashion can be automated and implemented in a CAD application.

Sketches can also be integrated with diagrams. A design is usually based on an hierarchical composition of elements; the hierarchy is not only formal but also of a functional and structural nature. The use of diagrams can provide an initial parti from which a three-dimensional model can be elaborated. A complete model of a work of architecture can be easily implemented if decomposed into submodels of its components (Bertol 1994). These submodels can be organized in a library, providing ready-made components to be assembled according to the initial diagram. The Matsushita kitchens demonstrate how an individualized design can be easily derived from a large selection of components. This could be broadened far beyond the kitchen example, extending to the design of complete building types and urban spaces.

An automated design system is easily implemented as a CAD application. In addition, VR can be applied as a final presentation and evaluation tool, using a CAD or modeling package. If alternative design solutions are suggested by the VR evaluation, they can be developed outside the immersive environment and translated to the CAD application. This process loses the strength of the solutions envisioned from the interactive and immersive evaluation. The implementation of an automated design in an immersive environment could translate a sketch into a functional model, which could be tested and evaluated at the same moment it is created. The immediacy of the process could enhance the creative act and instantaneously test the validity of a design solution.

Designing Using Two-dimensional Media and Scale Models

The design of architecture uses mainly two-dimensional media. Paper has historically been the main means of communication of ideas into constructable artifacts. Both presentation drawings as well as construction documents are two-dimensional representations of three-dimensional objects such as buildings. Even with computer-assisted technologies such as CAD, the output which is displayed on the screen or printed on paper is a two-dimensional view, an abstraction of the envisioned three-dimensional artifact: The act of design always happens from the *outside* of the designed object.

Physical scale models provide another option for the design and simulation of an unbuilt three-dimensional space. The scale of a physical model, however, limits the user's ability to experience the quality of the space because the model cannot be inhabited and perceived from the inside.

Designing in a Virtual Environment

Immersive design can be defined as the act of designing in a virtual environment, where the designer is inside the product of his designs. This process brings new approaches to the creative act.

Within an immersive design environment the creation of form in space becomes possible for the first time, without any intermediation. Like a magician, the architect's gesture can raise walls, cut openings, and adjust the slope of roofs. Floors and stairs can be added and subtracted according to the reaction and judgment provoked by the perceptual impact. If the design is based on volumes, Boolean operations of addition or subtraction can be utilized, allowing the molding of virtual space similar to the creation of a sculpture by a molding and carving motion.

Traditional compositional rules, such as symmetry and central organizations which are usually implemented in two-dimensional representations, assume different values when implemented in a three-dimensional immersive environment. Proportions between various architectural elements can be verified by inhabiting the space they define. The 1:1 scale of the immersive design environment gives the ability to perceive the designed space without the false assumptions which so often accompany two-dimensional representations.

Though to date, immersive design is largely unrealized, it is this aspect of virtual reality which will revolutionize the design of architecture. The architect must be open to discussion of the traditional act of designing, to adapt to the notion of sketching in space and being inside that sketch. New formal paradigms, unthinkable in the traditional design methodology, can arise from a direct experience of three-dimensional space.

REFERENCE

Bertol, Daniela. 1994. *Visualizing with CAD*. New York: Springer-Verlag.

Who Is Doing What?

The following chapters are based on papers which are representative of the state-of-the-art in virtual environments dealing with the subject of architecture. The contributions have been selected to represent the entire spectrum of research, from theoretical to more pragmatic projects. They cover conceptual projects, focusing on the morphology of abstract virtual spaces for their own sake, as well as technological developments in hardware, software, and effectors. The multiplicity of approaches is also reflected by the variety of interacting disciplines; teams of researchers from different fields, such as architecture, art, computer science, engineering, and psychology are involved in the development of VR systems.

Not surprisingly, the most interesting contributions in this specific field of VR belong to academic research. VR is generally not employed in the design and production process; it is still seen as an experimental technology by the architectural profession. However, all the presented projects clearly show the potential of this developing industry.

A theme shared by all the contributors was a sense of enthusiasm for the future of VR in design—a theme shared by this author. The only frustration comes from the fact that the depiction of this brave new world of rich visualization must be made with the two-dimensional images and text of a centuries-old technology, the book.

Architectural Applications and the Responsive Workbench

Jeff Feldgoise and Julie Dorsey
Massachusetts Institute of Technology

Maneesh Agrawala, Andrew Beers, Bernd Fröhlich, and Pat Hanrahan
Stanford University

INTRODUCTION

Today there are a number of virtual reality systems available for architectural applications. While such systems would seem to have broad applicability to the architectural design process, most of them have proven useful for presenting designs rather than developing them. Walk-through applications that allow architects to take clients on virtual strolls through unbuilt designs are representative of the types of tools that are commonly available (*Los Angeles Times* 1994). To directly impact the design process, the virtual reality application should provide the means by which the architect can *explore* design ideas. In practical terms, hardware and software ought to include design tools that will allow architects to move beyond explorations that are possible with traditional representations. While in the future, virtual reality devices might replace older modes of architectural representation, there also remains a need for new design tools to be compatible with traditional media. Rather than immediately supplanting older media such as freehand sketches, hard-line drawings, and physical models, the virtual reality device should add a new layer of design information.

The 3-D display of information in a virtual reality simulation responds well to the spatial complexity of architectural ideas. Traditionally, many architects have used physical models to test design proposals because 2-D paper representations were not sufficiently sophisticated for the accurate representation of architectural space. Likewise, virtual reality display devices move from static 2-D screen representations of CAD renderings to dynamically updated 3-D displays. Real-time updates available with a VR display enable a fluidity in the exploration of design ideas that is markedly absent from most CAD modeling systems.

This chapter describes the Responsive Workbench (Figure 8.1), which is a virtual environment that is an attractive vehicle for architectural design. We then discuss two interactive design programs in the context of the Workbench, which serve as examples of the many possible architectural applications for this virtual environment.

The Responsive Workbench (Krüger et al. 1995; Krüger and Fröhlich 1994) is a virtual reality system, which was developed for a certain class of users—physicians, engineers, and architects—who all have problems and tasks that require desks, tables, and workbenches. This basic supposition led to a non-immersive design, where virtual objects and control tools are located on a real workbench (Figure 8.2). The objects, displayed as computer-generated stereoscopic images, appear on or above the table top. A guide uses the virtual environment by wearing LCD shutter glasses while several

Figure 8.1   *The Stanford main quad.*

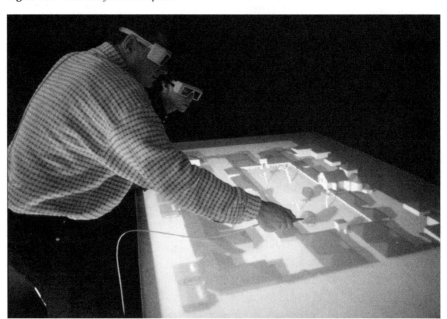

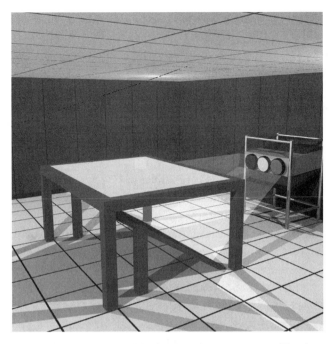

Figure 8.2 *Virtual objects displayed on the Responsive Workbench.*

observers can watch this person acting. To obtain correct perspective stereoscopic rendering from any location around the table, the computer keeps track of the guide's head position by using a 6 degree of freedom electromagnetic tracking system.

Most classical VR systems like the HMD (Head-Mounted Display), BOOM (Binocular Omni-Orientation Monitor), and the CAVE (Cave Automatic Virtual Environment, Cruz-Neira, Sandin, and DeFanti 1993) completely immerse the user in a virtual space. The Responsive Workbench is a non-immersive alternative to these classical systems. The non-immersive setup is advantageous, because the virtual scenery is integrated into the user's natural working environment. For many architects, the ability to transfer design information between different media is a necessary part of their design process. With the Workbench, it is possible for the user to place digitally scanned or physical drawings on the Workbench surface, thereby augmenting traditional media with virtual representations.

The workbench metaphor for image display is conducive to collaborative design. Although the stereoscopic images are view-dependent, it is possible to have several people concurrently viewing models on the Workbench.

As long as they stay close to the tracked user (e.g., by looking over his or her shoulder), additional observers can see the virtual objects with only slight distortions. In architectural design, the collaboration between architects, clients, engineers, contractors, and so on is often essential for a project's success.

Architects feel immediately comfortable designing on the Workbench because the virtual model sits on a horizontal surface much as a physical model sits on a table. The Workbench table top is at waist height, allowing a standing person easy access to the work surface. When working on the Workbench, one's viewpoint is generally a bird's-eye perspective. This orientation is similar to how architects typically view their models when working with traditional media. The immobile physical presence of the Workbench table provides a natural spatial reference frame for the virtual objects. The user operates with respect to the table, rather than in a free-floating virtual world found in many immersive VR systems.

Users interact with the virtual environment with their hands by wearing data gloves or pointing with a tracked stylus. These devices allow natural and intuitive interaction with the virtual model. The interaction is similar to dealing with a physical model, as most of the virtual objects are within reach of the user, enabling direct manipulation.

User interaction with a Workbench model of moderate complexity occurs in real-time. As the user's viewpoint or the model's geometry changes, the Responsive Workbench dynamically updates the display. For the site plan model (Figure 8.1) containing 18,000 polygons, there was a 12 frame-per-second display update with Gouraud shading and texture-mapping. When solar shadows were added, a 15 frame-per-second rate was achieved. In general, the Responsive Workbench was developed using commercially available hardware and software, including a Silicon Graphics Reality Engine 2 graphics workstation, SGI Performer and Iris GL, Crystal Eyes shutterglasses, Fakespace's PINCH glove system for gesture tracking, and Polhemus's Fastrak tracking system for head and hand tracking.

THE WORKBENCH FOR ARCHITECTURAL DESIGN

We have developed two representative software applications for architectural design on the Workbench. The "Architectural Site Planning" program demonstrates how the Workbench could be used for large-scale site design and evaluation. The "Kit-of-parts" application offers a way for architects to assemble building models with virtual material elements.

Architectural Site Planning

In architectural site planning, physical 3-D mock-ups are often constructed to gain a better understanding of the structure of a site. This kind of scenario is especially well-suited to the Responsive Workbench environment in which the user is naturally looking down at the table from an overhead viewpoint.

There are several advantages to using the Responsive Workbench in this way. The Workbench can display a site model from a typical 3-D CAD file shortly after modeling is completed. The virtual model is easy to manipulate, allowing the architect to view the model at various scales and levels of detail. Viewing a single building is as easy as viewing the entire site model, since the user can zoom in to look at a particular structure or zoom out to view the entire site.

It is also convenient to include support for level of detail (LOD) adjustments. For example, as the user zooms in to look more closely at a particular building, the building's geometry is represented with a more detailed polygonal model. When the user moves away from a building, fewer polygons can suffice. This approach gives the user fast display update rates for large site models, while still producing detailed models when necessary.

Furthermore, modeling changes can be rapidly incorporated into the site plan. As with physical mock-ups, the architect can easily pick up and reposition buildings in the virtual site plan, using the data gloves or the stylus. The advantage of the virtual site plan is that changes to the shape of individual buildings are easier to incorporate with a virtual model than with a physical model. Modifying the appearance of a CAD model of a building is relatively simple, whereas changing the appearance of a building in a physical site plan often requires an entirely new model.

The ease with which one can modify a Workbench CAD model is helpful when testing multiple building alternatives in the virtual site. The user can rapidly insert several variations of a building design into the site model. Or, the user can replicate the entire site model, insert the different building alternatives into each site model, and simultaneously view multiple versions of the site plan for side-by-side evaluation of design alternatives. Figure 8.3 shows two different landscape designs within the Stanford main quad.

The Workbench, like other visualization systems, is well-suited for sunlight and shadow analysis. Accurate solar orientation and shadows for the model can be visualized for any time of day and any day of the year (Figure 8.1). It is also possible to animate the solar position. The user can watch the shadows changing in real-time and visualize the full gamut of solar orientations.

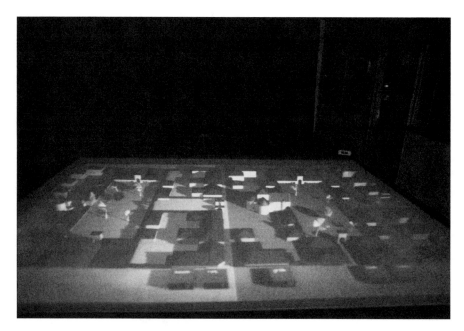

Figure 8.3 *Side-by-side evaluation of two landscaping designs.*

By connecting a database system to the virtual site model, one can use the Workbench for 3-D display of GIS or facilities management information. For example, the material, square-footage, and volume of a room, or the number of bathrooms in a building, might be stored in the database. A number of methods could then be used to visualize this information. For example, if the user wants to know which walls are made of brick, all of the appropriate walls might be colored dark red. Or the user might view the model through a virtual lens that causes all the brick walls within the lens that are thicker than two feet to appear blue. With such a system users can quickly and easily view exactly the information that they are most interested in, without being overloaded with unnecessary details.

"Kit-of-parts" Modeling Environment

While the site planning application is useful for large-scale design issues, the kit-of-parts program is helpful for designing individual buildings. This modeling environment offers a system for additive architectural design that supports the exploratory nature of architectural design modeling. One approach towards the design process suggests that building design begins as an assemblage of "primitive" elements in three-dimensional space. This theory grew out of such work as that by Friedrich Froebel, the German educator who developed the Kindergarten system of education. This system of instruction provides a pedagogical basis for this design method, as part of the Froebel method consists of sets of wooden building blocks called *gifts*. The gifts are assembled by students to create various patterns and designs. In his autobiography, Frank Lloyd Wright credited his Froebel Kindergarten gifts with the development of his spatial understanding (MacCormac 1974; Wright 1932).

We have developed a kit-of-parts design system that takes the Froebel idea of a limited set of repeated design elements and adds material qualities and dimensions. Selecting from among a palette of standardized building materials, the user can choose and assemble parts to model the design. Using the stylus, material parts can be picked up from the "stockpiles" on the Workbench surface and moved into place in the model. The modeling system includes tools for intelligent resizing and accurate placement of the modeling materials. Building materials come in a series of standard dimensions that can be encoded into the virtual parts. The kit-of-parts modeling system presents the user with the standard-unit-sized materials as the components for the building design.

The user may choose to resize a material element to better fit the design intention. Depending on the material, resizing is constrained to conform to the material's intrinsic dimensional properties. For instance, if the material is a 10-foot-long wooden 2 × 8 joist, then the element's 2-inch width and 8-inch height are constrained, while the length is changeable. The intelligence behind the constraints reflects how one would actually build with the material, helping to create architectural designs that are reasonably constructed.

To guide the placement of the material parts, there are tools, similar to those found on many CAD modeling systems, that aid in locating and aligning the pieces in 3-D space. To accurately position the part in space, one can introduce a 3-D constraining grid of user-defined dimension. The part vertices can be constrained to lie only on the array of grid points. In a similar fashion, the rotation of pieces can be constrained to angular increments to aid in angular alignment. One can also align an object's vertices with another object's vertices with virtual magnets. As one vertex is moved close to another vertex, a "magnetic" attraction drags one vertex on top of the other, making the two vertices coincident. For dimensional feedback, one can use the tape measure tool to ascertain distances and sizes of objects in the model.

Using this set of simple tools, one can quickly build up a well-constructed architectural model, such as this example of a house. The first story of the house consists of an 8-inch load-bearing concrete masonry unit (CMU) component. It is possible to build using larger pieces of 8-inch thick wall, or one can essentially build up the wall one block unit at a time (Figure 8.4), much like one would construct a physical block wall. In between the CMU wall sections are wood-framed infill panels and window units. The second story is a post and beam structural system, with wood-frame floor and roof systems.

At the Workbench, the user can introduce hand-drawn sketches into the design environment. For example, if the goal is to design an addition to an existing building, the user can scan in a drawing of the original house plan or simply place the physical drawing on the Workbench table surface for reference. The Workbench's flexibility in integrating and augmenting traditional design media allows each user to develop a design process that best suits the individual's preferred method of working. Unfortunately, not all types of drawings and models can be placed on the Workbench, as the virtual image can become obscured. This limitation can be avoided by using drawings that permit most of the Workbench's light to transmit though the drawing sheet.

To analyze the interior structure of a model, the sectioning-plane tool is used to cut away parts of the model to reveal any desired plan or section view (Figure 8.5). This type of interactive removal of parts of a model highlights one major advantage of using a virtual model over a physical model. To achieve this type of effect with a physical model would involve significantly more work, as one would have to repeatedly rebuild the model from scratch.

Figure 8.4   *Constructing a wall from a set of building blocks.*

Figure 8.5 *Sectioning the kit-of-parts model.*

It is also possible to allow the user to see the inside of the model by simply giving certain materials a level of transparency. For instance, to see the interior of the first floor, the roof and second floor materials could be made partially transparent. Any of the model's material properties can also be easily changed, and the user could experiment with different material combinations. For example, exterior wall materials could be changed from stucco to clapboard. Or, the user could change the color of the concrete to test compatibility with the color of the windows.

CONCLUSIONS AND FUTURE WORK

The Responsive Workbench is a non-immersive virtual environment that is especially well suited to architectural design applications. Unlike an HMD or a BOOM that require the user to wear or look into large cumbersome display devices, the Workbench requires the user to wear only a light pair of LCD shutterglasses. The non-immersive desk-like nature of the workbench is comfortable for architects and conducive to collaborative design.

We have built a site planning application that allows the architect to quickly visualize site designs. By providing a natural interface for picking and moving the virtual buildings, incorporating changes into a site plan is intuitive. The kit-of-parts application is useful for rapidly prototyping individual buildings. Structures are constructed from components with material-specific dimensional properties and are analyzed with the help of the sectioning tool.

There are a number of additional features that would be especially useful for these two architectural design applications. Gravity and collision detection could provide a much more natural setting for placing virtual objects. Currently, when a building is moved to a new location in the site planning application, it is often difficult to align it with the ground plane. With gravity and collision detection the building could simply be dropped slightly above the ground plane and it would "fall" into place.

While tactile feedback technology needs further development, it would add a new set of interactions to the Workbench environment. For example, using a PHANToM (Massie 1993; Salisbury et al. 1995), which provides a normal force at the fingertip, one could feel the roughness of a particular building material. It would also be possible to directly push parts around in the kit-of-parts environment and feel their mass. The attraction or resistance of two magnetic alignment constraints can be felt by pulling or pushing the user's finger through the PHANToM.

A networked pair of Workbenches opens up the possibility of remote cooperative design. Architects that are in two completely different physical locations could interact as if they were standing across a table from one another. Since both architects view and manipulate the same 3-D model on a Workbench, they would both be able to actively participate in the building's design.

The natural interaction and visualization capabilities of the Responsive Workbench have made it a valuable new tool for architectural design. Although this system is useful for many aspects of the design process, there is still much research to be done. In particular, the user interface could become more natural and intuitive. Technical improvements such as reduced latency and higher accuracy tracking would produce a more realistic virtual environment. Perhaps the most useful enhancement for architects would be the development of more architectural applications that provide for the specific needs of designers. There remains a great demand for devices that can address the unique visualization requirements of architects.

ACKNOWLEDGMENTS

Hans K. Pedersen and Larry Cuttler helped convert the models from Autocad to Wavefront, and Bill Lorensen helped with the tree models. GMD, the German National Research Center for Information Technology, developed part of the software which was used for this project. The project was supported by Interval Research Corporation.

REFERENCES

Cruz-Neira, Carolina, Daniel J. Sandin, and Thomas A. DeFanti. 1993. Surround-screen projection-based virtual reality: The design and implementation of the CAVE. In *Computer Graphics 27 (SIGGRAPH '93 Proceedings)*, edited by James T. Kajiya. (August): 135–142.

Krüger, Wolfgang, and Bernd Fröhlich. 1994. The responsive workbench. *IEEE Computer Graphics and Applications* (May): 12–15.

Krüger, Wolfgang, Christina-A. Bohn, Bernd Fröhlich, Heinrich Schüth, Wolfgang Strauss, and Gerold Wesche. 1995. The responsive workbench: A virtual work environment. *IEEE Computer* (July): 42–48.

MacCormac, R. C. 1974. Froebel's kindergarten gifts and the early work of Frank Lloyd Wright. *Environment and Planning B.* 29–50.

Massie, Thomas. 1993. Design of a three degree of freedom force—reflecting haptic interface. *SB Thesis. MIT EECS Department.*

Salisbury, K., D. Brock, T. Massie, N. Swarup, and C. Zilles. 1995. Haptic rendering: Programming touch interaction with virtual objects. *1995 Symposium on Interactive 3D Graphics.* 123–130.

Virtual reality raises dresden church from rubble. June 11, 1994. *Los Angeles Times.* B–4.

Wright, Frank Lloyd. 1932. *An autobiography, Frank Lloyd Wright.* London: Longman's, Green and Co.

Architectural Education and Virtual Reality Aided Design (VRAD)

Holger Regenbrecht and Dirk Donath
Computer Science in Architecture, Bauhaus University, Weimar, Germany

INTRODUCTION

Currently available computer-aided design systems are conceived with the purpose of generating a two-dimensional drawing and, eventually, attaching to it information and calculation sheets. The nature of the I/O of such systems (i.e., of the interaction techniques and of the two-dimensional output) both in the form of drawings and presentation tools, is therefore two-dimensional, although the data to which it refers is often three-dimensional (3-D). With the newly available Virtual Reality (VR) technology, it is nowadays possible to build a design system that allows full three-dimensionality in all stages of the design process. This chapter describes the conception of a new modeling system, based on VR techniques, which can be used during the early phases of the architectural design process. Such early phases of the design process are characterized by the shaping, in German "die Gestaltung," of the three-dimensional space into architectural forms. The system allows the user, in this case the architect, to experiment with new 3-D interaction and sketching techniques while being immersed in a virtual design space.

VR BASICS AND EXPLORATORY SYSTEMS

Virtual reality can be defined as the component of communication which takes place in a computer-generated synthetic space and that embeds humans (actors) as an integral part of the system. The tangible components of a VR system are the set of the hardware and software providing the actors with a three-dimensional, or even more-dimensional, input/output space, in which, at each instant, the actor can interact in real-time with other autonomous objects.

Under these premises, we define Virtual Reality Aided Design (VRAD) as computer-aided design using the methods of virtual reality. VRAD is nothing particularly new and can be seen as a new application of human-computer communication in VR spaces. In general, communication in virtual reality is characterized through individual differences between the actors, through the presence of a private sphere for each actor, through sensory-motor experiences, and through the relationship between information, navigation, orientation, and the different forms of user expression.

Thus, a virtual reality aided design system has to be configurable for each actor, to be separable into a public and a private sphere, and able to react in a sophisticated way, as well as to offer access to external information and, ultimately, to be navigable (i.e., made of recognizable cues, which are perceived as being non-chaotic and bear correspondencies to the real world).

One main design goal of an VRAD system should be the possibility for the actor to experience the space. This is, according to von Foerster (1991), not possible without active doing. Thus, an interaction space has to be provided in the real world which is large enough to move in an appropriate way, that is, an architecturally sized space. Current virtual reality systems do not provide these capabilities.

A great deal of development and research has been undertaken during the last few years to establish virtual reality techniques in architecture. Most of these systems are simply viewing programs, also known as walk-through systems. With the exception of viewing controls there is no real interaction. Other (research) systems attempt to provide information displays, computer-aided design or planning support in VR. To these belong interesting projects such as the Architectural Space Laboratory (ASL) in Zurich or the Virtual Design / Given project at the Fraunhofer Society / Germany to mention only a few.

Essentially, the geometrical methods that can be used to develop a VRAD system fall into three main categories. In a boundary representation model (BRep), an object is described by points, edges, and faces—by its boundaries. In the second category, constructive solid geometry models (CSG) build the objects from readily available simple geometrical objects. Finally, voxel space models partition the 3-D space into equal elements, each of which represents an atomic element of the space. An object is represented here as a connected set of voxels of the whole space. A BRep model requires a tedious process of construction before an object comes into existence, and therefore distracts from the real task of the first phases of architectural design, where creativity is most important.

CSG models don't allow sketching with 3-D shapes other than those pre-defined and are thus too inflexible for the task of shaping space. Voxel models instead look much more promising, since they allow sufficient fuzziness in the conception phase, but are also accurate enough to provide enough information for rendering on a VR output device.

A few voxel-based approaches are described in Williams (1990) and Galyean and Hughes (1991). The most recent work in voxel-based architectural design has been undertaken by Wang and Kaufman (1995). They use the metaphor of sculpting. A complex 3-D model is derived from a solid material by carving and sawing. This method is promising for the design of highly detailed objects. Through the use of interpolated voxels and textures, Wang and Kaufman attempt to generate realistic looking results. For our purposes such fine graduation in design is not necessary. Our approach is from the opposite end—the coarse, simply "bordered" model, the elementary form.

The previous approaches aim for "near photorealistic" virtual images. This brings with it the resulting well-known problems associated with rendering time, resolution, texturing, and so on. The second major criticism is the limited space of the user's action/movement. Most of today's VR applications are desktop-based, some allowing the user to interact on a one square-meter floor. We want to emphasize the space required for Doing, that supporting a 1:1 experience for the user/actor.

A NEW APPROACH TO SHAPING

Our aim consists of three components: to formulate, develop, and evaluate an architectural design support system through the use of VR space. The exploration and development of design intentions is supplemented by a new method of three-dimensional sketching.

A universal and definite theory that describes the exact *process* of architectural design does not exist. The direction and individual steps of a design are dependent upon the task at hand and the designated site, not to mention the mentality of the architect himself or herself. However, in direct contrast to the process of architectural design, much is known about the *techniques* applied in the design process, in particular with relation to form finding and external expression. The model (working or development model) and the sketch play the most important role as traditional methods of design exploration.

Sketching, in particular, has special importance as a design instrument. The sketch encompasses the entirety of a design, communicating the functionality of a floor plan in addition to its spatial definition. Sketches are the abstracted pictorial intentions of architects. In contrast to the finished architectural drawing, the sketch contains the thoughts and deliberations of the architect. This, as opposed to the drawing, is the early phase of the design process.

Sketching is at once the direct formulation and the description of new ideas. It represents as much a method of feedback and testing as of documentation. The sketch is also the discovery of the unintentional. It occurs as memo, half-formed idea, or thoughts of the moment. The architect Norman Foster describes it as follows: "How can you design the plan, section and facade of a building, without sketching the three-dimensional aspects in the margins, without feeling it through the pen. . . ." (Blaser 1992). Sketching is, therefore, an essential part of the architectural design process.

The developments of voxDesign choose not to exclude the model or the sketch. The possibility to directly and spatially (three dimensionally) design space *expands* the existing working methods of the architects with a third new design technique. The degree to which it will be used and the particular set-up in which it will be applied, is dependent upon the situation and the architect. The defined design environment of the experimental system aims to provide a 1:1 architectural interior space. Through the use of a 4m × 4m physically bound movement space, any form element or spatial situation can be directly described, observed, modified, or discarded.

The Project Atelier Virtual

This project began by setting up a multidisciplinary project group in autumn 1994. Four different disciplines are involved in the project: computer science, architecture, product design, and psychology. At first it was necessary to bring together the multiple views on virtual reality. The main topics of the discussion were:

- ◆ Investigations about real and virtual space including the coherencies
- ◆ Forms of communication and recognition in virtual worlds
- ◆ Navigation in virtual space(s)
- ◆ Interaction with virtual objects
- ◆ Information displaying
- ◆ Questions about ethics and social responsibility

Although the results of this discussion are not that spectacular, this kind of approach was necessary for establishing a workable group. The different and individual views and attitudes were expressed via 3-D modeling and animation tools (non-VR). Some problems are still unresolved, such as realistic versus symbolic information displaying and circumstances in which a private sphere is needed, to mention a few. The discussion and the results are documented in internal publication at the Bauhaus University Weimar (1995) and Weimar home-page. To establish a more precise idea of the possibilities and limitations of VR, two additional sub-projects were set up: the *platform* project and the *voxDesign* project.

VR Equipment

Setting up a high-end virtual reality system is very expensive and often exceeds the budgets of architects. We are using a minimal hardware configuration for virtual reality according to the definition of VR previously given.

The hardware basis is a Silicon Graphics Crimson VGXT with 64 MB of memory. The output is realized with a Virtual Research VR4 head-mounted display (HMD), a video-multiplexer RGB4, and a Commodore monitor for presentation purposes. The tracking system consists of a Polhemus controller unit with a long range transceiver, one HMD-tracker, and a Stylus (or 3Ball) as a pointing device.

The head-mounted display is operated in NTSC monoscopic color mode. The tracking system works with about 60 Hz for each tracker and can track a range of about 5 meters. All the wires are extended and modified for operating in such a large space. We assume that such a configuration will be available at reasonable prices in the next few years. At present the price falls somewhere in the graphics high-end entry/midrange pricing.

Platform

With particular regard to usability tests and other methods of experimental psychology and human-computer interface design it is necessary to provide an appropriate physical environment.

Today's VR research testbeds are characterized typically by unstable laboratory conditions, but for hci testing and development a (real) environment is needed that will free the user/actor from all the technical restrictions (like wires around the legs). Unfortunately, some things are not yet removable and still uncomfortable (especially the head-mounted display), but we are working on it.

To fulfill the desire of a large interacting room, the main design goal of the platform-project was to provide an almost unconstrained physical space of about $4 \times 4 \times 2.5$ meters^3. Within this space there are no obstructions to the movement of the actor. The second goal was to integrate all the technical equipment needed for the VR application (see VR equipment).

Thirdly, there must be an appropriate workspace for the operator and respective software developer. The platform should be used for both public and research presentations/tests and for system development.

The result of the design is shown in Figure 9.1. The actor interacts on a circular floor about 4 meters in diameter. The HMD and the tracker cables are led through a rod-like construction. Integrated into the whole system is all the equipment needed for demonstrations and development. When used for presentations, the audience can follow the interaction process of the virtual world via two additional monitors and an optional large screen.

voxDesign

The software solution "voxDesign" works together with the physical environment platform. Platform provides the free interaction space in the real world.

voxDesign is implemented in C/C++ based on the SGI Graphics Library GL. The main goals of voxDesign are (see also Figure 9.2):

- Realizing a simple (to use and to implement/modify) virtual reality aided design (VRAD) system for the early phases of the architectural design process.
- Providing an experimental system for studying human-computer interfaces in virtual worlds.
- Using the system in architectural and design education.
- Formulation and evaluation of relevant functionality in architectural design.
- Transferring a VR application from the laboratory to real usage.
- Public presentation of the possibilities and limitations of virtual reality.
- A testbed object/subject for multidisciplinary work in the future.
- Testing of software techniques for real-time-critic-systems.

voxDesign is based on the following premises. For architects among others, sketching is an elementary form of the expression of design thoughts. VR extends the traditional sketch methods through the fundamental addition of the third dimension for the design process.

Three-dimensional sketching is used as a medium for communication with other architects or nonprofessionals. The 3-D sketch in VR can, however, additionally be used for immediate reflection and feedback of the design process. The user can operate with the medium of the computer in an intuitive, game-like, experimental way.

(a)

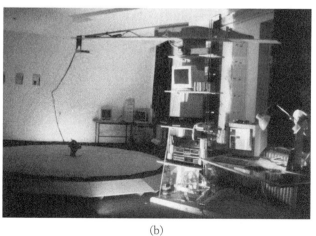

(b)

Figure 9.1   (a) platform as a computer model; (b) a photo of the result.

Figure 9.2 *The main goals of voxDesign.*

The early phases of the architectural design process are characterised by fuzziness, coarse structures and elements, and a trial-and-error process. Searching for form, shape (gestalt) is the principal goal of the designer.

Small cubes (voxels) are a sufficient minimum element for expression in these early phases. They are the virtual equivalent of the Lego brick in the real world. This is an intuitively comprehensible system for the user and avoids the need for extensive training before using the system.

The development of the software is separated into two phases: Phase 1, the so-called "voxDesign0" is already completed and allows the user to set and erase voxel-elements, choose one color of sixteen, load and save voxel spaces (see Figure 9.3). Even with this very simple functionality, it was possible to achieve reasonable design results. "voxDesign0" was necessary to test and evaluate some basic interaction techniques and to formulate the requirements for "voxDesign,1" which forms phase 2 (see Figure 9.4).

In the following section the functionality of "voxDesign1" will be described. "voxDesign1" allows the user/actor to place voxels (cubes with a volume of $2.5 \times 2.5 \times 2.5$ cm^3) into the virtual space. The virtual space is the same size as the real interaction space (i.e., about 40 m^3). A voxel is represented as an untextured, colored (true-color) element. To provide an appropriate design environment it is possible to import three-dimensional CAD models via DXF or pixel pictures (bitmaps) into the system. In addition to this, the platform provides an analog audio environment with loudspeakers. The virtual design space is lit by two ambient lights and two spot lights.

The designer can load and save the virtual model. For presentation purposes a snapshot function has been implemented. With this function it is possible to print out some views of the model after finishing or during the design session. With the platform environment it is also possible to record

three simple functions
set / erease
change color
save

evaluation
and formulation
for voxDesign 1

voxDesign o

usability tests

Figure 9.3 *Phase 1 of software development.*

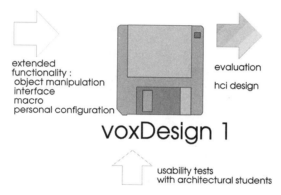

extended
functionality :
object manipulation
interface
macro
personal configuration

evaluation

hci design

voxDesign 1

usability tests
with architectural students

Figure 9.4 *Phase 2 of software development.*

the session on video tape. Changing the different modes and actions in voxDesign1 is very simple: You twist the pointing device toward your face. After twisting, a three-dimensional menu appears at the current position in virtual space. The actor chooses the desired option and continues the design process. All user-specific parameters are saved in a configuration file and can be overwritten with command-line options. An X-Windows-based starting interface is currently under development. This simple functionality allows initial design thoughts to be expressed in an easy-to-use way. Resulting examples are shown in Figures 9.5a, b, and c.

USING VOXDESIGN IN EDUCATIONAL TRAINING

It is still not usual practice at European universities to confront students with VR techniques in practice. We decided to provide such an opportunity to

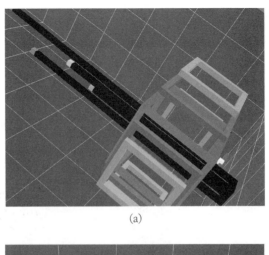

(a)

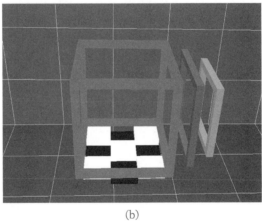

(b)

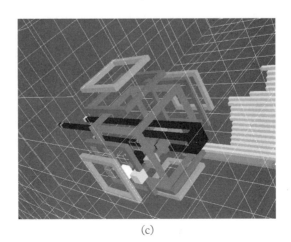

(c)

Figure 9.5a, b, c   *Three views of the virtual model.*

about a dozen senior and graduate students in architecture. Our intention was to give them a new tool to express their design ideas, not to teach them the basics of architectural design.

They had to solve an architectural design task in virtual space. The two main topics for the students were to describe their design thought with voxDesign and to reflect the process of the design variants using this new technology. One side effect of this course for us was the possibility of a first set of usability tests.

The given task was not that spectacular and actually not that important: to design a personal (individual) virtual student room with all communicational and housing structures only in the very early phases of the design process. The complete design was to take place in virtual space (the voxel room). For presentation purposes the students were allowed to edit the model or views of the model with external programs, although the design idea itself had to be developed in the voxel space.

Before entering the course most of our students had the following skills and knowledge:

- Knowledge of the basics of computer-aided architectural design (CAAD)
- Experience in architectural design using the traditional techniques and tools
- No knowledge of or experience with virtual reality
- Experience in setting up architectural models
- Readiness to explore a new terrain

One main goal was to give the students a feeling of what virtual reality can be. After finishing the course we wanted the students to be able to distinguish between the facts and fiction, to know the possibilities and limitations of this technique, and to estimate its influence on social life and especially on their own profession. For these reasons the course covered the following topics, in addition to practical work with the system:

- The fundamentals of virtual reality
- VR applications in general and especially in architecture
- The history of computer graphics and VR
- Basics in using workstations and local- and wide-area networks
- Basics in digital model and picture handling
- The social and psychological impact of virtual reality now and in the future

- Ecological aspects of virtual reality and computers in general
- Questions of perception and cognition using VR techniques
- Some philosophical aspects of (virtual) reality (especially radical constructivism)
- Some aspects of the theory of media

For more details on this course see http://www.uni-weimar.de/iar.

The discussions about the general and theoretical subjects were very fruitful for both staff and students. Thinking beyond one's own professional borders broadens one's field of view, not only in the context of virtual reality.

The practical sessions took place in our atelier (virtual) room. It is a 40 m^3 room with two workstations, two personal computers, and the platform, not to mention the coffee maker, a lot of literature, records and CDs, and presentation equipment with 24-hour room and Internet access, a conference table, and a lot of ashtrays. For special presentations a video-beamer was connected to the system so the inside of the virtual space could be displayed on a 4 × 3 m^2 screen; this was very impressive. For the auditory, the actor acted inside the virtual space.

The number of students and the *voxel-time* was limited because there was only one virtual reality system available. Each student used our VR system about seven hours in practice to realize the design task, each session lasting an average of one hour (between 30 minutes and 3 hours). Using the system longer than one hour led to simulator sickness in about one third of the students. The students liked the home-like ambience in our atelier and the close contact to the staff (tutor, assistant, professor) too. In general, the discussions about interdisciplinary subjects helped us to understand the complexity of this new technology.

The results of the design task were very different from traditional techniques (see student work results). In a very different way the students tried to use and explore the new medium. Most of them left pure real-world metaphors (like chair, table, wardrobe) and "played out" the other opportunities and properties of virtual space like the absence of gravity or static laws.

The first attempts of the students to go into design details or to express very accurate structures were not successful because of the coarse voxel structure (2.5 cm grid) and the limited functional features. In the actual use of the system our approach to sketching was very limited. So with this kind of usability experience it would be more accurate to talk about "bricking." At a certain number of set voxel, it is necessary to sketch with voxDesign like a three-dimensional pen; it is necessary to set voxel after voxel. Offering faster workstations to the students would solve this problem, but nevertheless, the attempt to support the early phases of the architectural design process is possible with this sketching/bricking method. Further results in brief were:

- The Stylus exhibited very good usability including the twist mode.
- Sometimes there were problems with the stability of the tracking system.
- Sixteen colors are enough for the design task.
- The system was slowed rapidly with applied textures as an environment; the textures were useful only for presentation purposes.
- Using sound as a design environment was very welcome.
- During long sessions the students tended to lay down on the floor during the design process.
- The most spectacular effect was to "experience" a virtual structure by just going around it.
- A stereoscopic head-mounted display is not that necessary; other depth cues are much more important.
- The students confirmed our assumed voxel size as fine enough for this phase of the architectural design process.
- The rendering method is absolutely unimportant for the usage of the system (flat, gouraud, phong).
- Unfortunately, there was not enough time to edit the voxel models inside another CAD or animation program.
- Primitive CAD functions were missed, like line, wall, circle.
- At about 2,000 voxel set into the virtual space the system was slowed down extremely.
- The selectable value for the field of view is very dependent on the individual (between 30 and 100 degrees).
- The estimated duration time by the student was shorter every time than the real-time.
- Most of the students were immersed (or at least involved) in the virtual voxel space during their design sessions.
- All the external controls of the program should be integrated into the virtual world, such as field of view control, loading and unloading textures, switching between different variants/models.
- For longer periods of usage the head-mounted display is not very comfortable.
- Using a pen metaphor as a pointing device seemed to be the right decision; the students associated it with sketching.

- As assumed, uncomfortable wires were no longer a problem for using the system (see platform).
- There should be more depth cues in virtual space, like fog (aerial pollution), reference objects, well-placed light sources, perhaps spatial sound applied to the objects and the space.

To give a better impression of the system discussed in this chapter, here are four examples of selected student work (Figures 9.6–9.9). These pieces are only selected snapshots of the students' work. Every student tried out many variants and situations. But this will give an impression to the reader what is possible if students work with such a system under the circumstances previously mentioned.

LIMITATIONS AND FUTURE WORK

We will continue teaching with voxDesign because of the positive feedback from our students. We are also proud to present this work at cebit '96, the

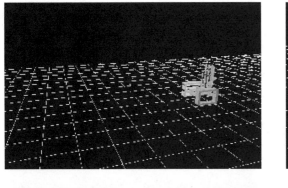
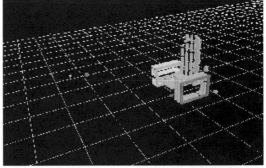
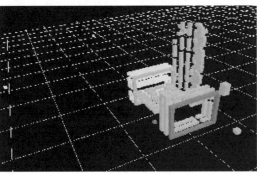
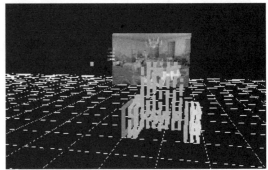

Figure 9.6   Michael Oelschlaeger.

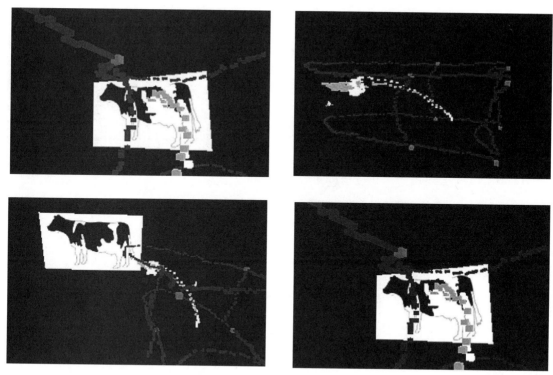

Figure 9.7   Birgit Felsch.

world's largest fair in computer science, this year to be held in Hannover, Germany. With this presentation we can give an example of and a starting point for discussion about using new technologies in university education.

The use of the system without any knowledge of a UNIX system would be desirable because the teaching time will be much more useful for learning the VRAD system. A lot of time was wasted in using DTP (desktop publishing) programs and network-wide file handling too. The environment of such a system should be useable in the same intuitive way as the VR system itself, but that is a very difficult task. It would be desirable, too, if every student in architecture could get the necessary education in using computer environments.

The architectural office of the future will not be as traditionally equipped as today. We believe making our attempt to teach students to work with virtual reality is both risky and necessary. On the one hand, only a few architectural offices are fully equipped with CAD stations, but on the other hand, using computer-aided design techniques, including virtual reality, will have a growing influence on more and more architects and living in general. One main task of a university is to prepare the students for the future and our con-

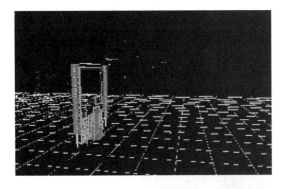
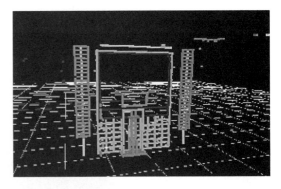

Figure 9.8 *Peter Bringt.*

tribution is only one piece of the puzzle. While introducing new technologies to the students, a feeling for social responsibility should be encouraged or even required by the teachers. Our attempt is very humble but we think it is a step in the right direction.

The system in its current manifestation cannot satisfy all the needs of the early design phases. A step-by-step approach is, however, necessary to explore and evaluate the right techniques and to formulate the right questions. Developing and testing human-computer interfaces is necessarily an experimental task. Our solution does not support multi-user-design (CSCW). It is doubtful whether there is a real need for this in the early formulative design phases.

More interesting are problems surrounded by the sensory-motor experience. How can we improve the immediate design feedback? We are looking for practicable, useable techniques. The state of the art in force, tactile, and auditory feedback is not yet satisfactory. More promising is perhaps the approach with graspable user interfaces as mentioned Fitzmaurice, Ishii, and Buxton (1995). We will try to adapt these methods to our VR system. The current size of the interaction space, and therefore the virtual space in a 1:1

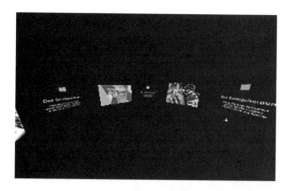

Figure 9.9   *Matthias Beyer.*

experience system, is also too small; the area of design tasks is reduced to the scale of product and interior design. We are attempting to extend this space using long-range tracking methods.

Not yet resolved are the problems associated with rendering speed and resolution with large numbers of voxels. We are currently working on an algorithmic solution. In addition to this, we hope that the graphics and machine power of the computers of the future will increase.

There are many more methodical and technological problems to solve. Our focus is set on defining a wider set of architectural form-generating functions. Some theoretical investigations have been undertaken on this subject. We have defined some general principles for object generation and manipulation, extending the voxel idea with elements from Brep and CSG models. In this case, an object is described by points, lines, and faces. Moving a point will generate a line, moving a line will generate a face, and so on (see Figures 9.10–9.13). We want to evaluate this hybrid way of acting through extensive usability tests. In addition to this, we are investigating the need for free-shape and unconstrained functionality in virtual space. Could this influence the real (buildable) design? Could this lead to a VR style in design?

An additional development is to integrate dynamic gesture recognition into voxDesign. This could dramatically improve the intuitive handling of the system.

We are trying to involve the potential user as much as possible in all stages of the developmental work. For this reason, most of the research is the result of multidisciplinary university courses. This has two major benefits: There is an immediate and constant feedback of research results; and secondly, the students are confronted with state-of-the-art technology.

Our next substantial steps are as follows:

- Extending voxDesign with more VRAD functionality: For this reason we applied for a research grant from the DFG (German Research Society)
- Academic research on immersion and abstraction in virtual worlds based on theoretical work and user tests
- The development of networked personal virtual worlds
- Investigations and implementations hopefully answering some special questions about navigation and displaying of informational structures in virtual space

Finally, the ethical and social questions that arise from VR are just as much an integral part of our work. We cannot and do not want to ignore these questions.

Figure 9.10 *Object described by points, lines, and faces.*

Figure 9.11 *Object described by points, lines, and faces.*

Figure 9.12 *Object described by points, lines, and faces.*

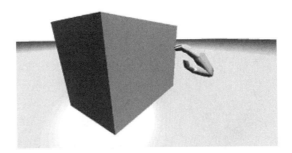

Figure 9.13   *Object described by points, lines, and faces.*

ACKNOWLEDGMENTS

We gratefully acknowledge the support of Charles Wuethrich. Furthermore, our current work would be impossible without the great efforts of all the members of the "atelier, virtual", especially of Martin Kohlhaas, Thomas Schubert, Thore Schmidt-Tjarksen, and Jan Springer. Tracy Bartholomew turned our German English into English, thank you. Thanks also to Joerg Lehmann for his contribution to this paper.

REFERENCES

Bauhaus University-Weimar WWW-home-page. http://www.uni-weimar.de

Blaser, E., ed. 1992. Norman Foster sketches. Birkhaeuser Verlag Basel.

Briefe an vradmin@. 1995. Internal publication at the Bauhaus University, Weimar.

Butterworth, J., A. Davidson, S. Hench, and T. Olano. 1992. 3DM: A three-dimensional modeler using a head-mounted display. *Proceedings*. 1992 Symposium on Interactive 3D Graphics. In *Computer Graphics*, (special issue 1992), ACM SIGGRAPH.

Coquillart, S. 1990. Extended free-form deformation: A sculpting tool for 3d geometric modeling. In *Computer Graphics* 24 no. 4 (August): 187–196.

Dagit, Charles E. III. 1993. Establishing virtual design environments in archi-tectural practice. ed. Flemming, van Wyk. *Proceedings of caad futures '93*. Elsevier Publishers.

DIVISION Ltd. Books to dVs and dVise. dvs2@division.demon.co.uk.

Donath, D., and H. Regenbrecht. 1995. Virtual Reality Aided Design (VRAD) in the early phases of the architectural design process. In *Proceedings of caad futures '95*. Singapore.

Encarnacao, J., M. Goebel, and L. Rosenblum. 1994. European activities in virtual reality. In *Computer Graphics and Applications* 14. no. 1 (January).

Fitzmaurice, George W., Hiroshi Ishii, and William Buxton. 1995. Bricks: laying the foundations for graspable user interfaces. *CHI '95*, Denver, Colorado: ACM Press.

Foerster, Heinz v. 1995. Entecken oder Erfinden. Wie laesst sich Verstehen verstehen? In Watzlawick *Einfuehrung in den Konstruktivismus* Frankfurt/M., Germany: Suhrkamp.

Galyean, Tinsley A., and John F. Hughes. 1991. Sculpting: an interactive volumetric modeling technique. In *Computer Graphics* 25, no. 4 (July).

HIT Lab Overview and Projects 1991. Human Interface Technology Laboratory Seattle/WA/USA Technical Report No. HITL-P-91-1.

Pentland, A., I. Essa, M. Friedmann, B. Horowitz, and S. Sclaroff. 1990. The ThingWorld Modeling System: virtual sculpting by modal forces. *Proceedings*. 1990 Symposium on Interactive 3D Graphics. In *Computer Graphics* 24 no. 2 (March 1990) ACM SIGGRAPH.

Regenbrecht, Holger. 1994. Virtuelle Realitaet und Design. *Diplomarbeit.* HAB Weimar.

Riedel, Oliver. 1993. Virtual Reality: Stand der Anwendung in Architektur, Buerogestaltung und Produktdesign. Proceedings Building Management 93 Symposium: *Virtuelle Realitaet-Technik & Anwendungen* (15.6.93).

Schmitt, Gerhard. 1993. Virtual Reality in architecture. In *Virtual Worlds and Multimedia,* edited by Thalman. New York: John Wiley & Sons.

Superscape VRT. 1993. *User Manual.* Reference Manual Dimension International Version 3 (21 May).

Thompson, J. 1993. *Virtual Reality—An International Directory of Research Projects* Meckler Westport.

Wang, Sidney W., and Arie E. Kaufman. 1995. Volume sculpting. 1995 Symposium on Interactive 3D Graphics. Monterey CA: ACM Press.

Williams, L. 1990. 3d paint. In *Computer Graphics* 24(2) (March): 225–233.

WorldToolKit for Windows. 1993. *Users' Guide,* Libraries Version 2.0 (Beta) Sense8 Corp. (Nov 19).

10

Architectural Realities

Virtual Reality Case Studies at Calibre Institute

Jo M. Mantelers
Calibre Institute, Faculty of Architecture, Urban Planning and Management
Eindhoven University of Technology, The Netherlands

INTRODUCTION

The Calibre Institute is an institute for research and development in the area of information technology and automation in the building industry. One of the main subjects has been the use of digital presentation media in the architectural design process.

For several years, the use of digital presentation media mainly focussed on the visualisation of architectural concepts using 3-D computer graphics. These (passive) media proved to be a powerful addition to existing presentation media. Unsurpisingly, one can determine a full acceptance of this type of media in the building industry.

One of the reasons for this acceptance has been the growing adaptation of CAD systems to the needs of the building industry, both in cost and functionality, and the resulting low threshold to introduce 3-D computer graphics as an additional facility in a building company. Another reason has been the familiarity with presentations using (3-D) graphics; hand-made artists impressions and scale models are almost as old as civilization. Three-dimensional computer graphics are in this perspective nothing more than a substitution.

Virtual Reality technology, on the other hand, is all but a substitution: It is an extrapolation and unification of several existing media. To obtain satisfactory results this medium puts a high demand on the hardware and software, as well as on an organization; therefore, steps towards acceptance are relatively hard to take.

In this, the Calibre Institute saw its task to develop tools and techniques by which existing CAD technology and Virtual Reality technology can be linked or merged, thus lowering the threshold of acceptance. Without hesitation, it can be said that during the time the Calibre Institute has been working with Virtual Reality technology, huge progress can be seen with respect to the practical applicability of this technology in the architectural design process. In the following paragraphs, several aspects of this development will be discussed in relation to case projects done by the institute over the last three years.

CASE STUDIES

ESPEQ: Design Presentation

PROJECT DATA

Date: January 1993
Client: Innovatiecentrum Alkmaar and ESPEQ Opleidingsbedrijven, Heerhugowaard, the Netherlands
Software: AutoCAD (modelling), Division dVS and custom software (VR)
Hardware: Division ProVision 200
Site location: Tuitjenhorn, the Netherlands
Architect: Zeeman Architecten, Hoorn, the Netherlands
Development time: 3 months

The ESPEQ case study was the development of a Virtual Reality presentation of a housing project (Figure 10.1). Although this presentation was initially aimed at people who had an interest in the project, those people who had an interest in Virtual Reality also came. The presentation was announced as a first Virtual Open House. Each person was able to walk through the 3-D design model and move the furniture and fittings.

During this case study consideration has been given to the relationship between the interfaces which exist between the user and the system, the level of detail of the model, and the speed of the representation. In consultation with the principal and the architect, the representation based on illumination simulation was assessed. After several adaptations to the model, the functionality of the system was tested before it was to be used by possible interested parties. Finally,

Figure 10.1 *The ESPEQ Virtual Open House.*

various illustrative sounds were linked to the design model which could be made audible in certain preprogrammed cases.

For the presentation of the design of the house the whole system was accommodated at a special location, which was where it was supposed to be built in reality. Interested parties got the opportunity to perceive the interior immersively with the aid of a head-mounted display and also walk around it with the help of a 6-DOF input device. In order to make the presentation more attractive, the users were able to move several items of furniture and also to pick up various articles.

The presentation was enthusiastically received and favourably judged by the principal, the designer, interested parties, journalists, and TV and radio.

Hertog van Lotharingen: Design Evaluation and Presentation

PROJECT DATA

Date: January 1994
Client: Woningstichting Hertog Hendrik van Lotharingen, Eindhoven, the Netherlands

Software: AutoCAD (modelling), custom software (VR)
Hardware: Sun Microsystems SPARCstation 10ZX
Architect: Groosman Partners BV Rotterdam, the Netherlands
Site location: Eindhoven, the Netherlands
Development time: 4 weeks

The case study of Hertog van Lotharingen focused on the use of Virtual Reality during a design process. The system was used for the evaluation of visibility and safety aspects for a housing project (Figure 10.2). The use of the system was initially only aimed at the designer and the principal. Based on their evaluation of the design in the end, different design modifications were effected. After this the system was also used for internal presentations, of applications as well as of technology. This application for the evaluation and presentation of an architectural design has been developed for a full-immersive and a partial-immersive system. The problem which played a part during this study was first a design problem and a technical problem in the second instance.

On the basis of design drawings, a 3-D computer model of the buildings and their immediate environment was produced. The emphasis here was on the exterior of the buildings and the designed underground parking since the principal and the designer were to

Figure 10.2 *Bird's eye view at the housing project.*

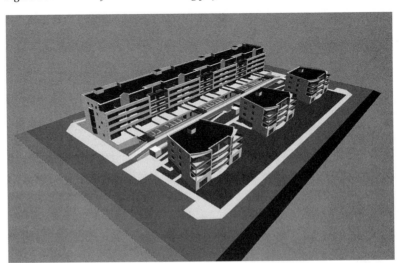

investigate some of the safety aspects of this parking provision. In doing this, they wanted in particular to evaluate the possible visual monitoring of the parking area and of the footpath between the parking garage and the houses. This meant that consideration had to be given to the lighting of the open spaces, the mass of the construction, and the facades of the buildings.

During the modelling, these visual and safety aspects were taken into account as much as possible. Furthermore, account was taken of the possibilities and the limitations of the Virtual Reality systems which were finally to be used. The computer model was provided with color and lighting characteristics, and was converted for use in the Virtual Reality system. The principal and the designer had control over the final design model.

The case study led to the situation where several expectations with regard to the impact of some design decisions were confirmed. By experimenting with the technology several other conclusions with respect to the design model were made, which led to some changes in the design: Virtual Reality had made a contribution to the quality of a design solution. Following the use of Virtual Reality for the evaluation of design solutions, several more presentations were made for the employees and relations of the principal. For this reason an additional interior model of one of the apartments was modelled and added. This additional model was converted for use within the partial-immersive Virtual Reality system. The possibility of putting the two types of Virtual Reality systems next to one another in practice raised interesting questions both for the research and for the presentation itself.

Office of the Future: Design Presentation

PROJECT DATA

Date: August 1994
Client: Kantoor van de Toekomst NV, Den Bosch, the Netherlands
Software: AutoCAD (modelling), custom software (VR)
Hardware: Sun Microsystems SPARCstation 20ZX
Architect: Esenso, Zeist, the Netherlands
Site location: Den Bosch, the Netherlands
Development time: 4 weeks

The Office of the Future is an exhibition center for innovative office and business technology (Figure 10.3). The office offers companies

Figure 10.3 *Interior view of the Office of the Future.*

that are involved in the office as participants an environment to exhibit and test products and concepts, and facilitates a platform for discussion.

The Calibre Institute contributed to the office via a Virtual Reality demonstration setup, showing state-of-the-art Virtual Reality technology in relation to the use in the building industry. The demonstration setup focused on two applications showing the use of Virtual Reality technology.

The first application showed the use of VR for guided and unguided walk-throughs of existing and nonexisting buildings. To enable multiuser walk-throughs, a stereoscopic projection system for active glasses was set up to project the images. Several *Virtual tours* were developed for the demonstration setup; among others was a tour through the Office of the Future, which showed not only the interior of the office, but also specific (behavioral) aspects of exhibition items presented in the office.

The second application demonstrated in the setup was the use of immersive Virtual Reality for single-user walk-throughs. For this application an interior model of a part of the Office of the Future was created in which the user could walk around and interact with interior elements through picking and relocating.

MIPIM '95

In January 1995 an elaborate research project started in partnership with the Dutch building engineering company Starke Diekstra. Starke Diekstra saw Virtual Reality as a tool to improve communication between the participants of the building process through objective design presentation and evaluation.

In order to make current and potential clients familiar with the possibilities of Virtual Reality, several representative applications were developed by the Calibre Institute and Starke Diekstra. The aim was to show the added value of Virtual Reality as a substitute for a design prototype for the evaluation of a design. The problem was defined by the required size and complexity of the architectural models in order to enable an adequate simulation and evaluation of several aspects of the building process, and by composing a Virtual Reality platform (hardware and software) that could meet the requirements.

The final result of the project consisted of two applications: the presentation, evaluation, and simulation of (aspects of) the head office of Schiphol Airport in Amsterdam, and a representation of the Taj Mahal in Agra, India. Both applications were presented at the MIPIM '95 conference in Cannes, France and an international conference on real estate.

NV Luchthaven Schiphol: Design Evaluation and Simulation

PROJECT DATA

Date: March 1995
Client: Starke Diekstra Project Managers, Nieuwegein, the Netherlands
Software: AutoCAD, 3D Studio (modelling), Sense8 WorldToolKit and custom software (VR)
Hardware: Silicon Graphics Onyx RealityEngine2
Architect: Architektenburo Quist BV, Rotterdam, the Netherlands
Site location: Amsterdam, the Netherlands
Development time: 2 months

In this application the focus was set on simulation of several visual, functional, and technical aspects of a design, the head office of Schiphol Airport (Figure 10.4). These aspects were a visual simulation via Virtual walk-throughs and Virtual wayfinding, functional

Figure 10.4   *Head office of Schiphol Airport: exterior.*

simulation via a Virtual fire drill and Virtual furnishing, and technical simulation via Virtual alterations and Virtual lighting.

VIRTUAL WALK-THROUGH

This application can be characterized by a low level of interactivity: The user can explore the surroundings and the entrence hall of the office building without constraints (Figure 10.5). The application is therefore purely a visual simulation of the building and its surroundings.

VIRTUAL WAYFINDING

In this visual simulation the key aspect is to evaluate the way signs are designed and located in the building to enable wayfinding (Figure 10.6). In the model several signs are located and evaluated by the user. In addition, auditive information is integrated in the application to assist the user during the exploration of the building.

VIRTUAL FIRE DRILL

One of the most powerful aspects of Virtual Reality is the presence of a (real) time dimension, with which time-dependent processes can be directed. One of the most common examples of such processes is gravity. In real life emer-

Figure 10.5 *The main hall of the head office of Schiphol Airport.*

Figure 10.6 *View of office interior during wayfinding simulation.*

gency situations the time aspect is often a major factor that determines the way processes take place: The longer a visitor is in a building in which a fire burns, the more his life is in danger.

These common characteristics are combined in the Virtual fire drill application (Figure 10.7). In this application the visitor has to find his way out of the building after a smoke alarm is activated. The longer it takes to do so, the more his vision is obstructed due to an increasing smoke density in time. With this functional simulation the quality of the design can be evaluated with respect to emergency routes.

VIRTUAL FURNISHING

This application shows possibilities to refurnish an office by relocating interior elements. The relocation is constrained based on ergonomical criteria. New furnishment situations can be evaluated on the spot.

VIRTUAL ALTERATIONS

In this technical simulation the design model itself can be altered by replacing building components or by changing the texture and color of building components. These alterations have to be predefined, which means that the designer

Figure 10.7 *View of an office room during fire drill simulation.*

has to develop design alternatives and implement the alternatives. In the Virtual alteration application the user can change the color of the carpet and replace a solid interior wall by a transparent glass wall (Figures 10.8 and 10.9).

VIRTUAL LIGHTING

Lighting situations can be simulated using various techniques that can be distinguished by the level of realism of the resulting lighting simulation model and the necessary performance of the hardware (Figure 10.10). In the Virtual lighting application, radiosity simulation techniques are applied that result in a very high level of realism, but at the same time put a high demand on the hardware in order to achieve an optimal respresention of the simulation model. Besides the high level of realism, the application is also characterized by several dynamic features: The user can dim separate light sources and replace a lighting situation by another, predefined, lighting situation.

Taj Mahal: Design Representation

PROJECT DATA

Date: March 1995
Client: Starke Diekstra Project Managers, Nieuwegein, the Netherlands

Figure 10.8 *Solid interior wall before alteration.*

Figure 10.9 *Interior wall after alteration.*

Figure 10.10 *Lighting simulation model.*

*Software: AutoCAD, 3D Studio (modelling), Sense8 WorldToolKit and custom
    software (VR)*
Hardware: Silicon Graphics Onyx RealityEngine2
Site location: Agra, India
Development time: 2 months

The Taj Mahal in Agra, India, is an impressive example of oriental
architecture. To explore this building using Virtual Reality was a
great challenge; therefore, the Calibre Institute and Starke Diekstra
decided to attempt to represent the mausoleum in all its aesthetic
quality. In co-operation with an Indian firm a 3-D computer model
was made, after which the elaborate texturing of the Taj Mahal had
to be applied. This latter proved to be the most complex aspect in
developing the application, since all necessary visual data, gathered
from different media, had to undergo elaborate modification in
order to achieve the desired visual result and desired real-time performance of 25 stereoscopic images per second.

The result is an atmospheric Virtual Reality application in
which the user can explore and experience the exterior and interior
of the Taj Mahal (Figures 10.11, 10.12, 10.13).

Figure 10.11   *Taj Mahal: exterior.*

Figure 10.12   *Taj Mahal: interior.*

Figure 10.13   *Bird's eye view on the interior model of the Taj Mahal.*

Augmented Reality Applications in Architectural Construction[1]

Anthony Webster
Associate Professor of Architecture, Graduate School of Architecture,
Columbia University and Associate Member, ASCE

Steven Feiner
Associate Professor of Computer Science, School of Engineering and Applied Science,
Columbia University

Blair MacIntyre
Graduate Research Assistant, Department of Computer Science, Columbia University

William Massie
Adjunct Assistant Professor of Architecture, Columbia University

Theodore Krueger
Adjunct Associate Professor of Architecture, Columbia University

INTRODUCTION

A variety of computer technologies and computer science techniques are now used by researchers aiming to improve aspects of architectural design, construction, and maintenance. Virtual reality systems are used to envision modified cityscapes, and to assess the impact of proposed buildings (Novitski 1994). Both virtual reality and conventional computer systems are currently used in demonstration testbeds to simulate complex construction operations.

---

[1] An earlier version of this article was published in the proceedings of the American Society of Civil Engineers' Third Congress in Computing in Civil Engineering as *Augmented Reality in Architectural Construction, Inspection, and Renovation.* It is reprinted here by permission of the American Society of Civil Engineers.

These systems promise to improve the optimization of construction operations and to allow checks of constructability and maintainability before building materials are ordered (Virtual 1995; Oloufa 1993); integrated structural, architectural, and mechanical building databases are being combined with engineering expertise to create knowledge-based systems for improving the design process (Myers et al. 1992). Robotics systems, mostly adapted from the automotive industry, have also been used recently in experimental and commercial attempts to automate various aspects of building construction (Webster 1994; Richards 1994).

AUGMENTED REALITY APPLICATIONS IN ARCHITECTURE AND STRUCTURAL ENGINEERING

Recent advances in computer interface design, and the ever-increasing power and miniaturization of computer hardware, have combined to make the use of *augmented reality* possible in demonstration testbeds for building construction, maintenance, and renovation. In the spirit of the first see-through head-mounted display developed by Sutherland (Sutherland 1968), we and other researchers (e.g., Robinett, 1992; Caudell and Mizell 1992; Bajura and Neumann 1995) use the term *augmented reality* to refer to enrichment of the real world with a complementary virtual world. The augmented reality systems we are developing employ a see-through head-worn display that overlays graphics and sound on a person's naturally occurring sight and hearing. By tracking users and objects in space, these systems provide users with visual information that is tied to the physical environment. Unlike most virtual realities, whose virtual worlds replace the real world, augmented reality systems enhance the real world by superposing information onto it. The spatial tracking capabilities of our augmented reality systems distinguish them from the heads-up displays featured in some wearable computer systems (Quinn 1993; Patents 1994; Smailagic and Siewiorek 1994).

As part of a program aimed at developing a variety of high-performance user interfaces, we have begun work on two augmented reality systems for use in structural engineering and architectural applications. The first, called "Architectural Anatomy," creates an augmented reality that shows users portions of a building that are hidden behind architectural or structural finishes, and allows them to see additional information about the hidden objects. We have built structural and architectural models of parts of Columbia's Schapiro Center for Engineering and Physical Science Research, including the Computer Graphics and User Interfaces Lab, which provide data for use in this "x-ray vision" demonstration system. The model is based on the as-built construction drawings provided by the building's architects. Our prototype application overlays a graphical representation of portions of the building's structural systems over a user's view of the room in which he or she is standing. A see-through head-mounted display provides the user with monocular augmented graphics and tracks the position and orientation of the head with an ultrasonic tracking system (Figure 11.1).

Figure 11.2 is a view of a corner of the Computer Graphics and User Interfaces Lab photographed through a version of our head-mounted display that is designed to be worn by a 35mm camera. The overlaid virtual world visible in this figure includes the outlines of parts of three support columns and the space between the structural concrete floor and the raised lab floor above it. The middle, larger column is inside the protrusion in the corner. The two other, smaller columns are actually located in nearby rooms. The mouse cursor is visible near the front right corner of the top of the desk. By clicking on a column with the mouse, our prototype allows the user to see more information. In Figure 11.3, the user has looked up and slightly to the right and has selected the middle column that contained the cursor in Figure 11.2. This causes the outlines of the other support structures to dim. (This project's display hardware is one-bit deep, so dimming is accomplished through the use of different line styles; in this case, dotted lines.) As shown in Figure 11.3, the re-bar inside the column is revealed and a structural analysis of the column is presented to the user. The analysis is provided by Dast, a commercially available structural analysis and design program (Das 1993).

Our prototype system is written in a combination of the C, C++, and CLIPS programming languages and runs on the UNIX operating system. Each component of the system runs in a separate process, allowing the computational work to be distributed over multiple machines. The graphics component runs on an Intel 486-based PC-compatible machine. The remaining components, such as the tracker controller, run on a wide variety of UNIX-based machines. Our head-worn display uses a Reflection Technology Private Eye display whose image is reflected by a mirror beam splitter. A Logitech ultrasonic tracker provides position and orientation tracking (the display and triangular tracker receiver are shown in Figure 11.1).

The display's graphics are rendered in software at 720×280 resolution and, in the application

Figure 11.1   The see-through, head mounted display and ultrasonic tracker used in our first architectural augmented reality system.

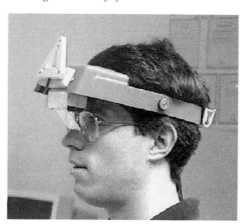

Figure 11.2 A corner of the Computer Graphics and User Interfaces lab as seen through the head-mounted display. Overlaid graphics show the outline of three columns and the space between the raised floor and the structural concrete floor below.

described here, include 3-D vectors without hidden-line removal. We provide support for 2-D applications such as the structural analysis of the column through a full memory-mapped X11 Window System (Scheifler & Gettys 1986) server. The X11 bitmap is treated as if it were projected onto a portion of the surface of a virtual sphere surrounding the user and is composited with the bitmap containing the 3-D graphics for presentation on the head-mounted display (Feiner et al. 1993).

Our augmented reality testbed allows an X11 window to be positioned so that a selected point on the window is fixed at an arbitrary position within the 3-D world. We refer to such windows as *world-fixed* windows to distinguish them from windows that are fixed to the display itself or to the body-tracked virtual sphere. Building on our work on knowledge-based augmented reality for maintenance and repair (Feiner, MacIntyre & Seligmann 1993), we are developing a knowledge-based system that will dynamically control which parts of the structural system are displayed to satisfy the user's goals in exploring the environment.

We have recently developed another augmented reality testbed system that addresses spaceframe construction. Spaceframes are typically made from a large number of components of similar size and shape (typically cylindrical struts and spherical nodes). Although the exterior dimensions of all the members may be identical, the forces they carry, and therefore their inner diameters, vary with their position in the structure. Consequently it is relatively easy to assemble pieces in the wrong position—which if undetected could lead to structural failure. Our augmented reality construction system is designed to guide workers through the assembly of a spaceframe structure, to ensure that each member is properly placed and fastened.

Figure 11.3 Detail of a column as seen through the head-mounted display. The column in the middle has been selected by the user, causing its re-bar to be shown, and a structural analysis of it to be displayed in a window.

Our prototype spaceframe structure, shown in Figure 11.4, is a diamond-shaped, full-scale aluminum system manufactured by Starnet International (Starnet 1995). We have created a 3-D computer model of the spaceframe, an ordered list

of assembly steps, and a digitized set of audio files containing instructions for each step. Undergraduate Computer Science, Engineering, and Architecture students helped develop the testbed as part of an NSF-sponsored educational grant in conjunction with the Columbia University Teachers College. The head-worn display used in this project is a *Virtual I/O* see-through stereoscopic color display with integral headphones and orientation tracker (Figure 11.5). Position tracking is provided by an Origin Instruments DynaSight optical radar tracker, which tracks small targets on the head-mounted display. The user interface also includes a hand-held barcode reader, which has an optical target mounted on it, and is also tracked by the DynaSight.

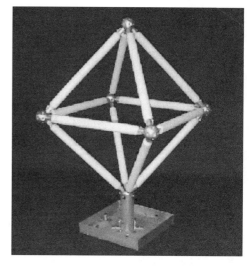

Figure 11.4 *Spaceframe structure used in our augmented reality spaceframe construction system.*

The spaceframe is assembled one component (strut or node) at a time. For each step of construction, the augmented reality system:

- Directs the worker to a pile of parts and tells her which part to pick up. This is currently done by playing a sound file containing verbal instructions.
- Confirms that she has the correct piece. This is done by having her scan a barcode on the component.
- Directs her to install the component. A virtual image of the next piece, with a textual description fixed near it, indicates where to install the component (Figure 11.6), and verbal instructions played from a sound file explain how to install it.
- Confirms that the component is installed in the right place by asking her to scan the component with the tracked barcode reader to verify its location.

Figure 11.5 *The see-through headworn stereoscopic color display, with attached optical tracker targets.*

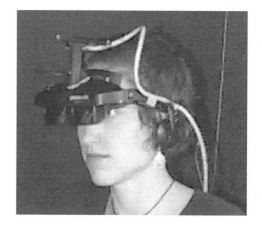

The testbed we are using for the spaceframe prototype is a multi-platform, distributed system that has been designed to allow a potentially large number of users to interact in a shared environ-

Figure 11.6 *Detail of partially assembled space-frame as seen through the headworn display. A virtual image of the next (topmost) strut to be installed is shown, along with written instructions.*

ment (MacIntyre and Feiner 1996). It runs on an assortment of hardware under UNIX, Windows NT, and Windows 95. The majority of the testbed was written in Modula-3, a compiled language that is well-suited for building large distributed systems. The remainder of the testbed, and the majority of the applications, are written in Obliq, an interpreted language that is tightly integrated with Modula-3. Application programmers are free to use either language or both. For this application we use shaded, hidden-surface–removed graphics supported by Criterion RenderWare running on a relatively inexpensive Diamond Stealth 2D graphics accelerator because of the relative simplicity of the models we are rendering. We provide support for 2D applications in a manner similar to that of our previous testbed, except that the windows are displayed using the native window system. This allows us to display X11 application windows on all platforms and native Windows NT/95 windows on those platforms.

We are currently developing a flowchart of the spaceframe construction steps and worker queries, which we will use as the basis for a rule-based system for assembly. The rule-based system will include context-sensitive help and will accommodate users with varying levels of experience. We also plan to incorporate a tracking system that will track each spaceframe component. This will allow better verification of the installation of each piece and ensure adherence to the proper assembly sequence.

CONCLUSIONS

We believe that the work described in this chapter demonstrates the potential of augmented reality's x-ray vision and instructional guidance capabilities for improving architectural construction, inspection, and renovation. Future augmented reality x-ray vision systems may enable maintenance workers to avoid hidden features such as buried infrastructure, electrical wiring, and structural elements as they make changes to buildings and outdoor environments. This promises to both speed up maintenance and renovation operations and reduce the amount of accidental damage that they currently cause. Future versions of augmented reality instructional systems may guide construction workers through the assembly of actual buildings and help to improve the quality of their work. Inspectors with augmented reality interfaces may be similarly guided through their jobs—allowing them to work without reference to conventional printed construction drawings and ensuring that every item which needs to be checked is in fact inspected.

The potential impact of augmented reality on architecture and structural engineering will increase as the technology is tied to other emerging technologies. For example, the addition of knowledge-based expert systems (Feiner & McKeown 1991; Myers 1992) to the core augmented reality technology described here could yield systems capable of training workers at actual construction sites while they work to assemble a real building. Such real-time at-site training systems could guide inexperienced users through complex construction operations. The continued evolution and integration of these and other technologies will yield systems that improve both the efficiency and the quality of building construction, maintenance, and renovation.

ACKNOWLEDGMENTS

Research on these projects is supported in part by the Office of Naval Research under Contract N00014-94-1-0564; NSF Gateway Engineering Coalition under NSF Grant EEC-9444246; the Columbia University Center for High Performance Computing and Communications in Healthcare, a New York State Center for Advanced Technology supported by the New York State Science and Technology Foundation; the Columbia Center for Telecommunications Research under NSF Grant ECD-88-1111; and NSF Grant CDA-92-23009. Starnet International Inc. provided the spaceframe. The undergraduates involved in development of the spacefame prototype were Rod Freeman (Mechanical Engineering), Jenny Wu (Architecture) and Melvin Lew (Computer Science).

REFERENCES

Bajura, M., and U. Neuman. 1995. Dynamic registration and correction in augmented reality systems. *Proc. Virtual Reality Annual International Symp. '95 (VRAIS '95)* Los Alamitos, CA: IEEE Computer Society Press. 189–196.

Caudell, T., and D. Mizell. 1992. Augmented reality: an application of heads-up display technology to manual manufacturing processes. *Proc. Hawaii International Conf. on Systems Science* 2: 659–669.

Das Consulting, Inc. 1993. *Dast User's Manual.* North Andover, MA: Das Consulting, Inc.

Feiner, S., B. MacIntyre, and D. Seligmann. 1993. Knowledge-based augmented reality. *Communications of the ACM* 36 no. 7 (July): 52–62.

Feiner, S. and K. McKeown. 1991. Automating the generation of coordinated multimedia explanations. *IEEE Computer* 24 no. 10 (October): 33–41.

Feiner, S., A. Webster, T. Krueger, B. MacIntyre, and E. Keller. 1995. Architectural anatomy. *Presence: Teleoperators and Virtual Environments* 4 no. 3 (Summer): 318–325.

Myers, J., J. Snyder, and L. Chirca. 1992. Database usage in a knowedge-based environment for building design. *Building and Environment* 27 no. 2: 231–241.

MacIntyre, B. and S. Feiner, 1996. Language-level support for exploratory programming of distributed virtual environments. To appear in *Proc. UIST '96 (ACM Symp. on User Interface Software and Technology)*, New York: ACM Press.

Novitski, B. 1994. Virtual reality for architects. *Architecture* (October).

Oloufa, Amr. 1993. Modeling and simulation of construction operations. *Automation in Construction* 1 no. 4: 351–359.

Patents: portable no-hands computer for consulting manuals. 1994. *The New York Times* (May 9) D2.

Quinn, R. 1993. 1990s jobsite fashion forecast: the computerized hardhat. *Engineering News Record* (March 29).

Richards, M. 1994. Automation in construction. *The Industrial Robot* 21 no. 4: 26–28.

Robinett, W. 1992. Synthetic experience: a taxonomy. *Presence: Teleoperators and Virtual Environments* 1 no. 2 (Summer).

Smailagic, A. and D. Siewiorek, 1994. *The CMU Mobile Computers: A New Generation of Computer Systems.* Engineering Design Research Center Report 18–48–94. Carnegie Mellon University.

Starnet International, Inc. 200 Hope Street, Longwood, FL 32750.

Sutherland, I. 1968. A head-mounted three-dimensional display. *Proc. Fall Joint Computer Conference 1968.* Washington, DC: Thompson Books. 757–764.

Virtual reality by Raytheon. 1995. *Engineering News Record* (May 29) 27.

Webster, A. 1996. Networked multimedia tools for architectural engineering. *Journal of Architectural Engineering.* In press, January.

Webster, A. 1994. *Technological Advance in Japanese Building Design and Construction,* New York: ASCE Press.

Community and Environmental Design and Simulation

The CEDeS Lab at the University of Washington

Dace A. Campbell
Virtual Architect, Human Interface Technology Laboratory

James N. Davidson, AIA
Lecturer, Department of Architecture

> *We shall not cease from exploration*
> *And the end of all of our exploring*
> *Will be to arrive where we started*
> *And know the place for the first time*
> T. S. Eliot

INTRODUCTION

The impact of digital media on society is being felt in all parts of our economic, cultural, and social lives. Every business has been affected by changes in how products are designed and manufactured, and how these processes are administered. The technical and research disciplines, as well as the arts, have seen incredible impacts on how work is conducted. For the professionals who design and help construct our built environment, the changes are remarkable.

From designer to building official, from client to subcontractor, all members of the construction industry are seeing irrepressible forces alter the communication infrastructure on which they rely. The blueprint is being replaced by a stream of digits; the legal, financial, and logistical repercussions of this change have yet to be resolved. This reconfiguration in-process is having a profound effect on what and how we design and build. There is a need to teach design students and professionals to have an understanding of these currents and help direct the flow of this cultural change through our endeavors.

All businesses and all disciplines rely on media of different types to exist. These media range from the simple to the complex, from the subtle to the obvious, from the vital to the exploratory. Whether analogue or digital, these media are used to generate, represent, communicate, and evaluate ideas pertaining to the content of any discipline. This is especially true for the design professions. In architecture, the design of experiential, three-dimensional space, designers create environments which have meaningful cultural, social, and symbolic content. Architectural space is designed and developed in a complex process, accomplished by various media of *simulation* or representation. While these media are chiefly used in the *process* of architectural design, they can also be used as the *product* of architectural content. This is true of all media of representation, including those digital media experienced with virtual interfaces and real-time rendering.

Simulation in the Design Process

The process of architectural design is a complex one, to the point of eluding a clear definition or description. However, at a rudimentary level, it can be described as the (re)iteration of the following three basic steps: (1) the generation or conception of an idea; (2) the documentation or simulation of this idea in a medium; and (3) the communication and analysis of that idea by the creator or by others. This analysis can lead to the acceptance or refinement of the idea or it can lead to new ones. The designer then starts over with the conception of a (refined) idea and the process reiterates.

An important factor which determines a designer's ability to communicate, evaluate, and refine an architectural idea is how well the idea is represented, or simulated, in a medium. This depends on many factors, but most importantly, it depends on the designer's skill with the medium and the ability of that medium to simulate the idea clearly. The unique characteristics of a simulation medium, be it one-dimensional (linear) text, two-dimensional imagery, three-dimensional models, or four-dimensional (kinetic) animation, determine its appropriateness to simulate an idea in order to communicate it to the designer or to others. Because each medium presents concepts and ideas with its own strengths and limitations, each one is appropriate to simulate architecture in a different way. A skilled designer who chooses the appropriate medium can communicate an idea effectively with a minimal effort.

Conceptualization

In the conceptualization of an idea, certain media have characteristics which allow an immediate feedback to the mind of a singular designer. Stereotypically, these are the "napkin sketch" and clay model of the architect. These "intuitive" media allow for a tight feedback loop between the designer and the media, as the media become transparent to the ideas they represent. Digital media, which offer the advantages of accuracy and recordability, have traditionally not been intuitive enough to the designer's thought process to support rapid development of design ideas (Campbell and Wells 1994). Rather, they have often found a place in the design process for the precise refinement and documentation of well-developed design ideas. With the advancement of virtual interfaces and real-time simulation, digital media offer a feedback loop tight enough to augment traditional conceptual design tools (Furness 1987). There is a need to explore the potential of digital media to aid in the conceptualization and generation of architectural design ideas.

Representation

Media for simulation are selected by how well they represent ideas. Influenced by market forces and the construction process, this is often measured by the clarity, precision, and reproducibility of the medium which represents architectural information. Due to the nature of reprographic (and xerographic) media, the entire construction industry, and the legal system with which it is deeply entwined, has demanded that architectural ideas be represented in a specific manner to be communicated to others. The diazo, or "blueprint" process, has been the dominant means of representing architecture in the twentieth century. Powerful industry and legal forces, combined with market pressures, have led to the dependence of design professions on a singular medium for the majority of architectural representations. In recent years, however, we have witnessed the use of computers as a valid medium to document architectural intentions. Computer technology has developed such that the time required to simulate architecture has shortened to "real" time, allowing nearly instantaneous representation and presentation of an architectural idea. The digital suite of media, from rastor graphics and CAD drawings, to models, animations, and immersive virtual environments, allows us to perceive architecture in new ways, enhancing our abilities to simulate and represent designs. "Interpreting spatial information using virtual interfaces is perhaps as simple and intuitive as it is to interpret real spaces" (Henry 67). However, the construction industry has been slow to embrace digital media as a valid means of conveying architectural intentions.

In time, this is likely to change as digital media become assimilated into the construction industry. The ramifications of this possibility are not yet completely understood and need exploration.

COMMUNICATION

The success of the design process also depends on how well architectural ideas are communicated and evaluated between many people. Specifically, it involves the *exchange* of ideas between multiple minds. The ideas are exchanged through visual media as varied as those for architectural presentation, along with media which support verbal communication. It is not possible, yet, to walk around a potential building site and imagine a building into being. Ideas must be developed over time by many people involved in the process. In architecture or in urban planning, the designer or the client gets an initial idea for a particular project; then that idea must be documented, formalized, critiqued, refined, and communicated between the designers, clients, patrons, consultants, contractors, and financiers. There exists a need to understand the relationship of the communication of ideas between multiple minds and the media which assist in that communication. Digital media offer new ways to communicate, record, and exchange ideas in a precise manner. With the introduction of distributed, multiple-participant virtual environments, this collaboration can take place intuitively and in real-time.

Simulation as Design Product

It is clear that media are used in architecture to aid in the process of design, whether in the generation, representation, or communication of design intentions. Certain media which represent architectural space have been used in the product of architecture as well. This recognition of design media as architectural content, having only recently grabbed the attention of popular culture in the digital design of cyberspace, is not new to designers.

An early example of the use of media representative of architectural space as an architectural product is Donato Bramante's Santa Maria presso San Satiro in Milan, Italy (1478). Due to site constraints, Bramante was unable to include a choir, so he contrived a "virtual" choir in fresco, using the relatively new technique of one-point perspective. This work is the, "first use of illusionistic architecture in the Renaissance" (Heydenreich 1996). Using a fresco as the media of simulation, Bramante simulated physical space to enhance the spiritual and symbolic content of the chapel.

Today, digital simulation media are being used in a similar manner. The unprecedented growth of the on-line culture, exemplified by the development of the Internet and its graphic interface, the World Wide Web, has led to a desire and a demand for three-dimensional content experienced through three-dimensional (even virtual) interfaces. This three-dimensional content of cyberspace needs to be designed, to be consciously shaped and constructed (Benedikt 1993; Best 1993), and architects as three-dimensional designers are being called to answer the challenge (Anders 1994). Leveraging the skills, understanding, and tradition accumulated over the centuries, architects are uniquely and ideally suited for this role (Campbell, *Virtual Architecture,* 1995). A new cadre of design professionals needs to be trained with the necessary skills to design and construct virtual spaces and they must be given the requisite insight to comprehend the social and cultural ramifications of these spaces.

THE CEDeS LAB

To research and respond to this influence of digital media on the way we design space, the Community and Environmental Design and Simulation Laboratory (CEDeS Lab) has been established at the University of Washington. The CEDeS Lab (pronounced "seeds") is sponsored by the Cascadia Community and Environment Institute, at the UW College of Architecture and Urban Planning (CAUP), and the Human Interface Technology Laboratory (HIT Lab), at the Washington Technology Center.

The CEDeS Lab was established in 1994 to bring virtual interface technology closer to the students and faculty of CAUP, and to bring spatial design expertise and sensibility into the research at the HIT Lab. The partnership between the HIT Lab and the Cascadia Community and Environment Institute allows each of the organizations to access the other's strengths, enabling joint research, application, and educational opportunities.

Mission and Objectives

The CEDeS Lab combines the use of digital media with the professional design disciplines of CAUP to create a center for research and teaching in advanced simulation for urban and architectural design, landscape design, and artificial virtual environments. The lab's mission is to confront the implications of digital technology for society in the design of human environments.

The mandate for the Lab has a three-fold emphasis on education, research, and community involvement. The goals for this mandate are: to educate students to be skilled, thoughtful, and critical designers; to research and develop new tools, techniques, and procedures for the design of inhabitable space; and to be a resource to the community in the design, planning and construction processes. This mandate directs specific objectives for the CEDeS Lab:

◆ Provide computer-aided design technology and instruction to enrich the professional curricula of the CAUP. A new "Virtual Environments" course has been added to the curricula at UW's CAUP. In this class, students are taught the skills required to build computer models suitable for real-time simulation and to apply these skills by developing virtual environments. In conjunction with specialized classes, the CEDeS Lab provides computer resources for existing CAUP classes, enabling design studios to be taught with digital media as a focus. All of these classes fit within the lab's pedagogical strategy to incorporate digital media in design education professionally, technically, and theoretically.

◆ Research and develop new tools and techniques for design by applying simulation technology to the design process. The CEDeS Lab is involved in a number of projects at the HIT Lab and in a global context which further design and design review. There is a need to understand how digital media, specifically virtual interfaces and real-time rendering, can and should be applied both in the design process and as architectural product; this research is central to the efforts by the staff and students at the CEDeS Lab.

◆ Initiate the development of a new professional discipline for the design of virtual environments which will not be constructed or inhabited in physical reality. The principal focus of architectural education is to teach an understanding of spatial solutions to functional needs given a gamut of technical, financial, and logistical constraints. Architects and planners have applied these skills to shape our physical environment for thousands of years. Now, we are looking ahead to an increase in the need for three-dimensional content on the Internet and other digital venues. The demand for well-designed digital content is answered by a specific educational emphasis on a new application for architectural education.

◆ Provide a resource for design, planning, and community development organizations. In the future, as the technology matures, advanced simulation will be applied in professional practice. Currently, the technology required to produce a virtual simulation is complex, expensive, and relatively scarce. As the hardware and software continues to advance, the CEDeS Lab will act as a resource for the community. It will continue to utilize the most advanced simulation technology available and it will direct the way this technology is transferred and incorporated into the business procedures of professional practice.

Projects

As indicated in its mission and objectives, the goals of the CEDeS Lab pertain to education, research, and community involvement. These are accomplished by projects relating digital media and architectural design, with specific emphasis on the integration of virtual interfaces and real-time rendering in the architectural design process and as architectural product. A number of these projects are described in the remainder of the chapter.

DIGITAL MEDIA IN ARCHITECTURAL CONCEPTUALIZATION

The design and development of virtual environments for real-time rendering is an expertise- and labor-intensive endeavor, often requiring the generation of digital models using standard CAD hardware and software followed by the simulation of this data in real-time. Current technology requires the translation and editing of data in several formats and file types in order to construct complex environments like those of architectural subject matter. Furthermore, the generation of data with traditional CAD interfaces is awkward and does not lend itself to the rapid development of conceptual design. Recognition of these limitations has encouraged research into the development of software which allows immersive, real-time generation of virtual environments.

The Blocksmith Project

The Blocksmith Project, based on the HIT Lab's GreenSpace software platform for distributed, networked simulation of virtual environments (described later), is meant to enable rapid, immersive virtual world-building. Blocksmith is intended to empower designers with the ability to generate, evaluate, and modify conceptual architectural design in real-time with advanced virtual interfaces. Such software can allow architects to rapidly create and compare alternatives, and to visualize data in ways not previously possible (Schmitt et al. 1995). It can empower a designer with the ability to study designs as rapid as one thinks, limited only by one's imagination.

Preliminary research into Blocksmith has indicated that the three-dimensional interface for accessing and using its tools immersively should be only loosely based on two-dimensional graphical user interface. Widgets and icons representing tools should be clustered around a configurable worktable at which the designer works. The metaphor of a drafting table or worktable is a strong one for designers, and will be implemented as a virtual worktable in Blocksmith. The interface of tools and icons on the virtual desktop will be enhanced with voice commands and auditory feedback as well.

Blocksmith, currently in its early stages of development, is intended to allow a designer to create simple objects and modify them extensively along a variety of constraints. By selectively constraining translation and rotation, data topology (point, line, plane, volume), grid snaps, and angle snaps, Blocksmith can allow designers to edit objects or portions thereof in a limitless yet controllable number of combinations. Designers will also be able to color, copy, cut/delete, and paste single or multiple objects to allow rapid construction of elements in the virtual environment. Furthermore, Blocksmith will enable designers to change their scale relative to the data. This will enable the designer to study a model at any number of scales, ranging from an exocentric, omniscient scale to an egocentric, full-sized scale. Lastly, Blocksmith will be able to load and save data to file formats supported by open standards.

After Blocksmith is initially developed and tested, its capabilities will be expanded to include features found in the mature CAD packages in today's market. This will include layers, instances, and advanced tools and constraints for creating and editing primitives. Eventually, it is anticipated that Blocksmith will be able to incorporate extended features such as: the three-dimensional visualization of abstract data like building and zoning codes, lighting information, and materials specifications; the linking and embedding of information from architectural databases pertaining to specific site conditions or materials; and the integration of artificial intelligence and software agents to aid in the gathering and presentation of information relevant to the design.

By developing the Blocksmith project, the CEDeS Lab hopes to research and document how virtual interface technology can be used specifically to aid in the architectural design process. While the software will primarily be used for research and educational purposes, it is anticipated that the project can eventually aid in the development of commercial software packages which enable architects to design sophisticated virtual environments in real-time.

DIGITAL MEDIA IN ARCHITECTURAL REPRESENTATION

To teach the issues related to the use of virtual interfaces and real-time rendering in the representation of architectural design, the CEDeS Lab has developed several complex virtual environments in the context of a "Virtual Environments" class. Students in the class have constructed virtual environments which represent designs ranging from architectural interiors, to building restorations, to proposals for urban neighborhoods. The content created is then used for design review or presentation by various clients, firms, or institutions. Of the environments created at the CEDeS Lab, a few exemplary ones are described here.

Seattle Commons

The City of Seattle is considering a proposal for the development of an urban design near its downtown. The proposal involves the creation of a 61,000-acre park connecting the central business district with Lake Union. Although the Seattle Commons has the support of the local media and the mayor, it remains a controversial proposal due to its high cost and the concerns for the business already in the area which would be displaced by the park. In a referendum in November of 1995, the citizens of Seattle voted down a proposal for a tax increase which would fund the Seattle Commons. The project continues to be pursued by interested parties; it is possible that a proposal for the Seattle Commons may one day be accepted and implemented.

In the summer of 1994, in the context of the pilot "Virtual Environments" class—eight graduate students in architecture, landscape architecture, and urban planning—the CEDeS Lab developed a virtual environment representing the Seattle Commons. This virtual environment was simulated in real-time using virtual interface technology at the HIT Lab to aid in review of the proposal and its evaluation by the citizens of Seattle (see Figures 12.1 and 12.2).

Westin Guest Room 2000

In winter of 1995, staff and students at the CEDeS Lab undertook a project simulating an architectural interior for Westin Hotels. Westin Hotels is interested in the design and development of hotel rooms tailored to the business traveler of the twenty-first century. They provided a design of a guest room, which the CEDeS Lab modeled and simulated as an animation (see Figures 12.3 and 12.4). The guest room features a large bathroom complete with an exercise area, a bed which folds to a sofa for daytime use, and glass of variable transparency controlled by the hotel guest.

Virtual Venice

The CEDeS Lab has also collaborated with Telecom Italia to develop virtual environments. Telecom Italia, the Italian phone company, is interested in

Figure 12.1   *An aerial view of the Seattle Commons proposal, represented as a virtual environment.*

Figure 12.2   *Another view of the Seattle Commons.*

Figure 12.3 *A view within the Westin Guest Room 2000, as seen from the entrance.*

Figure 12.4 *Another view within the guest room, featuring the main living space.*

using virtual interface technology as a means of communication. To promote the technology, it sponsored the development of a virtual environment representing the Arsenale, an historic naval shipyard in the city of Venice. The Arsenale was the largest industrial complex in Europe in the fifteenth century, capable of constructing and storing parts for over a hundred naval galleys. The Arsenale complex was able to build one ship per day; in 1436 a Spanish visitor to the Arsenal witnessed the completion of 10 fully armed galleys in six hours (Thubron 1980).

The focus of the CEDeS Lab's simulation of the Arsenale is the Squadratori, currently under reconstruction. The simulation also features a proposal for a new bridge designed by Professor Augusto Burelli of the Architecture University of Venice (see Figures 12.5 and 12.6).

DIGITAL MEDIA IN ARCHITECTURAL COMMUNICATION

The development of virtual environments to teach the representation of architectural space in digital media is a significant focus of the CEDeS Lab. As well, the CEDeS Lab supports research into the development of virtual interface tools and methods to aid in the communication and evaluation of architectural design ideas. Such communication as a collaborative effort to critique and improve a design is fundamental to the making of architecture. The participation by the CEDeS Lab in this research includes the Virtual Design Studio project and the HIT Lab's GreenSpace project.

Virtual Design Studio

The Virtual Design Studio (VDS) is a project based on the premise that spatially distributed design collaboration can and should take place using digital tools. Since 1993, architectural institutions world-wide, including MIT, the University of British Columbia, Hong Kong University, Cornell, and the University of Toronto, have used a number of computer and telecommunications tools to facilitate long-distance collaboration between students and design faculty on common design problems (Davidson 1995). "Consistent with the actual experience of design practice, it recognizes that discussion and negotiation processes are a necessary complement to technical problem solving processes and accepts that these should be supported effectively by the computational environment in which the design tasks are engaged" (Mitchell 1995). This effort recognizes that communication of architectural design is not only a technical process, but is also fundamentally a social one.

Personnel from the CEDeS Lab have been involved with the Virtual Design Studio project since its inception. In 1995 and again in 1996, the

Figure 12.5   *A view of the Venice's Arsenale, featuring the Squadratori.*

Figure 12.6   *Another view of the Arsenale, featuring a proposed bridge.*

CEDeS Lab participated directly in the review of VDS projects. This included the exchange of email, contributions to World Wide Web pages, and participation in teleconferencing to evaluate and critique designs by students from around the globe. In addition to these media typical to VDS interactions, the CEDeS staff and students used virtual interfaces and real-time simulation equipment at the HIT Lab to investigate digital models that other students had created. The simulations of the student work (as experiential virtual environments) was then transferred long-distance using simple teleconferencing software *back* to the student designers across the globe. This real-time feedback from a simulation across the network proved to be a powerful way to investigate and communicate design ideas. These VDS explorations and endeavors were then incorporated into the HIT Lab's GreenSpace project.

GreenSpace

To empower people to collaborate over long-distances more efficiently and intuitively than by traditional means, the HIT Lab has been researching the GreenSpace project (Mandeville 1995). Begun in 1993, the GreenSpace project has served as a venue developing distributed, networked virtual environments for collaboration by multiple participants. After a first phase of development, an historic demonstration of this technology took place in November 1994 in which a trans-Pacific virtual environment was inhabited by participants immersed in Seattle, Washington and Tokyo, Japan. The event demonstrated that people can interact over long distances in real-time to accomplish a task. In the case of the demonstration, the task was to work together to "herd" dynamic "creatures" into a "corral."

The second phase of the HIT Lab's GreenSpace project began immediately following the initial demonstration; it was demonstrated in February and March of 1996. Incorporating ideas from the Virtual Design Studio project, GreenSpace II (GS2) was implemented to explore and demonstrate the utility of distributed virtual environments in architectural design review. The staff and students from the CEDeS Lab worked closely with the HIT Lab GS2 team to develop the application software and the content for experimental demonstrations. The prototype software, based on Silicon Graphics Open-Inventor 2.1, effectively demonstrates that distributed virtual environments aid in the communication of design ideas using virtual interfaces in real-time simulations.

To demonstrate the GS2 application in architectural design review, the CEDeS Lab designed and developed a number of hotel guest rooms. This program was selected because the content was simple to implement and represent, yet allowed enough variety of design to enable effective demonstration of the GS2 application tools. Along with a vestibule and hallway, three hotel guest rooms were designed and built. Each of the guest rooms was represented as several design alternatives: an empty, flat-shaded space; an empty space with "realistic" lighting; and a number of furnishing and lighting alternatives (see Figure 12.7). The participants, represented as "avatars" with heads and hands, could interact with each other in real-time to evaluate and critique the designs (Figure 12.8).

The GS2 application provided a "worktable" in each design alternative on which scale models and tools were placed for use by the participants. The tools, implemented to facilitate interaction between participants, enabled navigation within and between alternative designs, communication between participants, and manipulation of the environment itself. Navigation within the environment was accomplished using standard Inventor tools and with virtual interfaces including six-degree-of-freedom controllers, magnetic trackers, and head-mounted displays. Navigation between room alternatives

Figure 12.7   *A view within one of the hotel guest rooms used as GreenSpace content.*

Figure 12.8 *A view of multiple participants greeting each other within the GreenSpace vestibule.*

was implemented with hyperlink technology: Hyperlinked doors switched participants between adjacent rooms and icons on the worktable "transported" participants between noncontiguous spaces.

Audio communication between the participants was enabled to aid in the critique of the designs and scaled models of the hotel guest rooms were placed on the worktable for visual reference. Each of the models was surrounded by a "cutting" tool, which when picked up could clip the model in plan or section (see Figure 12.9). This proved to be an effective tool to supplement the full-scale investigation of each virtual environment, as it recalls traditional media of scale models and orthographic projection drawings for the critique of architectural ideas.

In traditional design reviews, there is rarely manipulation of the design (representation) itself. Feedback is often limited to a gestural and verbal critique. However, given the ability to edit digital data in real-time, participants find it advantageous to modify the environment during the critique of the design. To allow minor modification of the environment itself, the GS2 appli-

Figure 12.9   *A view of the GreenSpace section-cutting tool in use on a model at the worktable.*

cation enabled participants to move and (re)color furniture in each of the guest rooms (see Figure 12.10).

The experimental demonstrations of the GreenSpace project have indicated several new directions for further study in the application of digital technology in architectural design review. The GS2 application software is now being tested in conjunction with the Virtual Design Studio project. This will demonstrate and test the use of real-time digital simulation technology in a global context to aid in the communication and evaluation of architectural design.

DIGITAL MEDIA AS ARCHITECTURAL PRODUCT

The CEDeS Lab is integrating digital simulation technologies with the design professions by researching and implementing tools for the conceptualization, representation, and evaluation of architectural ideas. In keeping with its mission, the CEDeS Lab is also interested in exploring the use of advanced digi-

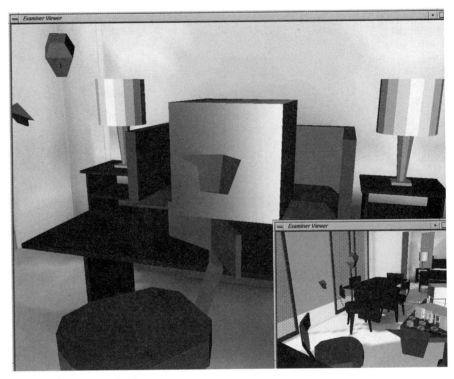

Figure 12.10 *A view featuring GreenSpace participants changing the color of a chair.*

tal media as architectural product. In this way, simulation media become the inhabitable, experiential content.

Virtual Architecture

Architecture is the making of a place by the ordering and definition of meaningful space, as developed in response to a need or program (Ching 1979). It is also described as the expression of society or culture in spatial, experiential form (Campbell, *Virtual Architecture*, 1995). These definitions describe architecture as a concept or idea which can be embodied in both physical and virtual forms. *Virtual architecture*, realized with polygons and texture maps and experienced via virtual interfaces, is a three-dimensional, inhabitable expression of electronic society or culture (Campbell, *Design,* 1996). It is the embodiment of data on the Internet as three-dimensional content and is not meant to be built in the physical world.

Virtual architecture as expressed in electronic form is a relatively new phenomenon. From the maps used to orient participants in MUDs and

MOOs, to Fujitsu's Habitat project (Club Caribe 1996; Morningstar and Farmer 1990), to Marcos Novak's "Liquid Architecture" (Novak 1990), most examples of virtual architecture have one thing in common: They use the metaphor of physical architecture to one degree or another in order to represent electronic information. "The architectural metaphor of cyberspace validates the designer's work: just as spatial cues help to orient us in a real building, they also offer a visual structure for abstract information, revealing relationships and hierarchy" (Anders 1994). The metaphor of physical architecture is a valid, though limited, one for the design of virtual environments as content (Campbell, *Design,* 1996). The research by staff and students at the CEDeS Lab is breaking new ground in the exploration of virtual architecture.

Virtual architecture, like physical architecture, uses architectural parti to organize information and it strives to create meaningful place by ordering elements in Cartesian space in response to a socio-cultural context. Virtual architecture lacks physical constraints of gravity, climate, and geography, yet it responds to its own set of technological constraints (Campbell, *Nature of Cyberspace* 1996) and human factors like cognition and perception become strongly pronounced in absence of physical factors (Furness 1987). The virtual realm enables the designer to deny the physics of time, space, light, and materiality (Campbell, *Design,* 1996). Furthermore, the hyperlink technology of the virtual realm enables designers to break free of even more constraints, such as the geographic nature of physical architecture bounded by a site. Study needs to be done into the expression of liquid, dynamic architecture which responds to a participant's movements and interactions with other participants or with the environment itself (Best, *Virtual Environments,* 1993). "A liquid architecture in cyberspace is clearly a dematerialized architecture. It is an architecture that is no longer satisfied with only space and form and light and all the aspects of the real world. It is an architecture of fluctuating relations between abstract elements. It is an architecture that tends to music" (Novak 1990). Virtual architecture can be as responsive to the individual's needs and actions as the complexity of the technology will allow.

One example of virtual architecture explored at the CEDeS Lab is a gallery for the organization and demonstration of virtual environments created at the HIT Lab (Campbell, *Design,* 1996). The gallery, intended for exploration using virtual interface and real-time simulation equipment at the HIT Lab, now exists as a VRML repository for on-line exploration on the World Wide Web (*VRML Gallery*) and includes a vestibule, main circulation spine, active gallery space, archives, and a main hall for the gathering of multiple participants on-line (see Figures 12.11 and 12.12).

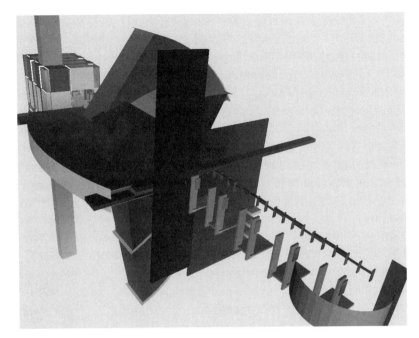

Figure 12.11 *The HIT Lab Gallery, an example of virtual architecture, as seen from the exterior.*

Figure 12.12 *A view of the circulation spine of the HIT Lab Gallery.*

This research at the CEDeS Lab, as well as research by others, is leading to the birth of a new design profession: virtual architecture. In time, virtual designers will be educated side-by-side with the designers of the physical realm, learning to design three-dimensional space in a studio setting. Their technological education, their equivalent of "construction," however, will be that of computer science and programming (Benedikt, *Cyberspace,* 1990). The architects of the virtual realm will design architecture every bit as valuable and interesting as their counterparts of the physical. Without a doubt, there will be much confusion in the near future regarding the similarities and differences in roles the "sister" professions will have in society of the twenty-first century (Campbell, Virtual Reality, 1995). There is a need to continue to explore the role of design—and the designer—in both the physical and the virtual realms. This exploration is being undertaken by the CEDeS Lab in order to provide designers with the skills needed to create both physical and virtual architectural content.

CONCLUSIONS

The profession of architectural design is changing dramatically. Our reliance upon the drawing as the dominant means to represent and communicate architectural intentions is being replaced by the encapsulation of design ideas in digital media. This digital data can be represented as drawings or models, similar in appearance to conventional media. However, they are fundamentally different from their analog counterparts by virtue of their malleability, accuracy, and accessibility. This digital data used to represent architectural intentions can be simulated in real-time with virtual interfaces, empowering all involved in the design process to visualize ideas intuitively. These simulations can be used to aid in the conceptualization, representation, and communication of design ideas as part of the design process.

The social and cultural ramifications of digital media in the design of architectural space needs to be addressed at research and educational institutions of architecture. The CEDeS Lab, established for this purpose, directly confronts these cultural changes by teaching designers to be fluent in the use of digital tools in design and cognizant of their social and spatial repercussions. Projects like Blocksmith, real-time simulations of architectural spaces, and GreenSpace endeavor to investigate the role of digital media in architectural design; they provide an opportunity to direct the use of the media in an academic and professional practice setting. This is appropriate, as these digital media will inevitably become the graphic and technological infrastructure of the design professions.

Moreover, digital media introduce the possibility of a new architectural venue: the design and construction of virtual spaces. The rapid growth of the Internet has demanded the use of digital media to design and develop digital content. The CEDeS Lab, in an effort to prepare designers with the skills to construct virtual environments, is pioneering the creation of a new design profession, virtual architecture. The effects of the developing telecommunication infrastructure and the growth of virtual architecture as inhabitable content are not yet fully understood. The urban forms and spaces of our cities, continually influenced by communications and transportation media, will likely change with the continued integration of digital media and content into our everyday social interactions. Designers of physical and virtual spaces alike must come to understand the social and cultural implications of digital technology on the built environment.

REFERENCES

Anders, Peter. 1994. The architecture of cyberspace. *Progressive Architecture* (October): 78–81, 106.

Benedikt, Michael, ed. 1990. *Cyberspace: First Steps.* "Introduction" and "Cyberspace: Some Proposals." Cambridge, MA: MIT Press.

———. 1993. Unreal estates. *Architecture New York* (Nov./Dec.): 56–57.

Best, Kathryn. 1993. *The Idiot's Guide to Virtual World Design.* Seattle: Little Star.

———. 1993. *Virtual Environments in Architecture.* Glasgow: University of Strathclyde.

Campbell, Dace A. 1996. *Design in Virtual Environments Using Architectural Metaphor: A HIT Lab Gallery.* Seattle: University of Washington.

———. 1996. The nature of cyberspace in *Vers Une Architecture Virtuelle . . .* Ser. *CRIT 35* (Winter): 26–28.

———. 1995. Virtual architecture in *Vers Une Architecture Virtuelle . . .* Ser. *CRIT 34* (Fall): 14–15.

———. 1995. Virtual reality: destroyer or savior of architecture? in *Vers Une Architecture Virtuelle . . .* Ser. *CRIT 36* (Spring): 20–21.

Campbell, Dace A., and Maxwell Wells. 1994. *A Critique of Virtual Reality in the Architectural Design Process.* <http://www.hitl.washington.edu/projects/architecture/R94-3.html> (Accessed March 1996).

Ching, Francis D. K. 1979. *Form, Space & Order.* New York: Van Nostrand Reinhold.

Club Caribe. 1996. *Caribe Pages—Images Page.* <http://www.islandnet.com/~crazy/ccimages.html> (Accessed March 1996).

Davidson, James N. 1995. Aspects of asynchronous and distributed design collaboration and digital pinup board—the story of the virtual village project. *Virtual Design Studio.* Edited by Jerzy Wojtowicz. Hong Kong: Hong Kong University Press.

Furness, Thomas A. 1987. *Designing in Virtual Space.* Seattle: University of Washington.

Henry, Daniel. 1992. *Spatial Perception in Virtual Environments: Evaluating an Architectural Application.* Seattle: University of Washington.

Heydenreich, Ludwig H. 1996. *Architecture in Italy, 1400 to 1500.* New Haven, CT: Yale University Press.

Human Interface Technology Laboratory. 1996. *CEDeS Lab.* <http://www.hitl.washington.edu/projects/cedes/> (Accessed April 1996).

————. *The GreenSpace Project.* 1996. <http://www.hitl.washington.edu/projects/greenspace/> (Accessed April 1996).

————. *VRML Gallery.* 1996. <http://www.hitl.washington.edu/vrml/gallery/> (Accessed April 1996).

Mandeville, Jon et al. 1995. *GreenSpace: Creating a Distributed Virtual Environment for Global Applications.* <http://www.hitl.washington.edu/publications/p-95-17/>

Mitchell, William J. 1995. The future of the virtual design studio. *Virtual Design Studio.* Edited by Jerzy Wojtowicz. Hong Kong: Hong Kong University Press.

Morningstar, Chip, and F. Randall Farmer. 1990. The lessons of lucasfilm's habitat. *Cyberspace: First Steps.* Cambridge, MA: MIT Press.

Novak, Marcos. 1990. Liquid architectures in cyberspace. *Cyberspace: First Steps.* Edited by Michael Benedikt. Cambridge, MA: MIT Press.

Schmitt et al. 1995. Toward virtual reality in architecture: concepts and scenarios from the architectural space laboratory. *PRESENCE: Teleoperators and Virtual Environments.* 4: 267–285.

Thubron, Coli. 1980. *The Venetians.* Alexandria, VA: Time-Life Books.

RECOMMENDED READING

Baudrillard, Jean. "Simulcra and Simulation." *The Body, in Theory Histories of Cultural Materialism* Ser. Ann Arbor: University of Michigan Press, 1983.

Bell, Gavin, Anthony Parisi, and Mark Pesce. *The Virtual Reality Modeling Language Version 1.0 Specification (Draft).* <http://www.eit.com/vrml/vrmlspec.html> November 1994.

Bender, Gretchen, and Timothy Drucker, Eds. *Culture on the Brink: Ideologies of Technology.* Seattle: Bay Press, 1994.

Borgmann, Albert. "Hypermodernism." *Crossing the Postmodern Divide.* Chicago: University of Chicago Press, 1992.

Davidson, James N. "The Machine and Architectural Value." *Digital Folio,* edited by Jerzy Wojtowicz. Vancouver: University of British Columbia, 1992.

Gibson, William. *Neuromancer.* New York: Ace Books. 1984.

Heidegger, Martin. *The Question Concerning Technology and Other Essays.* New York: Harper & Row, 1977.

Human Interface Technology Laboratory. *On the Net: VRML Resources, Sites and FAQs.* <http://www.hitl.washington.edu/projects/knowledge_base/vrm.html> (Accessed March 1996).

MacDonald, Lindsay, and John Vince, Eds. *Interacting with Virtual Environments.* New York: John Wiley and Sons, 1994.

Mitchell, William J. *City of Bits.* Cambridge, Mass: The MIT Press, 1995.

Pearce, Martin, and Neil Spiller, Guest Eds. "Architects in Cyberspace." *Architectural Design Profile No 118.* London: Academy Group, 1995.

Pesce, Mark. *VRML—Browsing and Building Cyberspace.* Indianapolis: New Riders, 1995.

Pesce, Mark. *VRML Visions.* <http://vrml.wired.com/concepts/visions.html> (12 June 1994).

Rheingold, Howard. *Virtual Communities.* Reading, MA: Addison-Wesley, 1993.

Taylor, Mark C., Guest Ed. "Electrotecture: Architecture and the Electronic Future." *Architecture New York* (Nov./Dec. 1993): 44–53.

Wexelblat, Alan, Ed. *Virtual Reality: Applications and Explorations.* Boston: Academic, 1993.

Conceptual Design Space— Beyond Walk-through to Immersive Design

Doug A. Bowman
Graphics, Visualization, and Usability Center, College of Computing
Georgia Institute of Technology

INTRODUCTION

From the beginnings of virtual reality research and technology, the architectural walk-through has been a driving application. Using a head-mounted display, trackers, and rendering software, an architect or designer can become immersed in a three-dimensional environment which provides realistic perspective and head-motion cues. By moving through this environment, the user can gain an understanding of the structure in a way not possible with blueprints, CAD drawings, or even 3-D models.

But how does this knowledge help the architect? Obviously, one can produce new versions of a design fairly cheaply and quickly, then put them into a walk-through for verification. Hopefully the design is then more complete and closer to the final product when construction is ready to begin.

Consider, however, the process that a designer might perform after a walk-through. The walk-through most likely prompted some changes to the design. How did the architect note those changes while immersed in the environment? When the desired changes have been recorded, the architect must leave the immersive environment and make the changes in a more traditional modeling or CAD program. Can one accurately remember the perceptions and sensations from the virtual environment in order to make the correct modifications? Assuming so, the new model must then be put into a format that can be used by the walk-through software—a process which can in some cases take hours or even days of tweaking and combining. Finally, the cycle begins again with another walk-through.

Work has been done to make this cycle tighter and easier to manage, but the fact remains that one must leave the immersive environment to make even the simplest of changes, such as the color of bricks in a wall. Therefore, it is only natural to ask whether the virtual environment application can be extended, so that it becomes active, rather than passive. We would like the former walk-through to become instead a design session, where models can be changed and created, not only viewed. This is the concept of **immersive modeling.**

In attempting to address some of these issues, we have developed an application called the Conceptual Design Space (CDS). CDS is a fully immersive, real-time virtual environment in which designers can view, walk through, modify, and create models. It is an ambitious step towards the possibilities of immersive modeling, while still retaining links to the normal design cycle previously described. CDS has been used and tested by professional architects and architecture students, and has provided a testbed for research on virtual environment interaction techniques. Some of the capabilities and implementations of the system, personal experiences with real-world users, and some general comments about the future of immersive design are presented in the following paragraphs.

CDS SYSTEM CAPABILITIES

The Conceptual Design Space system begins with functionality equivalent to any walk-through package. Users can load models which have been produced in a common modeling program and walk or fly through and around them in real-time. The models are rendered in full color, can be texture-mapped, and can be shaded. Here, however, the similarity to most VR walk-throughs ends.

CDS provides a very high level of functionality beyond simply navigating through the environment. One area of this functionality is the ability to modify existing 3-D designs. While still immersed, the user can apply simple geometric transformations (translate, rotate, and scale) to any model, so that elements of a design can be changed in position, orientation, or size. CDS also provides methods to change aesthetic qualities of a model, such as its color or texture.

The system goes further to provide users the ability to create new models while immersed in the three-dimensional environment. This can be accomplished in one of two ways. First, users can create primitive shapes, such as cubes, spheres, cylinders, cones, and planes. These can be modified, transformed, and grouped together to form a simple model. CDS also allows the creation of simple building units. The user specifies vertices on the ground plane, then a height value for each vertex (Figure 13.1). From this specification, the system creates walls and a ceiling to form a simple unit. These can then be moved, reshaped, and combined to create more complex structures.

It is in this creation area that we wish to stress the notion of *conceptual* designs. With current technology and the inherent limitations that arise when the user is wearing a head-mounted display (HMD), the models that can be created within CDS are necessarily rough and imprecise. The idea, however, is to allow the designer to "sketch" a design idea in three dimensions (Figure 13.2), then refine that idea within a more traditional desktop modeler (any CDS model can be saved to a common CAD file format). Hopefully, the ability to spatially experience a design as it is being created will allow architects greater freedom and new possibilities for the creative process.

Figure 13.1   *To create a simple building unit, the user specifies vertices and heights, which combine to make building walls.*

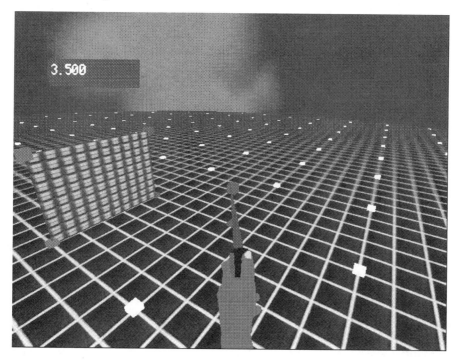

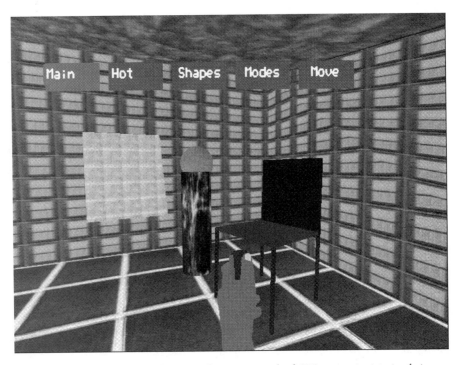

Figure 13.2 *Users can use the shaping and positioning tools of CDS to examine interior designs as well as other architectural structures.*

CDS IMPLEMENTATION

The implementation of these high-level concepts in the CDS system was difficult and challenging. As already noted, there are some inherent limitations to working within a head-mounted display, without the help of a mouse or keyboard. In fact, walk-throughs quickly became very popular as a VR application precisely because they require little action on the part of the user. A walk-through needs only some method of travel, so that the user can move her view from place to place in the virtual environment.

Since HMD users need freedom of movement, most VR applications are limited in their choice of input device. We felt that current glove technology and gesture recognition did not provide the precision, ease-of-use, or flexibility that we would need for our system, so we decided to use a 3-D mouse. This is simply a 3-button device with a tracker attached to it. Thus, the mouse can be located by the system at a unique position and orientation in three-dimensional space (it has six-degrees-of-freedom—three translational and three rotational). Two of the buttons on the device are used for navigational purposes, so we were left with a single button with which to perform all other interactions. That is, every other capability in the system previously described had to be accessible through this button.

To accomplish this, we made use of a single, universal interaction metaphor throughout the system. To be specific, we utilized **ray-casting**, in which a "light ray" of infinite length emanates from the end of the 3-D mouse in the virtual environment. This ray is used to select objects, issue commands, specify transformations, and so on (Figure 13.3). The ray-casting metaphor is quite useful, especially since the object the user is attempting to select with the ray can be at any distance from the user. If users were required to "touch" the objects directly, a great deal of time would be wasted in traveling to the desired location, especially when the environment is on the scale of a large architectural structure. With ray-casting, large-scale movements of objects become simple.

One of the defining features of virtual reality is the ability to interact *directly* with the objects in the environment, rather than indirectly, through commands. In CDS, all transformations can be carried out directly. To mod-

Figure 13.3 *By attaching the light ray to an object, its position and orientation can be naturally specified. User hand movements are all that is required.*

ify an object's position and orientation with complete freedom, the user simply has to point at the object, which attaches it to the ray until the button is pressed again. If more precision is needed, a user can select one of the transformation widgets attached to each object (Figure 13.4), then move his hand to translate the object in a single dimension. Other transformations, such as rotations and stretches, can also be performed directly using these widgets.

This type of direct manipulation suffices for simple transformations, but it is often unclear whether other types of operations can be done directly or if this is even desirable. For example, how would an abstract operation such as a texture change be done directly? For these types of actions, we felt it necessary to include a more indirect interface to the functionality of CDS. Since 2-D desktop applications have been developing this type of interface for many years, we simply adapted many of their techniques to work in a 3-D virtual environment. Virtual pull-down menus, then, which work in a way similar to menus in desktop systems, are used for many abstract tasks in CDS, such as

Figure 13.4 *Two types of tools are used in CDS: direct manipulation widgets, such as those attached to the cube, and adapted 2-D interface elements, such as the color palette and the coordinate information box.*

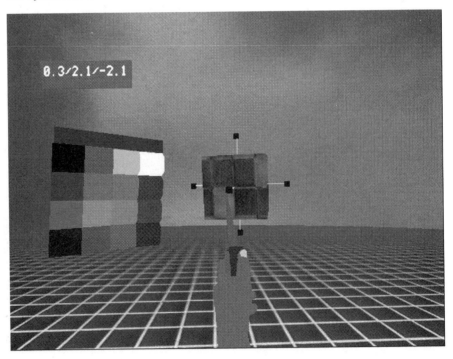

loading a model, changing the transformation mode, or setting the speed of travel (Figure 13.5). We have also implemented and used palettes, scrolling lists, and information dialog boxes (Figure 13.4).

Another important auxiliary task for CDS was to provide proper cues so that designers would be able to understand and manipulate their models properly. Most importantly, users need the ability to appropriately perceive scale and depth. In the real world, we use shadows, stereo vision, relative size, and many other perceptual cues to judge scale and depth, but in a virtual environment, real-time constraints force us to sacrifice most of the more subtle things. In particular, accurate lighting models and shadows cannot be rendered in real-time using today's technology. Stereo is possible, but since it would result in an unacceptable frame rate for our system, we opted to make CDS a monoscopic application.

To make up for this loss of cues, we had to provide some more mundane aids for the user. To judge relative scale, then, we provide a human figure which can be placed anywhere in the environment. A 3-D grid and coordi-

Figure 13.5 Abstract operations such as loading a model can be performed via the virtual pull-down menus.

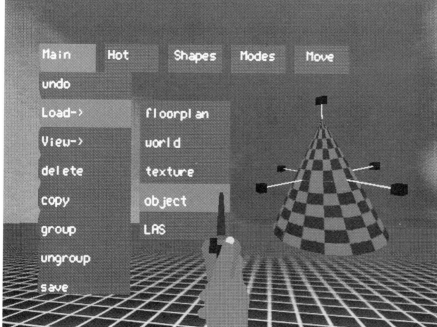

nate information are used so that objects and their movements can be measured, rather than subjectively judged. Finally, a graphical gauge tells the user how far she is above the ground plane. These artificial cues require some thought on the user's part, but do allow the user to judge scale and depth more accurately.

EXPERIENCE

The Conceptual Design Space system has not only encouraged research into innovative interaction techniques for virtual reality, but has also been tested extensively in the domain for which it was developed: architectural design. Both professional architects and students of architecture have used the software for real-world projects. The most important part of this experience was a collaboration with a graduate design studio in the College of Architecture at Georgia Tech. Five students used CDS to help complete their quarter design project.

This experiment highlighted many promising aspects of our approach to immersive design, but also showed that much work is still to be done in this area. Even though our focus was on moving beyond walk-throughs, CDS proved to be most helpful to these students as a visualization and "experience" tool. They gained better spatial understanding of their models through its use. Since models could be loaded and deleted from within the immersive environment, students could compare and contrast competing versions of a structure easily, without a great deal of setup time.

The participants also benefited from being able to make simple modifications while still immersed. Large-scale position and orientation changes and aesthetic modifications proved to be especially easy using CDS, and students received instant verification of the changes, since they felt present in the 3-D environment throughout the modification process.

More complex operations, however, proved to be quite difficult in most cases. Because of the imprecision of the trackers, the difficulties of pointing and acting in three dimensions, and the physical limit to the amount of time one can easily work in an HMD, most participants were not able to create any significant models within CDS. There were at least two occasions when the creation functions were used to gain a conceptual understanding of a proposed design. Primitive shapes or the simple building units described earlier were used as "place holders," or rough equivalents, of a structure being considered by the designer. The models themselves were of little further use, but the experience of visualizing in a conceptual fashion the spatial impact of a design allowed the users to return to their desktop modeling packages with a greater sense of direction.

In the final analysis, the difficulties users had with CDS arose mainly because of two issues: too many physical constraints and too few artificial constraints. That is, the physical situation was too encumbering to the user, while the virtual environment did not limit or guide the user's actions enough. We have already mentioned the fact that users simply cannot use the HMD for extended periods of time because of its weight and confinement. Most sessions were about 30 minutes, with 45 minutes being the maximum. Also, the mechanics of pointing in 3-D space and holding the input device at odd angles is physically challenging. On the other hand, there were a lack of constraints on the software side. When a user is placing an object, for example, there are simply too many degrees-of-freedom to control all at once. We provided constrained object motion to help with this problem, but getting the pieces of the model in the correct position was still a problem. Also, as we have noted, users lacked the real-world constraints provided by gravity, shadows, and object impenetrability. This freedom is often seen as an advantage of VR, but in applications such as immersive design, it is usually a hindrance.

FUTURE DIRECTIONS

What is in store for immersive design applications in the future? Is it possible to create, modify, and evaluate a design completely within a virtual space? The answer will depend on research in several key areas of virtual reality.

First, the physical system components must be improved. Head-mounted displays, if they are to be used, must be lighter and have higher resolution and field of view. Input devices which are less cumbersome and more natural must be developed. Trackers must be made more precise, with a greater working range. Many research centers are working on these issues, as well as alternatives to the common hardware. For example, projection-screen systems might be better suited to this application, especially if it is to be used for extended time periods.

Secondly, virtual reality systems in general must become faster and more realistic. For immersive design, it will eventually be necessary to incorporate better lighting models, shadows, gravity, collision detection, and other features of the real world. This will depend on bigger and faster machines with more specialized hardware, as well as improved and more complex software.

Finally, interaction and interface techniques for VR applications must be researched. We need to interact in a natural, straightforward manner with the objects in the environment, yet still retain the ability to perform complex and abstract operations with ease. This is perhaps the most challenging of the three research areas, since greater technology alone will not provide a solution. We feel that although direct techniques will always be at the forefront of VR interaction, the indirect methods we borrowed from 2-D interfaces are also useful and flexible. One intriguing possibility is that the user carry a 2-D, desktop-style interface with him in the virtual environment. Its menus, sliders, and buttons could be used for complex and symbolic functions and it could be put away when not needed, allowing an unobstructed view into the 3-D world.

The CDS project made it clear to us that technology and techniques are not advanced enough that complete immersive design is viable for today's architects. However, we have shown that VR is not restricted to being a passive tool for visualization and walk-through. Simple changes to the position, orientation, size, color, or texture of models can be made in the immersive space fairly simply. With this in mind, we are pursuing another research avenue that could help to make the design cycle shorter and more manageable: a real-time link between a CAD program and an immersive VR view. The idea is that changes made either at the desktop workstation or in the immersive environment would automatically be reflected on the other side. Thus, a single user could switch between the two, making simple changes immersively as needed, or going to the workstation for more complex actions. Also, two operators could use the system, allowing collaboration and reducing the need to put on or take off an HMD.

Immersive design is still a very young idea. There are many advances to be made before it could be widely used and accepted, in both technological and methodological areas. We believe that the Conceptual Design Space project has taught us a great deal about these challenges and brought us closer to a more active role for virtual reality in architecture.

ACKNOWLEDGMENTS

The author would like to acknowledge the help and support of his advisor on the CDS project, Dr. Larry Hodges, and the other members of the CDS project group: Brian Wills, Tolek Lesniewski, Harris Dimitropolous, Jean Wineman, Terry Sargent, Hamish Caldwell, Scott O'Brien, Tom Meyer, and Tom Browne. He would also like to acknowledge the creators and maintainers of the Simple Virtual Environment (SVE) toolkit, on which CDS was built.

For more information on the CDS project, visit its World Wide Web site at **http://www.cc.gatech.edu/gvu/virtual/CDS/**.

RECOMMENDED READING

Angus, I., and H. Sowizral. Embedding the 2D interaction metaphor in a real 3D virtual environment. *Proceedings SPIE, Stereoscopic Displays and Virtual Reality Systems,* 2409, 1995: 282–293.

Bowman, D. WiMP design tools for virtual environments. video *Proceedings of Virtual Reality Annual International Symposium,* 1995.

Brooks, F., et al. Final Technical Report: Walkthrough Project. Report to National Science Foundation, June, 1992.

Bukowski, R., and C. Séquin. Object associations: a simple and practical approach to virtual 3D manipulation. *Proceedings 1995 Symposium on Interactive 3D Graphics,* 1995: 131–138.

Darken, R. Hands-off interaction with menus in virtual spaces. *Proceedings SPIE, Stereoscopic Displays and Virtual Reality Systems,* 2177, 1994: 365–371.

Ferneau, M., and J. Humphries. A gloveless interface for interaction in scientific visualization virtual environments. *Proceedings SPIE, Stereoscopic Displays and Virtual Reality Systems,* 2409, 1995: 268–274.

Hinckley, K., R. Pausch, J. Goble, and N. Kassell. A survey of design issues in spatial input. *Proceedings ACM UIST 94 Symposium on User Interface Software and Technology,* 1994: 213–222.

Jacoby, R., and S. Ellis. Using virtual menus in a virtual environment. *Proceedings SPIE, Visual Data Interpretation,* 1668, 1992: 39–48.

Mine, M. Virtual Environment Interaction Techniques. UNC Chapel Hill Computer Science Technical Report TR95-018, 1995.

Mine, M. ISAAC: A Virtual Environment Tool for the Interactive Construction of Virtual Worlds, UNC Chapel Hill Computer Science Technical Report TR95-020, 1995.

Nielsen, J. Noncommand user interfaces. *Communications of the ACM* 36, no. 4 (April) 1993: 83–99.

Norman, D. *The Design of Everyday Things.* New York: Doubleday, 1990.

Pausch, R., T. Burnette, D. Brockway, and M. Weiblen. Navigation and locomotion in virtual worlds via flight into hand-held miniatures. *Proceedings SIGGRAPH 95,* in *Computer Graphics,* 1995, pp. 399–400.

Smets, G., P. Stappers, K. Overbeeke, and C. van der Mast. Designing in virtual reality: implementing perception-action coupling with affordances. *Proceedings VRST,* 1994: 97–110.

Sowizral, H. Interacting with virtual environments using augmented virtual tools. *Proceedings SPIE, Stereoscopic Displays and Virtual Reality Systems, 2177,* 1994: 409–416.

Stoakley, R., M. Conway, and R. Pausch. Virtual reality on a WIM: Interactive worlds in miniature. *Proceedings ACM SIGCHI Human Factors in Computer Systems,* 1995: 265–272.

Genetic Algorithms and Evolving Virtual Spaces

Eric J. Bucci
Advanced Design Research Group, University of Texas at Austin

The recent emergence of cyberspace as a realm of architectural design raises questions regarding effective design methods for virtual environments and their potential implications for the architectural community as a whole. The search for valid architectures in cyberspace will become increasingly important as the technology which allows its existence becomes more pervasive.

Concurrently, the continuing development of computer technology has enabled the use of algorithms, most recently *genetic algorithms,* as an avenue for addressing problems in a wide range of disciplines, including biology, economics, and reluctantly, architecture. The use of the genetic paradigm, with its mechanisms of mutation, fitness evaluation and selection, offers a mode of design with distinct differences from traditional methods.

In the pages that follow, the genetic paradigm as a model for the design of virtual spaces will be considered at length and a genetic algorithm which has been constructed and used to evolve virtual spaces will be presented, with emphasis on its potential as a robust method of spatial design. The focus will be on the use of the genetic algorithm as both a means of traversing large ranges of design possibilities and as a methodology for producing structures which continue to emerge over time. This is part of an ongoing body of work of the Advanced Design Research Group, a program in the School of Architecture at the University of Texas at Austin directed by Marcos Novak, which is concerned with algorithmic design, virtual environments, and the architecture of cyberspace.

THE GENETIC ALGORITHM MODEL

The use of the genetic algorithm as a model for investigating evolutionary behavior has its roots in the 1960s. While evolutionary models were being studied before this, it was John Holland in 1975 who presented the genetic algorithm (GA) model as a computational abstraction of the actual biological process; it is here summarized by Mitchell and Forrest:

> Holland's GA is a method for moving from one population of "chromosomes" (e.g., bit strings representing organisms or candidate solutions to a problem) to a new population, using selection together with the genetic operators of crossover, mutation and inversion. Each chromosome consists of "genes" (e.g., bits") with each gene being an instance of a particular "allele" (e.g. 0 or 1). Selection chooses those chromosomes in the population that will be allowed to reproduce and decides how many offspring each is likely to have, with the fitter chromosomes producing on average more offspring than less fit ones (Mitchell and Forrest 1994, 26).

The three genetic operators referred to represent a highly effective way to provide the great number of potential offspring variations which facilitates the evolutionary process. **Mutation** is the random change of values at single positions (**alleles**) in the chromosome. **Crossover,** in contrast, exchanges the locations of contiguous strings of genes—effectively, a sort of large-scale mutation. And **inversion** retains the values of the alleles, but takes the positions of one contiguous string of genes and reverses them. With all three genetic operators at work, the number of potential outcomes is clearly quite high, a condition not lost on architects.

The bitstrings representing the chromosomes are information which, when conveyed to a **development process,** will shape the physical characteristics of the offspring, the **phenotype.** It is this interface between the genes and the physical development processes which they regulate that is critical to the robustness of the evolutionary path taken by the algorithm. This is the part of the algorithm which allows the collection of gene values, the **genotype,** to manifest itself at two levels:

> In nature, the genotype contains (1) information that is descriptive, through the action of development and the environment, of a range of possible phenotypes, and (2) information encoding the development process itself, i.e.,

how to go about making a phenotype from a genotype. Both kinds of information are of course inherited and subject to variation and natural selection (Stewart 1989, 158).

Within the mechanics of the genetic algorithm model, the development process stands at a threshold: It is through development of offspring that genotypical information used for *transferral* of attributes is transformed into phenotypical information used for *evaluation* of those attributes. Development is the vehicle for the revelation of a genotype's significance within an evolutionary path:

> The particular effects that genes have are not intrinsic properties of these genes. They are properties of embryological processes, existing processes whose details may be changed by genes, acting in particular places and at particular times during embryonic development (Dawkins 1987).

Development, then, leads us to the second critical part of the genetic algorithm: *selection*. The algorithm must possess the ability to evaluate the fitness of each member of the population of the current generation in order to determine the degree to which each genotype will be passed down the evolutionary path via inheritance. To the extent that this "fitness function" is a set of some kind of explicitly stated, favored attributes constituting fitness, it departs from the genetic model found in nature; in natural selection, the notion of a "fitness function" per se is largely irrelevant:

> The important point is that nature doesn't need computing power in order to select. In nature, the usual selecting agent is direct, stark and simple. It is the grim reaper. Of course, the reasons for survival are anything but simple—that is why natural selection can build up animals and plants of such formal complexity (Dawkins 1987, 62).

In simulating a natural selection process within a genetic algorithm, then, one approach is to delineate certain preferred characteristics which constitute fitness and rank each phenotype in the generated population against them. With sufficient fitness criteria, there will be a sufficient degree of rigor in the selection process to allow the pursuit of a meaningful evolutionary path. An alternative is to follow more closely the biological model by creating an "environment" against which the fitness of each phenotype of the generation is played out. In lieu of explicitly identifying the criteria which contribute to fitness, the environment provides an arena in which the ability to perform certain tasks or evade certain dangers constitutes a high fitness value, regardless of any specific set of attributes which may have *facilitated* the performance of those tasks.

Modeling an environment in which to evaluate the behavior of phenotypes provides the opportunity to add a degree of complexity to the algorithm. For instance, John Koza points out that the environment affecting any single phenotype is more than just the arena in which its behavior is evaluated:

> The environment in nature actually consists of both the physical environment (which is usually relatively unchanging) as well as other independently acting biological populations of individuals which are simultaneously trying to adapt to "their" environment. The actions of each of these other independently acting biological populations (species) usually affects all the others. In other words, the environment of a given species includes all the other biological species that contemporaneously occupy the physical environment and which are simultaneously trying to survive (Koza 1992, 620).

The theme emerging here is that there is enough variability in the components of various genetic algorithm models to produce a large continuum of possible configurations. In the context of designing virtual spaces, this translates to a range of potential design process variations from which to select, a notion which will be revisited throughout the following pages.

With the addition of the selection procedure to the development process, a defining symmetry of evolution via genetic algorithm is established. In development, the robustness of the genotype determines the characteristics of the surviving phenotype; in selection, the robustness of the *phenotype* determines the characteristics of the surviving *genotype*.

When employing the genetic algorithm model for evolving a solution to some problem, it is usually the phenotype which is the desired goal. In the case of architecture in cyberspace, it is the evolved virtual structure that is of value, not the genetic code which was responsible for it. While many applications of genetic algorithms are concerned primarily with producing phenotypes of some kind, this is not always the case. In the genetic *programming* paradigm, for instance, the code itself is used in the fitness evaluation process; it functions as both genotype and phenotype. Genetic programming is one of the applications of the GA model which will be discussed shortly.

The final link in the cycle of the genetic algorithm model after development and selection is replication. This is the point at which the favored genotypes belonging to the selected phenotypes reproduce to allow for the development of new phenotypes and the beginning of a new genetic cycle.

This is also the phase at which the various forms of mutation mentioned earlier come into play.

The rate of mutation involved in the replication phase of the genetic algorithm is closely tied to the rate of evolution:

> If there is no natural selection, we might expect that there would be no evolution. Conversely, strong "selection pressure," we could be forgiven for thinking, might be expected to lead to rapid evolution. Instead, what we find is that natural selection exerts a braking effect on evolution. The baseline rate of evolution, in the absence of natural selection, is the maximum possible rate. That is synonymous with the mutation rate (Dawkins 1987, 125).

It would be prudent to consider what is meant here by "evolution." If we consider all of the various phenotypic attributes being determined by a set of gene values, then we can consider that evolution as a trip through the multidimensional space of all possible combinations of all possible attributes determined by all possible combinations of gene values. In a situation where there are no fitness criteria (the total absence of a selection process), the rate of movement through this space is as fast as the rate of change of the combinations of genes, that is, the mutation rate. When we introduce a selection process, the rate of movement through this set of possibilities is slowed. However, this decrease in the rate of movement is accomplished through providing direction for movement, which is what a selection process does. Since the goal of a genetic algorithm is usually movement towards something which satisfies criteria, either explicit or coincidental (e.g., "anything producing behavior which facilitates survival"), evolution is a tradeoff between speed and precision.

We have now outlined the complete cycle of the genetic algorithm model. Before discussing some of the current applications for which genetic algorithms are being constructed and employed, there remain a few remarks to be made about the two primary segments of the model: the development process and the selection process.

As noted earlier, the development process commences with the gene set itself. The values contained therein affect the various developmental processes according to their magnitudes. They contribute a higher level of embryological complexity, however, by acting together through a phenomenon called **epistasis.** Epistasis is the regulation of a developmental procedure by combinations of gene values or alleles as they are termed.

John Holland, the first person to delineate rigorously the framework of adaptive systems, stresses the importance of epistasis:

> In general, the fitness of an allele depends critically upon the influence of other alleles (epistasis). The replacement of any single allele in a coadapted set may completely destroy the complex of phenotypic characteristics necessary for adaptation to a particular environmental niche (Holland 1975, 10).

Clearly, the potential size of the genetic space of phenotypic development (in architecture, the number of design possiblities) expands greatly with the introduction of epistasis.

This notion of the assignment of combinations of genes to phenotypical characteristics via epistasis can also be considered within the counterpart of development, the selection process. In the biological world, there are numerous components of fitness, some probably much more important than others, but all nonetheless affecting the overall fitness of a given phenotype. In natural selection, where there are only two possible ultimate outcomes, survival or death, it is not possible to pinpoint the degree to which each fitness criterion contributed to the degree of demonstrated fitness that allowed for survival. Indeed, there are a multitude of potential combinations of fitness criteria interwoven into the overall ability of a phenotype to survive and reproduce.

In a constructed genetic algorithm where explicit fitness criteria are dictated, epistasis can be employed to value *combinations* of attributes. For example, the presence of three particular attributes together may contribute significantly to the overall fitness of a phenotype, whereas having only two of the three present may contribute nothing. This has familiar implications for architecture, where a combination of structural or spatial attributes may lose all of its value by removing only one of its parts. In this manner, a multitude of possible combination schemes can be considered within the selection process. Just as epistasis expands the potential phenotype in development, so it increases the potential variability of evolutionary pathways within selection.

While research regarding the use of the genetic algorithm model has been occurring for a relatively short time, a number of applications have begun to command attention. As a prelude to considering the specific application of evolutionary design to virtual spaces, three examples of current genetic algorithm uses are presented here.

One of the applications enjoying the most attention is the field of genetic programming of computers themselves. Rather than using the algorithm to produce a phenotypic result, the genotype itself becomes the desired product.

In the genetic programming paradigm, the individuals in the population are hierarchical combinations of functions and arguments of various sizes and shapes. Increasingly fit hierarchies are then evolved in response to the problem environment using the gentic operations fitness proportionate reproduction (Darwinian survival and reproduction of the fittest) and crossover (sexual recombination) (Koza 1992, 603).

In the genetic programming paradigm, the genes are program fragments which are joined in strings to form programs. Through mutation, the structure of these programs is changed just as in biological mutation, producing a large space of potential programs. These programs are evaluated against a given test and the best reproduce. For example, John Koza constructed a model whereby a computer-generated "ant" was required to traverse a grid laced with "food" in the shortest possible number of steps (Koza 1992, 603).

The genetic programming paradigm represents a leap forward in the ability to optimize computer programs in a wide array of fields. It is a unique departure from the standard genetic algorithm model in that it circumvents the need for a phenotype. As we have seen, it is the phenotype that is usually responsible for providing the context for fitness evaluation. In contrast, the genetic programming paradigm uses the genotype for fitness evaluation; in some sense, the chromosomes are phenotypic in that they possess the ability to engage an environment in some way.

Another, more readily apparent application for the genetic algorithm is the study of ecological systems. Natural phenomena such as resource flows, flocking, and co-evolution are prime candidates for this type of investigation.

Collins and Jefferson have constructed a computer program called "Ant-Farm" which employs a genetic algorithm to explore the actions of collective foraging among real ants (1992). Their interests include the chemical communication that ants use to organize their search (the depositing of pheremones), the co-evolutionary effects of food gathering in the vicinity of multiple ant colonies, and the evolution of cooperation among large numbers of individuals. In this case, the genetic algorithm is used to simulate evolution of ants based on ability to successfully find food, but the object of focus is the *behavior* evolved in turn by those evolving ants rather than the ants themselves.

A third area of application for genetic algorithms is the subject of learning processes and their relationship to evolution. The genetic algorithm provides a phenotype with a set of inherited characteristics with which its fitness in its environment will be determined. But there remains an entire set of *learned* characteristics which also affect fitness. The question of the interaction between these two sets of traits provides an opportunity for the use of the genetic algorithm.

Ackley and Littman have constructed an algorithm called ERL (evolutionary reinforcement learning) which combines the effects of evolution and learning (1992, 487). The genotype contains two types of data: an "evaluation network" which contains a fixed code for weighing the fitness of a phenotype in the environment (evolution) and an "action network" which changes over time through reinforcement learning. This arrangement allows the investigation of the extent to which and the consistency with which learning alters the evolutionary path.

The ERL model, in examining this potential interaction of evolution and learning in phenotypes, addresses a fundamental theme in the relationship: the *Baldwin effect*. It is evident that what is learned cannot be directly genetically passed on to one's offspring (the Lamarckian fallacy). But the possibility for an *indirect* relationship can be considered:

> The idea behind the so called Baldwin effect is that if learning helps survival, then organisms best able to learn will have the most offspring, and increase the frequency of the genes responsible for learning. If the environment is stable so that the best things to learn remain constant, then this can lead indirectly to a genetic encoding of a trait that originally had to be learned (Mitchell and Forrest 1994, 270).

Having discussed some of the issues for which genetic algorithms are currently being employed, we come to the convergence which constitutes the topic at hand: the application of genetic algorithms to the evolution of virtual environments. There are several characteristics of cyberspace which welcome the use of algorithmic design. After these are addressed, an example algorithm can be introduced.

The very existence of a virtual environment is algorithmic. The graphics engine which produces the visual space is constantly updating the model according to data produced by interactions of inhabitants and structures of the environment. This temporal dimension of cyberspace suggests a desire for designs which are capable of unfolding and evolving, since the emphasis upon, and potential for, dynamic interactions of structures in cyberspace is so significantly higher than in the terrestrial built environment. Michael Benedikt has described the dynamism of cyberspace as follows:

> Its corridors form wherever electricity moves with intelligence. Its chambers bloom wherever data gathers and is stored. Its depths increase with every image or word or number, with every addition, every contribution,

of fact or thought. Its horizons recede in every direction; its breathes larger, it complexifies, it embraces and involves (Benedikt 1992, 2).

This description reminds us of one of the primary functions of virtual environments: they function as the spatialization of information. Cyberspace provides a world in which to give form and texture to entities that are invisible in the physical world: transactions, ideas, databases. Certainly, the ability to experience the *changes* in these information structures over time (themselves constituting new information) is at least as important, and often more so, than seeing a static image of them, hence the desirability of being able to employ evolutionary design.

In functioning as an information space, a virtual environment necessarily acts as an arbiter of complexity. The benefit of visualizing information comes from the ability to bring a degree of comprehensibility to an otherwise unwieldly body of data. The structure of the genetic algorithm model, with its interrelated fitness criteria and large range of potential phenotypic outcomes, provides a vehicle with which to engage complexity; indeed, there is a wide continuum of potential algorithm configurations, from fairly simple to quite complex.

We now come to the consideration of an example genetic algorithm coded for the purpose of evolving virtual spaces. Written in the *Mathematica* programming language, it employs gene sets which are used to develop a population of structures containing several different elements. These resulting elements are evaluated against a fitness function, involving several geometric fitness criteria, to select the structure possessing the highest fitness. The genes corresponding to the fit structure are then reproduced, using mutation, to produce a new population, and the process is repeated. In this manner, it produces a three-dimensional model of an environment, complete with all of the textures that characterize the various structural elements contained therein. A diagram of the logic of the algorithm appears in *Figure 14.1*.

As mentioned earlier, this example occupies a position within a continuum between relative simplicity and potential complexity. At the very simple end, one can construct an algorithm that relies solely on the characteristics of the phenotype for evolution; there are no explicit genetic bitstrings, but rather, the genetic information is implicit within the phenotypes. Effectively, this would be a sort of "non-genetic" genetic algorithm. Mutation takes place within the development process rather than through replication of gene sets. In addition, the fitness function at this level is fairly simple, without the large number and combinations of attributes typically associated with both the genetic paradigm and the production of architecture; it operates primarily at the level of the individual elements of the structure rather than the total structure itself. Since there are no multiple fitness criteria, there is no weighting of criteria, which would constitute an increase in potential outcomes of the algorithm.

As we move along the continuum of genetic models towards increased complexity, multiple fitness criteria can be introduced, weighted within the selection process. This provides an opportunity to employ *epistatic* behavior, although only at the level of the phenotype, by considering combinations of criteria in addition to each individually.

The introduction of genetic bitstrings (chromosomes) constitutes a significant increase in the possible complexity of the evolutionary path. First, there is the explicit occurrence of genetic mutation, including crossover and inversion; the more varied the potential mutation of a genetic bitstring, the greater the area of potential phenotypes which can be more quickly navigated by the workings of the genetic algorithm. This point in the continuum is the "standard" manifestation of the genetic algorithm and the one embodied by the example presented.

As discussed earlier, the interface between the genes and development of phenotypes can be greatly enhanced by the use of epistasis. Making combinations of genes responsible for phenotype characteristics increases again the number of potential evolutionary paths.

Finally, the genetic algorithm model can use a simulated environment as the fitness test for selection rather than explicit criteria. In this scenario, fitness is measured in the ability to perform a given task within an environment, a task that could rely on any number of fitness criteria weighted in any number of ways. In this case, the phenotypes don't develop towards a known combination of criteria, but rather towards a demonstrated ability to perform or survive.

Like the three research applications of the GA model discussed earlier, then, the example discussed here occupies a particular place on this continuum of possible variations of the genetic algorithm model. In using this model to produce virtual spaces, the designer's selection of which variation to use is a decision with considerable implications for the course of their evolution.

Before proceeding, a final thought should be offered regarding the vocabulary of the genetic paradigm. Words such as "fitness function" and "selection process" often come attached with rather unpleasant Darwinian connotations of mechanistic, unthinking division between that which will survive and that which will perish. These images seem inconsistent with the depth and nuance associated with an endeavor such as architectural design. However, the constant evaluation and selection at work in the genetic paradigm produces a well-considered route for a design to follow, allowing it to refine itself, traverse a wide range of possibilities, and increase in value. Up to this point, an attempt has been made to show the variety and versatility of the genetic algorithm model; it is useful to remember it as such while considering an actual example.

AN EXAMPLE GENETIC ALGORITHM

The genotypic algorithm in Figure 14.1 introduces the standard genetic algorithm framework. A population of genotypes is produced from a parent set of genes; each in turn causes the development of a corresponding phenotype;

Figure 14.1 *Logic diagram of genetic algorithm.*

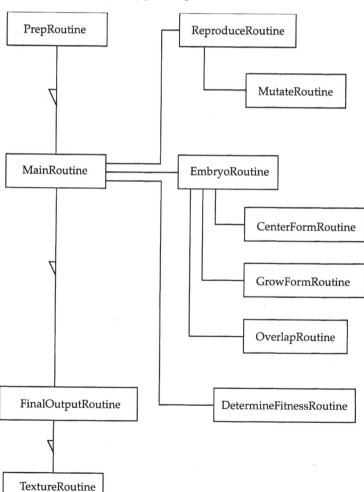

and the phenotypes are evaluated for fitness, either explicitly or otherwise, to determine the successful parents which will replicate to begin a new iteration of the process. Each genotype consists of 10 genes, with each gene possessing an integer value between 1 and 10.

The phenotypic structures produced in this algorithm consist of four geometric elements, with each being involved in the fitness evaluation routine; each exhibits "behaviors," relationships with the other elements, which are "rewarded" or penalized within the determination of the overall fitness of the phenotype. In addition, the textures of each of the four structural elements are produced; while they are not evaluated for fitness, they do reflect the evolution of the successful genotype. Views of the phenotypes produced by the algorithm can be found in Figures 14.2 through 14.5.

The first of the structural elements, *BoundaryForm,* is a regularly distorted sphere whose form is constant from generation to generation; it has the appearance of a cube with rounded edges and forms a boundary around the other three elements.

The second element, *GrowForm,* is another distorted sphere which is evaluated according to its volume; its continued expansion is favored in the evaluation of fitness. A third element, *CenterForm,* is composed of orthogonal

Figure 14.2   Evolving virtual space at initial configuration.

Figure 14.3   *Evolving virtual space after 30 generations.*

Figure 14.4   *Evolving virtual space after 60 generations.*

Figure 14.5 *Evolving virtual space after 90 generations.*

units which are derived from a distorted sphere of the same type as Grow-Form; its form is a cage-like structure. As its name would suggest, the proximity of CenterForm to the center point of the bounded space is favored in the fitness evaluation routine. The final element, *ConnectForm,* is derived from the two spherical forms, GrowForm and BoundaryForm; it is composed of cubic units derived from the lines that connect corresponding points of the two spheres. Like the textures produced in the algorithm, ConnectForm is not evaluated for fitness, but it does reflect the evolution of the virtual space as the relationship of the other structures changes.

Two parts of the fitness evaluation have been mentioned; there are others. First, although the expansion of GrowForm is favored, its extension outside of BoundaryForm is penalized. Second, as CenterForm and GrowForm each pursue differing behaviors, any instance of their volumes overlapping is penalized. The working of the fitness evaluation will be further elaborated upon as the individual routines of the algorithm are discussed.

The algorithm begins with a PrepRoutine, in which functions to be used later by other routines are initialized. In addition, it is here that the genotype of the first parent originates, prior to the iterations of the genetic algorithm. Most of the functions contained in PrepRoutine are used in the construction of the four elements of the phenotype.

The main module of the algorithm, MainRoutine, executes one full revolution of the genetic model each time it is invoked: the reproduction of genotypes by a selected parent, the creation of phenotypes for each child, the evaluation of fitness for each phenotype, and the selection of the next parent. In this particular algorithm, crossover of chromosomes is not employed (for processing considerations) and only one parent is required to produce the next generation. Each generation contains five offspring. Following the outline of MainRoutine, we can thus follow the progress of the rest of this algorithm by dividing the remaining routines into three relevant segments: reproduction, development, and selection.

ReproduceRoutine produces the five offspring genotypes of each generation. It calls MutateRoutine once for each of the four offspring. It is at this point that mutation is employed to alter 5 of the 10 genes in each genotype. Note that, unlike some of the genetic applications discussed previously, inversion and crossover are not used as forms of mutation here. Further, the Gene-Mutate function which calculates the mutation is skewed to ensure that there is the same number of possible mutated values for each gene, regardless of its present value.

With the set of five offspring genotypes established, the phenotypic development phase of the algorithm begins. For each of the gene sets, EmbryoRoutine calls the routines to produce the GrowForm and CenterForm portions of the phenotype, as described earlier. In addition, it invokes OverlapRoutines to detect whether the volumes of these two structures intersect one another, a condition relevant to the determination of overall fitness. In this instance, "volume" is simplified to denote the rectilinear space defined by the area between the maxima and minima along each axis of each form. OverlapRoutines uses these approximations to detect an intersection between GrowForm and CenterForm.

The last segment of the iteration of MainRoutine is the evaluation of fitness of the newly generated structures. This occurs in DetermineFitness-Routine, which ultimately produces a ranking of the five offspring and chooses the most fit as the subsequent parent. When this part of the genetic sequence is reached, four fitness values for each offspring have already been recorded: volume of GrowForm, CenterForm's proximity to the center, status with regards to boundary, and condition of intersection of CenterForm and GrowForm. In addition, a fifth criterion, the sum of the three orthogonal values of CenterForm, is also retained in the event of a tiebreaker; this rationale will be discussed shortly.

Calculation of fitness ranking begins by sorting three of the fitness sets, those for GrowForm's volume, CenterForm's proximity to the center, and the sum of its dimensions; in each of the three cases, each offspring receives a ranking of 1 through 5, with 1 being the most fit. These numbers are then squared, yielding the five possible values of 1, 4, 9, 16, and 25. This has two ramifications. First, it reduces the number of possible ties when the rankings are summed to give a final fitness distribution. Second, it creates an implicit value judgment within the algorithm: Overall lack of weakness constitutes higher fitness than specific presence of strength. For example, ignoring for the moment all other fitness criteria, if one offspring has the best GrowForm fitness and the third best CenterForm fitness, it is less fit (has a higher fitness score) than one which has the second best of each, losing 10 to 8. (Alternatively, if one wished to reward specific strength over general, the square roots of the five values could be taken instead; two second places would lose to a first and third in that case). While it is not the intention here to declare superiority of one of these two ranking methods over the other, it is a subject for future consideration.

The two other fitness criteria, overlapping and boundary fitness, are binary in nature, with 0 being given for fitness and 8 for non-fitness. As such, there is no need for sorting or replacing a quantity with a ranking. The value 8 is large enough to negate a first or second place ranking in another category; it ensures that that particular offspring will only be selected if every member of the population exhibits the same non-fitness in the particular category, rendering it neutral in the selection process.

With all values in place, then, the total fitness value for each offspring is arrived at. The preliminary ranking consists of four of the five criteria, excluding the sum of the maximum height, length, and width of Center-Form. In the event of a tie, this quantity is then added to the preliminary ranking to produce a winner. The choice of this value as a tiebreaker has to do with the factors that are driving the evolution of this virtual space. CenterForm *wants* to move as close to the center as possible, GrowForm wants to increase in volume, and the intersection of the two is penalized. If the dimensions of CenterForm are compact, there would seem to be a greater chance of gaining higher fitness in both criteria without penalty for intersection; CenterForm can move that much closer to the center without intersecting GrowForm as it expands. Obviously, there is no guarantee of this, as the algorithm is always subject to the whim of mutation. But this *potential for future fitness,* like the potential of a child to be a great gymnast or musician, is valued, and hence acts to determine greater fitness between otherwise equal offspring.

Even with the tiebreaker, there is the rare chance that a tie could still exist; this is attributable to the small population size selected for purposes of computer processing time. In the interest of preserving the algorithm's flow, in the event of an enduring tie, the first of the tied occurrences within the TotalFitnessSet is selected.

Once a parent has been selected, the full genetic iteration within Main-Routine is complete. The last two modules comprising the algorithm, Final-OutputRoutine and TextureRoutine, are responsible for producing the files containing the three-dimensional model data and textural data for the four components of a given phenotype. Since they are dependent only upon a given set of genes, the phenotype of any parent at any point along a given evolutionary pathway can be ported to a rendering program and its results viewed. A future direction would be to configure the algorithm for rendering in real-time.

Figures 14.2 through 14.5 show four views of the space, seen from the same vantage point within the space, at zero, 30, 60 and 90 generations. In addition to depicting the movements of CenterForm and GrowForm (and the resultant changes in the *strands* of ConnectForm), the evolution of the textures is also apparent.

In producing and running this algorithm, two things have occurred together: the evolution of a design and the design of an evolution. As much virtual architecture is dynamic, the space exists in an ongoing evolutionary state. The *design* of its evolution is complete, but the evolution itself is ongoing; a finished virtual space is unfinished, although not incomplete. An interesting next step would be to design the algorithm in such a manner that *it* could evolve along with the virtual space. This could potentially result in a higher degree of one learning from the algorithm's workings just as the algorithm "learns" from its author. While these various levels of interaction don't truly constitute humans talking with computers, they do embody the kind of benefit to be gained by architects from intelligently exploiting the strengths of computer processing without becoming enslaved by it.

GENETIC DESIGN OF VIRTUAL ENVIRONMENTS

Architectural design, either physical or virtual, is a search for value in a vast space of possible combined attributes: structural, spatial, visual, textural, and phenomenological. It comprises a journey along an evolutionary route; what is found along the way is mediated by the degree of *accessibility* to new vistas of possibilities granted by the path.

The use of the genetic algorithm model in the evolution of virtual spaces actively engages this abstract notion of accessibility. The algorithm presented here and its use in evolving virtual spaces have tested the feasibility of a paradigm for design with new implications for the theory and practice of architecture.

First, genetic design of virtual environments reconsiders access between the act of design and the act of construction in architecture. The twentieth century has witnessed a widening disparity between design and building, even questioning the relevance of one to the other. In the GA model, as we have seen, each iteration represents the evaluation of a completed construction. Genetic design encompasses a continuous informing of design by construction and construction by design, pointing towards a heightened effectiveness and value of each in the course of producing architecture.

In the example algorithm, the development process which evolved the virtual structures was dependent upon devising construction procedures to make this evolution possible. For example, the various routines which produced the elements of the phenotype employed a system of propagation rules, placing new units in a specified arrangement with regards to each other according to instructions from the genotype; this construction routine was, in effect, used as a tool for design, while the evolving *design* continued to inform the process of *construction*. The two were considered as one encompassing entity rather than as two separate stages in the production of the virtual space.

Another implication genetic algorithms bring to spatial design is access to a high degree of complexity in architecture. They provide a framework for combining and evaluating a large number of diverse characteristics of a space, and in a more consistent manner than through traditional design. Additionally, the interactions of design criteria within a genetic algorithm provide a large number of potential design variations, even when the number of these factors is quite small.

The algorithm here was constructed using a very controlled number of design variables. However, the framework that it employs has the capability of encompassing a far larger array of criteria. Indeed, the number of design considerations that can be incorporated into genetic algorithms is limited only by the processing time available and the thoughtfulness of the designer in translating design elements into the language and structure of the algorithm itself.

Although the scope of this algorithm was kept relatively narrow for the purpose of illustration, it was still capable of producing an evolutionary path which yielded a demonstrable variety of structural and textural configurations. The interaction of the various design elements occurring within the process of fitness evaluation provides a mechanism for comparing *combinations* of these elements on a scale that is inaccessible when working with traditional design methods under traditional time constraints.

Finally, genetic algorithms represent a means of access into an environment foreign to the one we traditionally inhabit. Cyberspace comes with a unique set of constraints; with regards to design, it demands the same adherence to these functional, cognitive, and aesthetic constraints as aquatic space or outer space. Genetic algorithms, by specifically addressing the temporal and evolutionary aspects of cyberspace, provide us with the access to new environments and the ability to design complex and meaningful spaces within them. The algorithm presented here, even with its very simple set of criteria, produces spaces which can continue to exist and evolve indefinitely, in keeping with this temporal dimension of virtual environments. The example space will continue to exhibit the preferences of certain structures to grow or seek the center of the space in precisely the same way that a tree in the physical world will seek to grow towards light and clouds will continuously be shaped by winds.

The wide range of potential configurations of the genetic paradigm discussed here provides numerous directions for future implementations of these algorithms in both virtual and physical architecture. The genetic algorithm suggests a new liaison between design and construction, is an efficient generator and arbiter of architectural complexity, and provides a valid means with which to pursue inhabitable architectures of cyberspace.

REFERENCES

Ackley, David, and Michael Littman. 1992. Interactions between learning and evolution. In *Artificial Life II,* edited by C. G. Langton, et al. Redwood City, Cal.: Addison-Wesley.

Arnheim, Rudolf. 1977. *The dynamics of architectural form.* Berkeley, Cal.: University of California Press.

Bachelard, Gaston. 1969. *The poetics of space.* Boston: Beacon Press.

Benedikt, Michael, ed. 1991. *Cyberspace: first steps.* Cambridge, Mass.: MIT Press.

————. 1987. *For an architecture of reality.* New York: Lumen.

Brand, Stewart. 1987. *The media lab.* New York: Viking Penguin.

Collins, Robert J., and David R. Jefferson. 1992. AntFarm: towards simulated evolution. In *Artificial Life II,* edited by C. G. Langston, et al. Redwood City, Cal.: Addison-Wesley.

Dawkins, Richard. 1987. *The blind watchmaker.* New York: Norton & Co.

Foley, James D. 1990. *Computer graphics: principles and practices.* Reading, Mass: Addison-Wesley.

Harvey, David. 1992. *The condition of postmodernity*. Cambridge, Mass: Blackwell Publishers.

Heidegger, Martin. 1977. *The question concerning technology*. New York: Harper & Row.

Heim, Michael. 1993. *The metaphysics of virtual reality*. New York: Oxford University Press.

Holland, John H. 1975. *Adaptation in natural and artificial systems*. Ann Arbor: University of Michigan Press.

————. 1995. *Hidden order: how adaptation builds complexity*. Reading, Mass.: Addison-Wesley.

Holtzman, Steven A. 1994. *Digital mantras: the languages of abstract and virtual worlds*. Cambridge, Mass: MIT Press.

Kalawsky, Roy S. 1993. *The science of virtual reality and virtual environments*. New York: Addison-Wesley.

Kauffman, Stuart K. 1993. *The origins of order*. New York: Oxford University Press.

Koza, John R. 1992. Genetic evolution and co-evolution of computer programs. Langton, C. G. et al. ed. *Artificial Life II*. Redwood City, Cal.: Addison-Wesley.

Langton, Christopher G., ed. 1989. *Artificial life*. New York: Addison-Wesley.

Langton, Christopher G. et al., ed. 1992. *Artificial Life II*. Redwood City, Cal.: Addison-Wesley.

Lefebvre, Henri. 1991. *The production of space*. Cambridge, Mass.: Blackwell Publishers.

McLuhan, Marshall. 1988. *Laws of media: the new science*. Toronto: University of Toronto Press.

Mitchell, William J. 1977. *Computer-aided architectural design*. New York: Petrocelli/Charter.

————. 1987. *The art of computer graphics programming*. New York: Van Nostrand Reinhold.

————. 1990. *The logic of architecture*. Cambridge, Mass.: MIT Press.

Mitchell, M., and S. Forest. 1994. Genetic algorithms and artificial life. Langton, Christopher G., ed. *Artificial Life 1*, no. 3. Cambridge, Mass.: MIT Press.

Negroponte, Nicholas. 1975. *Soft Architecture Machines*. Cambridge, Mass.: MIT Press.

Negroponte, Nicholas. 1995. *Being digital.* New York: Alfred A. Knopf.

Novak, Marcos. 1995. Transmitting architecture. *Architects in Cyberspace: Architectural Design* 65, no. 11/12. Cambridge: VCH Publishers.

Perez-Gomez, Alberto. 1990. *Architecture and the Crisis of Modern Science.* Cambridge, Mass.: MIT Press.

Pickover, Clifford A. 1990. *Computers, Pattern, Chaos and Beauty.* New York: St. Martin's Press.

Rheingold, Howard. 1991. *Virtual Reality.* New York: Simon and Schuster.

Shlain, Leonard. 1991. *Art and Physics: Parallel Visions in Space, Time and Light.* New York: William Morrow.

Sims, Karl. 1994. Evolving 3D morphology and behavior by competition. Langton, Christopher G., ed. *Artificial Life,* 1, no. 4. Cambridge, Mass.: MIT Press.

Steadman, Philip. 1979. *The Evolution of Designs.* Cambridge: Cambridge University Press.

Stevens, Gary. 1990. *The Reasoning Architect.* New York: McGraw-Hill. New York.

Thom, Rene. 1983. *Mathematical Models of Morphogenesis.* New York: Halsted Press.

Thompson, D'Arcy W. 1952. *On Growth and Form.* Cambridge, Mass.: Cambridge University Press.

Wilson, Stewart W. 1989. The genetic algorithm and simulated evolution. Langton, Christopher G., ed. *Artificial Life.* New York: Addison-Wesley.

Haptic Interface and Virtual Environment

Hiroo Iwata
University of Tsukuba

INTRODUCTION

Force sensation plays an important role in the manipulation of virtual objects. Haptic interface is a feedback device that generates skin and muscle sensation, including sense of touch, weight, and rigidity. Compared to visual and audio displays, haptic interface is a premature technology. Visual and auditory sensations are obtained by specialized organs: eyes and ears. On the other hand, haptic sensation occurs at any part of the human body and is inseparable from physical contact. Those characteristics make it difficult to develop haptic interface. Visual and audio media are widely used in everyday life, although very little application of haptic interface is used for information media.

We have been researching haptic interface in virtual environments for a number of years and have developed various force-feedback devices and their applications. This chapter presents our current work in those research activities. The aim is how haptic interface can be used for general information media and how human abilities in recognition and creation can be extended.

FORCE DISPLAY

Force display is a mechanical device which generates reaction force from virtual objects. Research activities in force display are rapidly growing, although the technology is still in a state of trial-and-error. There are three approaches to implement force display: exoskeleton, tool-handling type, and object-oriented type. Exoskeleton uses mechanical linkages attached to user's finger tips or hand. Those linkages apply independent forces to the attached points. Tool-handling type has a grip which a user grasps. Object-oriented type has deformable and movable interface separated from a user. The user's hand puts nothing on while the interface traces it.

Exoskeleton

In the field of robotics research, master manipulators are used in teleoperation. Most master manipulators, however, have large hardware with high cost, which restricts their application areas. In 1989, we developed a compact master manipulator as a desktop force display (Iwata, *Artificial Reality with Force,* 1990). The manipulator generates reaction force to the palm and the fingers of the operator. Figure 15.1 shows an overview of the device. The core element of the force display is a 6-degree-of-freedom parallel manipulator, in which three sets of pantograph link mechanisms are employed. Force sensation contains six dimensional information: three-dimensional force and three-dimensional torque. The top platform of the parallel manipulator is fixed to the palm of the operator by a U-shaped attachment, which enables the operator to move the hand and fingers independently. Three actuators are set coaxially with the first joint of the thumb, forefinger, and middle finger of the operator. The last three fingers work together. DC servo motors are employed for each actuator.

The users of the first prototype felt uncomfortable by restriction of their fingers. The device has only one-degree-of-freedom for each finger. In order to overcome the drawback, we have developed a new force display which allows 6-DOF (degree-of-freedom) motion for independent three fingers: thumb, index finger, and middle finger (Iwata and Hayakawa 1995). The device has three sets of 3-DOF pantographs at the top of which 3-DOF gimbals are connected. A thimble is mounted at the center of the gimbals. The thimble is carefully designed to fit the finger tip and is easy to put on or take off. Figure 15.2 illustrates the mechanical configuration of the force display. The device applies 3-DOF force at each finger tip. The user can grasp and manipulate a virtual object using three fingers.

Tool-handling Type

Virtual world technology usually employs glove-like tactile input devices. Users feel troublesome when they put on or take off these devices. If the glove is equipped with a force-feedback device, the problem is more severe. This

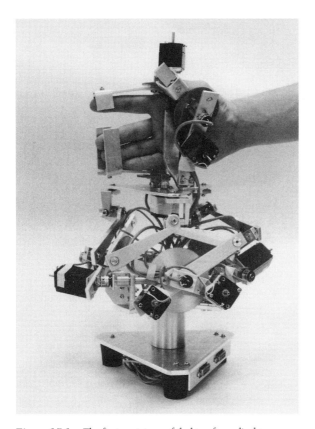

Figure 15.1 *The first prototype of desktop force display.*

disadvantage obstructs practical use of force displays. Tool-handling type force display is free from fitting it to the user's hand. It cannot generate force between the fingers, but it has practical advantages.

In 1993, we developed a 6-DOF force display which has pen-shaped grip (Iwata, *Pen-based,* 1993). Users are familiar with a pen from their everyday lives. Most intellectual works are done with a pen. We use spatulas or rakes for modeling solid objects. These devices have stick-shaped grips similar to a pen. In this aspect, the pen-based force display is easily applied to the design of 3-D shapes.

We also developed a 6-DOF force display which has a ball grip. We demonstrated it in SIGGRAPH'94 (Iwata 1994). The device is called "Haptic-Master" and is commercialized by Nissho Electronics Co. Figure 15.3 shows an early version of the HapticMaster. The HapticMaster is a high-performance force-feedback device for desktop use. This device employs a

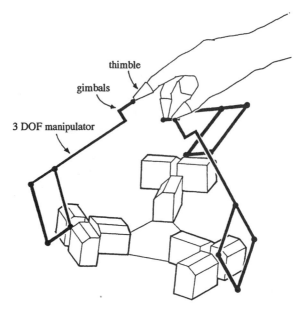

Figure 15.2 *Force display for three fingers.*

parallel mechanism in which a top triangular platform and a base triangular platform are connected by three sets of pantographs. The top end of the pantograph is connected with a vertex of the top platform by a spherical joint. This compact hardware has the ability to carry a large payload. Each pantograph has three DC motors; the total number of motors is nine, which is redundant for 6-DOF manipulator. The redundant actuators are used for elimination of singular points. Parallel mechanisms often include singular points in working space. The inertia of motion parts of the linkages is so small that compensation is not needed. The working space of the center of the top platform is a spherical volume whose diameter is approximately 40 cm. The maximum payload of the HapticMaster is 2.1 Kgf. Exchanging the top platform of the HapticMaster into three gimbals with thimbles, it is easily modified to an exoskeleton as mentioned previously.

Object-oriented Type

Object-oriented type is a radical idea for force display design. A user of the device can make contact with a virtual object by its surface. The type allows natural interaction compared to exoskeleton and tool-handling type. However, it is fairly difficult to implement; furthermore, its ability to simulate virtual objects is limited. Because of these characteristics, object-oriented type is

Figure 15.3 *HapticMaster.*

primarily effective for specific applications. We focused on 3-D shape modeling as an application of our object-oriented type force display and used an
elastic body made of rubber and force sensors for the force display (Iwata and
Arai 1994). A user of the device feels elasticity by handling the rubber. Deformation of the virtual object occurs according to the force applied by the user.
Figure 15.4 illustrates mechanical configuration of the force display. Four
strings are connected to the elastic body, which changes the shape of the
body. The body is mounted on a 6-DOF manipulator and it moves corresponding with the user's hand.

LOCOMOTION

Locomotion in virtual space is one of the key technologies in the field of virtual
reality. A head-mounted display (HMD) provides a 360-degree image of virtual
space. However, the walkable area of the virtual space is strictly limited according to the sensing range of the motion tracker and walkable space in the real
world. A possible method for exploring virtual space is hand gesture. The current system for virtual reality uses the index finger to point in a direction. In
terms of natural interaction, haptic feedback for walking motion is essential to
exploration of virtual space. The primary object of our research is presenting a
sense of walking while the position of the walker is fixed in the physical world.

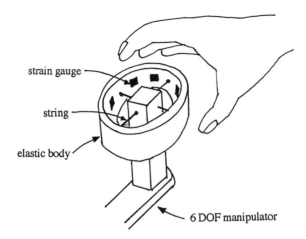

strain gauge

string

elastic body

6 DOF manipulator

Figure 15.4   Object-oriented type force display.

We have developed several prototypes of interface devices for walking around virtual space. The point of our research is changing direction according to the walker's feet. Controlling a steering bar or joysticks is not intuitive in locomotion. The motion of a twisting waist on a pedaling device is not natural. In 1989, we developed the first prototype for walking in virtual space (Iwata, *Artificial Reality for Walking*, 1990). Users of the system wore a parachute-like harness and an omni-directional roller skate. The trunk of the walker is fixed to the framework of the system by the harness. An omni-directional sliding device is inevitable in changing the direction of the feet. For this purpose, we developed a specialized roller skate equipped with four casters which enables two-dimensional motion. The walker could freely move his/her feet to any direction. Motion of the feet was measured by ultrasonic range detector. From the result of measurement, an image of the virtual space is displayed in the head-mounted display corresponding with the motion of the walker. Direction of locomotion in virtual space was determined according to the direction of the walker's step. We also tried the presentation of a virtual staircase by pulling the feet by strings (Iwata and Matsuda 1990).

The walkers of the first prototype, however, felt uncomfortable with the pressure of the parachute-like harness. We therefore replaced the harness with a belt around the waist (Iwata and Matsuda 1992). We put a brake pad at the toe of the roller skate to increase the stability of the walker. While the walker steps forward, the break pad generates friction force at the backward foot.

Our former system has two major problems: (1) the waist belt restricted the up-down and turnaround motion of the walker's body, and (2) the weight and height of the roller skate spoiled the natural motion. In order to overcome those problems, we developed a new frame and sliding device (Iwata and Fujii 1996). A hoop is set around the walker's waist in which he/she can physically walk and turn around (Figure 15.5). Diameter of the hoop is 70 cm. The walker can freely change the direction of walking. Novice users of the system can hold the hoop so that they can easily keep the balance of their bodies. Trained users can push their waists against the hoop and walk fast or even run. Since we don't use any harness, the walker's body has no restriction. We developed a new sliding device by using a rubber sandal in stead of a steel roller skate. Low friction film is put at the middle of the sole (Figure 15.6). The rubber sole at the toe serves as a brake pad. Material of the floor sheet is selected in accordance with the low friction film and brake pad.

The scene of the virtual space is generated in correspondence with the results of motion-tracking of the feet and head. The motion of the feet and head is measured by a magnetic sensor (Polhemus FASTRACK). The device measures 6-DOF motion. The sampling rate of each point is 20Hz. Two receivers are set at the toe of the sandals. The sandals are equipped with touch sensors. The touch sensor detects whether the foot steps on the ground. The length and direction of a step are calculated by the data from those sensors. Viewpoint in virtual space moves corresponding with the length and direction of the steps. We demonstrated the newest device at SIGGRAPH'95. During the five-day conference, 235 people experienced the device and 94 percent of them could walk freely in virtual space.

SOFTWARE TOOL

Virtual world technology usually employs various types of input/output devices. In most cases of haptic interface, the software of the virtual environment is tightly connected to the control program of force displays. This problem is a hazard for the development of further application of haptic virtual environment. We therefore developed a software tool for programmers of the haptic virtual environment, in which the control program of force display, description of virtual space, and user application are divided into modules (Iwata and Yano 1993). The system is called VECS (Virtual Environment Construction System). Various types of force displays can be plugged into VECS. The

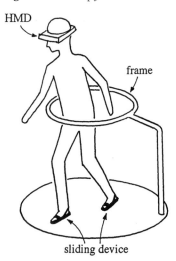

Figure 15.5   Hoop frame.

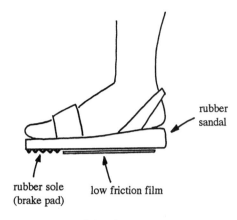

rubber
sandal

rubber sole
(brake pad)

low friction film

Figure 15.6   Sliding device.

system supports multiple haptic interface by using socket interface and IP multicast. Two or more users can simultaneously interact in the same virtual environment. This function enables easy construction of a groupware program. VECS is currently implemented in Silicon Graphics workstations.

Physical laws for the virtual world are contained in VECS. Gravity, elasticity, and viscosity are currently implemented. Collisions between virtual objects are detected in real-time. Shapes and attributes of virtual objects are defined in the user application module. Users of VECS program the methods for interaction between virtual objects and operators.

VECS is composed of the following three programs:

1. Program for object data—supervising behavior of virtual objects
2. Program for device data—communication with force display
3. Program for application data—detection of user intention and updating virtual environment

Dividing into these programs, force displays and physical laws in a virtual environment are easily reconfigured.

VECS is composed of two processes: kernel and user application. The kernel of VECS determines behavior of virtual objects and generates a graphic image of the virtual environment. This process runs autonomously. The user application determines the methods for interaction between virtual objects and operators. Shared memory is used for communication between these processes. The required update rate of force-feedback is much higher than that of visual feedback. VECS enables a high update rate of force display in complex virtual environment.

APPLICATION OF HAPTIC INTERFACE

Design of 3-D Shapes

Design of 3-D shapes is a major application area of virtual reality. We realized the direct manipulation of a free-form surface by pen-based force display (Iwata, *Pen-based,* 1993). The user can make 3-D shapes by embossing a plate in virtual space. In this case, the shape of the object is originally determined by a human designer. We have proposed an alternative approach of 3-D shape design in the virtual environment. Designers are often inspired by shapes of living creatures. We therefore implemented a virtual object which autonomously changes its shape (Iwata and Yano 1993).

Interaction with autonomous virtual objects can be done through following three parameters:

1. Time: Our virtual environment has a time clock which is supervised by the kernel of VECS. Growth or autonomous deformation occurs according to this time clock. The user can freely change the speed of time and he/she can also reverse it.
2. Congenital characteristics: Autonomous 3-D shapes have congenital characteristics which determine their morphological process. The user can arbitrarily change the congenital characteristics, which results in different shapes. Manipulation of congenital characteristics leads to an unexpected form of virtual objects.
3. Acquired characteristics: Acquired characteristics are obtained by direct manipulation of virtual objects by the user. The user can deform autonomous virtual objects at any time.

The user of our system can interact with an autonomous object in its morphological process. Controlling these parameters, autonomous shape and intentional shape are mixed. A similar design process in the real world is found in traditional Japanese art work called "bonsai." We implemented virtual bonsai by using VECS (Iwata and Yano 1993).

Industrial designers often make simple mockups using urethane or styrene boards in order to study the theme of the form at the early stage of design development. This process is called form study. We developed an autonomous free-from surface in a virtual environment as a tool for the form study (Iwata and Yano 1994). The basic theme of the form is created through deformation of the surface. Figure 15.7 shows an example of form study.

Collaboration in a Haptic Virtual Environment

Existing communication media supports only visual and auditory information. We have tried to use haptic information as a tool for communication. We used the network capability of VECS to connect two force displays in the same virtual environment (Yano and Iwata 1995). The two users of our system feel reaction force simultaneously. They can cooperatively manipulate virtual objects. One user can grasp the other user's virtual hand and they feel force applied from the other user. This function is beneficial for trainer-

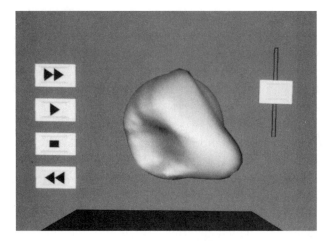

Figure 15.7 *Deformation of a free-form surface.*

trainee interaction. In the case of using the internet as a communication line, there is a time delay between the two force displays. We developed visual and haptic aid for compensation of the time delay.

Data Haptization

Scientific visualization is one of the major application areas of virtual reality. Visual information essentially consists of two-dimensional images. A three-dimensional scene is recognized by binocular parallax cues or motion parallax. Visualized volumetric data are often difficult to comprehend because of occlusion. Moreover, volume data which consists of higher-dimensional values, such as 4 or 5, are difficult to visualize.

The major objective of our research is representation of volumetric data by force sensation (Iwata, *Volume,* 1993). Force sensation contains six-dimensional information: three-dimensional force and three-dimensional torque. Therefore, higher-dimensional data can be represented by force sensation. The basic idea of "volume haptization" is mapping voxel data to force and/or torque (Figure 15.8). A HapticMaster is used for this application. The force display is combined to a real-time visual image of volume data.

Navigation in Four-dimensional Space

Higher-dimensional space enhances the intellectual activity of human beings. Three-dimensional graphics contain much more information than 2-D graphics. We proposed visual and haptic representation of four-dimensional space (Iwata 1995). Our 4-D space is generated by scanning a 3-D cube. The user's

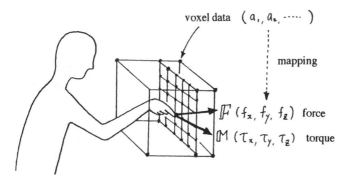

voxel data $(a_1, a_2, \cdots)$

mapping

$\mathbb{F} (f_x, f_y, f_z)$ force

$\mathbb{M} (\tau_x, \tau_y, \tau_z)$ torque

Figure 15.8 *Basic idea of volume haptizaion.*

hand can essentially move in 3-D space. We therefore use rotational motion of the hand for scanning a 3-D cube in a 4-D cube. The 3-D cube is a cutting volume of the 4-D cube. A cursor is indicated in a cutting volume, which moves corresponding with translational motion of the user's hand. The cutting volume moves by rotational motion around the roll axis of the user's hand. Figure 15.9 illustrates the basic idea of the 4-D cube. Force display presents a potential field which indicates the roll axis. The user can easily separate rotational motion from translational motion by force-feedback. Since rotational motion has three axes, the 4-D cube can be extended to a 6-D cube.

FUTURE WORK

We have clarified the possibilities of haptic interface through experimental prototypes. Our future work will be developing practical and serious application of the haptic interface. We are currently pursuing the following projects:

1. Refuge simulator for emergency: Locomotion by walking motion is intuitive and is inevitable in a study on human behavior in virtual environments. We are planning to apply our interface device for locomotion to research on a human model of refuge in case of emergency. We are working with Ship Research Institute (Ministry of Transportation, Japan) to develop a mathematical model of human behavior in case of fire accidents in ships. The

Figure 15.9 *Navigation in a 4-D cube.*

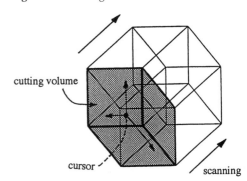

cutting volume

cursor

scanning

model will be constructed through observation of human behavior in a virtual ship.

2. Surgical simulation: Laparoscopic surgery requires training in a virtual environment. We are collaborating with the Olympus Co. to develop a training simulator for Laparoscopy. Two specialized HapticMasters are used for both hands.

3. Haptic browser for image database: Presenting referred data in 3-D space is effective for users of a database. We are working with Electric Technology Laboratory (Ministry of Trade and Industry, Japan) to develop a haptic user interface for navigation in a 3-D browser.

REFERENCES

Iwata, H. 1990. Artificial reality with force-feedback: development of desktop virtual space with compact master manipulator. ACM SIGGRAPH *Computer Graphics* 24, no. 4: 165–170.

Iwata, H. 1990. Artificial reality for walking about large-scale virtual space. *Human Interface News and Report* 5, no. 1: 49–52.

Iwata, H. 1994. Desktop force display. SIGGRAPH'94 Visual Proceedings: 215.

Iwata, H. 1993. Pen-based haptic virtual environment. Proc. of IEEE VRAIS'93: 287–292.

Iwata, H. 1995. Scientific haptization (in Japanese). *Proc. of Symposium on Graphics and CAD* 95, no. 4: 53–54.

Iwata, H. 1993. Volume haptization. *Proc. IEEE Symposium on Research Frontiers in Virtual Reality:* 16–23.

Iwata, H. and T. Arai. 1994. Interface device for shape modeling with force sensor and elastic body (in Japanese). Proc. of 10th Symposium on Human Interface: 183–186.

Iwata, H., and T. Fujii. 1996. Virtual perambulator: a novel interface device for locomotion in virtual environment. Proc. of IEEE VRAIS'96.

Iwata, H., and K. Hayakawa. 1995. Development of a glove-type force display for handling virtual object (in Japanese). Proc. of 11th Symposium on Human Interface: 395–400.

Iwata, H., and K. Matsuda. 1990. Artificial reality for walking about uneven surface of virtual space. Proceedings of 6th Symposium on Human Interface: 21–25.

————. 1992. Haptic walk-through simulator: its design and application to studies on cognitive map. Proceedings of ICAT'92: 185–192.

Iwata, H., and H. Yano. 1993. Artificial life in haptic virtual environment. Proc. of ICAT'93: 91–96.

————. 1994. Interaction with autonomous free-form surface. Proc. of ICAT'94: 27–33.

Yano, H., and H. Iwata. 1995. Cooperative work in virtual environment with force-feedback. Proc. of ICAT'95: 203–210.

16

Real Buildings and Virtual Spaces

Myron W Krueger
Artificial Reality Corporation

INTRODUCTION

Virtual reality has recently made its appearance as a mainstream concept. It is based on the observation that the synthetic worlds created with computer graphics are becoming so real that we are tempted to step through the computer screen and enter them. We imagine that once there we should be able to interact by using our bodies exactly as we do in the real world. In the ultimate expression of virtual reality, any fantasy that can be imagined could be experienced.

In the most visible form of virtual reality, users wear special goggles to see the virtual world, and instrumented gloves and clothing to help the computer track the movements of their bodies. These displays cut the participants off from their real environment. However, the division between the real world and the virtual one need not be so absolute. It is possible to take the ideas of virtual reality and apply them to the real world, so they become part of life rather than an escape from it.

RESPONSIVE ENVIRONMENTS

In 1969, when I first began thinking about virtual reality, I considered the current form of virtual reality implemented with goggles and gloves, and rejected it. I did not think that I wanted to interact with any world, whether real or imagined, through scuba gear. I thought in terms of what I called a *computer-controlled responsive environment,* which I defined as a space in which everything that you saw and heard was a response to what you did. In the extreme, this is the same concept as virtual reality. However, the constraint that I set for myself was that the participant would always be completely unencumbered by electronics and certainly not tethered to the computer by an umbilical cable. Thus, I considered a continuum of intermediate technologies that would seek to make the real world virtual. Since the goal of this activity was always to create magical environments, the design of interactive spaces might be considered a branch of architecture.

The general form of this technology comprises perceptual systems that analyze the movements of visitors through the space, environmental scale auditory and visual displays that deliver the space's responses to the visitor, and computerized decision-making that decides how the displays should respond to particular actions.

Psychic Space

In a 1971 environment titled *Psychic Space,* I used a sensory floor to detect the movements of participants about a gallery. Using this form of perception, it was quite easy to respond to the visitor's footsteps with sounds. The relationship between the person's footsteps and the sound responses was completely programmable, so that the space would sound different each time you walked through it. Architects typically think of creating a single space; while the space may look different under different lighting conditions, they do not think of physical space as a dynamic medium of expression. From the beginning, I thought of responsive environments, which I started calling *artificial realities* in 1973, as an aesthetic medium in which the interactive relationships might change from moment to moment. For instance, each footstep through the space could have easily triggered the replay of a recorded word instead of a musical tone, leading to the creation of a unique poem.

At one end of the *Psychic Space* environment was a rear-projection screen. At times, a simple three-dimensional scene was projected on that screen. As a visitor walked around the physical space, the view of the virtual scene changed to reflect what he or she would see from his or her perspective if the scene were real.

In 1993, I permitted visitors to navigate the world depicted on the screen by pretending to be children pretending to fly. Holding their hands out to their sides to make wings, they could steer to the left or right. Lowering their hands made them descend to skim the surface. Raising their hands caused them to ascend above the mountain tops. Keeping their hands raised made them soar into orbit, so they could see that they were flying around a graphic planet. *Small Planet* was the name of the piece (Figure 16.1a and b).

The Cave

While economics never permitted me to use more than one screen, the plan was always to use multiple screens on all walls as well as the floor and ceiling to completely define the participant's visual environment. A colleague of mine from the 1960s at the University of Wisconsin, Dan Sandin, working together with Tom Defante and students at the Electronic Visualization Laboratory at the University of Illinois at Chicago Circle have been demonstrating such a multisided projection environment which they call a CAVE since 1993. They use stereo projection of three-dimensional graphics to provide the most compelling view of virtual worlds achieved to date.

Screens and Spaces

While screens of all kinds are a familiar part of our real environment, the distinction between the screen and its surroundings is usually as obvious as the

Figure 16.1 *Small Planet. The projection screen becomes the windshield of a vehicle that is flying through a graphic world. You control your flight by holding your hands out to the sides and pretending to fly. It works just the way you thought it would when you were a child.*

distinction between what is inside a picture frame and what is not. We seldom think of screens as defining an environment as opposed to existing in one. Even murals that offer the same possibility seldom completely fill a wall from floor to ceiling. As we approach a time when video projectors will decline in cost and flat panel displays will increase in size, we will be able to think in terms of using computer graphics to alter a physical space much the same way we use murals, windows, and mirrors today.

If these computer images were to depict a static scene, they would go little beyond what could have been achieved with projected slides years ago. At the very least, the scene can be animated. It can also contain the visitor's live video image much as a mirror would contain his reflection. Moreover, the screen can reflect the visitor in a virtual space in which his image is joined by the images of other people in remote locations and by animated graphic creatures that inhabit the virtual space (Figures 16.2 and 16.3). Thus, when a person passes through the space, he can choose to stop and interact through his image in the simulated world or he can interact very briefly as he pass through, going about his business. Such environments have been treated as friendly presences when we have placed them in offices.

Figure 16.2 *TINY DANCER. This was a performance piece in which the shrunken image of a dancer performed on the giant image of my hands. I could wait patiently as she moved or I could throw her image into the air. If I tilted my hand and forearm, her image would cartwheel down the slope. If I squeezed her between my thumb and forefinger, she popped up like a watermelon seed.*

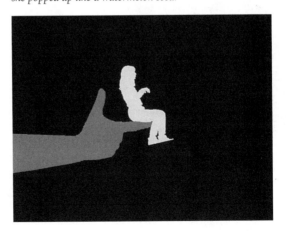

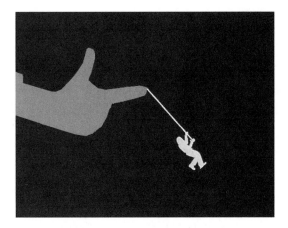

Figure 16.3 *HANGING BY A THREAD is a two-way interaction between a participant in the VIDEOPLACE and a second participant at the VIDEODESK. By moving her body, the small participant in the VIDEOPLACE is able to make her image swing on the graphic string held by the person at the VIDEODESK.*

VIDEOPLACE

I call the virtual space displaying the person's video image on a projection screen "VIDEOPLACE" (Figure 16.4). It is a composable medium with a wide range of aesthetic and practical applications in its own right. It builds on the better part of a century of tradition of identifying with the experiences of other people's images on both movie and television screens. People regard their own images as extensions of their identities. What happens to their image happens to them. What touches their image, they feel. Thus, when they see their images knocked over, or cut in half, or able to fly around on the screen, they are transported into the fantasy world (Figure 16.5). They can play with a graphic creature called CRITTER or interact with the images of other people on the screen (Figure 16.6). Alternatively, they can paint with the image of their bodies and leave a dynamic visual creation that decorates the space until the next person comes along and decides that she would like to make her own creation (Figures 16.7, 16.8, and 16.9).

Graphic Floor

The displays used do not need to be based on traditional formats. In the SIG-GRAPH Art Show in Dallas in 1991, I did an environment I called *Step Lightly*. This 16 foot by 16 foot space was covered with a new version of the 1971

Figure 16.4 *VIDEOPLACE Installation. The participant stands in front of a backlit translucent screen. The video camera sends information about the participant's position and behavior to the computer system. A composite image of the participant interacting in an artificial reality is displayed on the video projection screen.*

Figure 16.5 *Parachuting into an Artificial Reality. A participant parachutes into a graphic world.*

Figure 16.6 *Leapfrog. A participant plays leapfrog with CRITTER, a graphic creature that perceives your movements and engages your video image in a whimsical interplay. CRITTER affords a playful metaphor for one of the central dramas of our time: the encounter between humans and machines.*

Figure 16.7 *INDIVIDUAL MEDLEY. These images are from a family of interactions collectively called INDIVIDUAL MEDLEY. They were created by the participant's actions.*

Figure 16.8 BODY SURFACING. *The participant's actions create abstract three-dimensional patterns of pulsing light.*

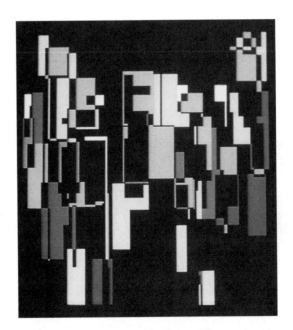

Figure 16.9 Broadway Boogie-Woogie. *The participant's actions create compositions of shifting rectangles.*

sensory floor comprising 4,000 individual hand-made pressure sensors. The computer scanned the floor 60 times a second and, based on the participant's movements, used a ceiling-mounted laser graphic system to depict a graphic fish on the floor (Figure 16.10). As visitors stepped onto the floor, the fish came careening after them at high speed. Their reaction was to laugh and run away from it. Often, several people would tease the fish by circling around it. Some people would stand on the side of the floor and dip their foot in, as if it were a pool. A baby crawled after the fish on her hands and knees. When we made the fish a little larger, she crawled away from it.

While the laser floor was set up as a standalone exhibit in a segregated space, it could just as well have been integrated with a permanent space. We can easily imagine the design of spaces that are inhabited by graphic creatures that lurk in the hallways, just out of sight, and which only venture forth when the building is relatively empty.

INTERACTIVE BUILDINGS

The outside of the building offers similar possibilities. While there has been some tendency to think of the illumination on a building at night as part of its design, there are no buildings that animate that lighting. Similarly, while many buildings are dominated by animated signs, these screens are still objects on the building. No one has thought of the entire building as a

Figure 16.10   *Step Lightly. A sensory floor detects your footsteps around the room and a ceiling-mounted laser draws a graphic fish on the floor that chases you.*

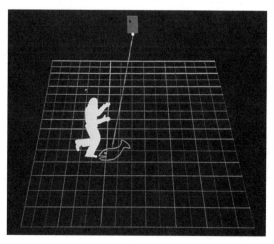

sign from its inception. Also, while the idea of buildings that respond to the goings on in their environment goes back to Nichlos Schoffer's Cybernetic Tower, the nature of such responsiveness is always general rather than individual.

Since 1972, I have proposed a number of interactive buildings that would react much more personally. In that year, I proposed taking over the lights in the individual offices in the administration building at the University of Wisconsin where I was then a graduate student. There was to be a single location on the hill across the street where a person could stand and control the pattern of lights by waving his hands. Rather than reacting to the general activity in its environment, this building would respond to the very specific actions of one person. The individual's control over the impersonal institutional edifices in his environment would be the point.

More recently, I suggested a more composable version of the interactive building for the new Ars Electronica building planned for Linz, Austria. The outside of the building would be a screen for a laser projection of computer-generated patterns. When one person approached the building, his outline would be drawn with a laser beam on the side of the building. This outline would be capable of flying around the side of the building. If a second person were to appear, her image would float across the building and interact with the other person's representation. When their images approached each other, one could orbit the other or one could engulf the other's image.

Painting the Town

The idea of a single interactive building could be expanded to an interactive skyline. We have simulated such an interaction using the New York City skyline (Figure 16.11). In this interaction, a participant's silhouette appears superimposed on the skyline. When the image of a finger touches a window in one of the buildings, the window lights up. Each time the participant turns the lights on in a particular building, the pattern is stored so that a sequence of patterns is defined for each building. Those patterns repeat on their own after the participant leaves.

RESPONSIVE ENVIRONS

The next logical step is to expand the scope to create responsive environs. Another 1972 proposal was to create a five-mile-long light display called Binary Icescape on frozen Lake Mendota in Madison, Wisconsin. That proposal has been revised to fit a number of situations over the intervening

Figure 16.11   *Painting-the-Town. Your fingertips turn on the lights in the buildings. This is a simulation of a real interaction in which the movements of a person's body would control the lights in the buildings of a city. It was first proposed in 1972.*

years—most recently at the request of Mercedes Benz for the new Munich airport. I proposed that people standing in the waiting room would be able to control the giant display around the airport by the moving their bodies. The display itself was designed to be seen from the air in anticipation of its becoming the symbol of the city.

CONCLUSION

This chapter has described a model of interactivity that has not been applied to architecture. The responsive art of the 1960s was characterized by general responsiveness to events in the environment. My own work has always argued that interactivity is not simply an interesting conceptual idea, but that it can be used to create a pleasing relationship between a person's body and the effect on his environment. In this case, general responsiveness is not enough. It is important that the participant be absolutely certain exactly how he is affecting the changes he sees. It is equally important that observers also be able to understand how the participant is controlling the environment. For the point of the work is not that the building is interactive, but that one individual can control it. Once this relationship is believed, someone viewing the building from a distance will see it differently because the giant organization that created the building respects the individuals who must live around it.

While the design of interactive spaces is currently considered a separate activity from the practice of architecture, the opportunity clearly exists to conceive buildings as defining environments that are playfully alive rather than as sterile objects and empty spaces.

REFERENCES

Krueger, M. W. 1983. *Artificial reality.* Addison-Wesley.

————. 1991. *Artificial reality II.* Addison-Wesley.

————. 1974. *Computer-controlled responsive environments.* Ph.D. diss., University of Wisconsin.

————. 1977. Responsive environments. NCC Proceedings: 375–385.

————. 1985. VIDEOPLACE—an artificial reality. SIGCHI '85 Proceedings (April): 35–40.

A Few Observations about the Future of Architecture in a Digital World

In the previous chapters we covered the heart of our topic, giving an overview of what is happening in architecture and digital media and focusing on the technology presently available. We have witnessed how major changes have been undertaken by the architectural profession not only at the design stage, but also in its delivered artifacts. A series of questions arise about a possible shift in the task of architecture. Will the new media affect not only the design but also the final built environment? How will architectural language be affected? Will the impact of the latest technology bring a redefinition of the architectural profession? Is cyberspace a visible sign in the image of our cities? These questions are asked not with the presumption that they be answered in the course of one chapter; nevertheless, a discussion of the latest technology in architecture will not be complete without bringing these issues to the forefront. The discussion of these questions is not meant to provide prophetic answers from a futurologist, but merely observations from a designer who has been involved with the digitalization of space for the last two decades.

THREE ISSUES RAISED BY DIGITAL ARCHITECTURE

Digital architecture as defined in Chapter 4 is not just a style, but is strictly related to the major transformations and developments which globally affect our cities and places of social interaction. Expanding bandwidth and computing power will increasingly affect our lives and be manifest in the presence of digital artifacts in our physical environment. By shifting the focus from the generic definition of "digital" architecture to more specific virtual environments, we can envision three main areas of investigation.

1. The area most directly related to the present state of virtual reality covers the potential technological developments in design media. The majority of VR applications in architecture are comprised of simulations and immersive walk-throughs. An integration between VR and CAD or between CAD and Geographic Information Systems could be envisioned as a major future development.
2. Another area for development is in the relationship between virtual environments and "solid" architecture. With the exception of certain cases such as projections or CAVE-type displays, the majority of VR applications use devices which are more a piece of body clothing than part of the external environment. Current widely used devices, such as head-mounted displays or the BOOM, tend to be obtrusive, isolating the participant in the virtual world. Future development might use less obtrusive systems and more projection displays: This would allow integration with the actual architectural space.
3. A third area for development is in virtual environments which exist for their own sake. Free of real-world constraints, virtual environments can aid in formal explorations and can create space for managing the new digital world.

The development of VR for architects involves the actual space as well as its virtual counterpart. The integration of virtual environments into a built context cannot be ignored or underestimated, but should become an active part of the designer's task.

IS THE ARCHITECTURE PORTRAYED IN VR EXPLORATION INDICATIVE OF NEW FORMAL DEVELOPMENTS?

The novelty of a medium is often not recognized by the contents expressed by that medium. This is often the case for CAD and other digital media used in architectural design which allow better design control over materials. Deformations and other forces can be easily visualized, enabling the designer to express the best potential of the material. Volumes and surfaces can be intersected, twisted, and transformed to generate quite elaborate shapes, whose structural properties can be easily verified, thanks to computer simulations. Nevertheless, in spite of the complexity of forms which can be explored, architectural projects designed and drawn using CAD often use very traditional elements and forms. The majority of VR applications similarly stress technological exploration while overlooking content. Software demos often feature traditional building forms in spite of the many possibilities offered by VR in the creation of space. The contrast between the aesthetics of the new technological media and the design content becomes striking when you see traditional houses, very conventional interiors, or postmodern facades displayed on the computer screen or head-mounted display.

IS ARCHITECTURE LOSING PERMANENCE?

Every time I return to Rome—the city of my childhood—I walk, as though part of a daily ritual, from my parents' house to St. Peter's cathedral. I walk to the piazza, through the colonnade, and sit at the foot of a column where I can enjoy the different perspectives of this seventeenth century work by Bernini. Both the piazza and the cathedral immediately convey a sense of permanence, strength, and grandness. When they were designed and built, the intention was that they last forever, as testimony to the Catholic church's everlasting power.

Permanence has always been a principal characteristic of architecture (Figure 17.1), perhaps as expression of the human desire to achieve immortality, if not in the body at least in the man-made transformations of the environment. Quoting Mies van der Rohe, "Architecture is the will of an epoch translated into space." Civilization leaves architectural artifacts as one of the main traces of its existence. Ruins can tell us stories about past life. A building does not just represent a temporary involucre to be disposed of after use, but is an expression of the life contained within it. Architecture has been used as the image of a society and as the expression of the political power of the state. Prominent examples are the urban planning of Pope Sisto of Rome, Haussman's plan for Paris, and the development of Brasilia.

The notion of permanence seems to contradict the ephemeral character of digital places. When the majority of individual and social functions are extensively delivered by a network of computers and terminals which can be

Figure 17.1 *Architecture and permanence: The temple of Hera in Paestum (450 B.C.).*

conveniently located in our living rooms, where does one find the permanent manifestations of architecture? Can electronic files—of any comunication, transaction, or interaction—be considered footprints of our collective and individual history? William Mitchell in his book *City of Bits* (Mitchell 1995) expresses the transition of architectural typologies from permanent artifacts to ephemeral places in computer networks:

> Not so long ago, when the world seemed simpler, buildings corresponded one-to-one with institutions and rendered those institutions visible. Architecture played an indispensable representational role by providing occupations, organizations, and social groupings with their public faces. Firehouses were for firefighters, schoolhouses were for scholars, and jailhouses were for jailbirds. The monarch's palace at Versailles, like the Forbidden City of Beijing or the Red Fort in Delhi, housed the ruler and his court, and its in-your-face form unambiguously expressed established power; it was where the ruling got done, and it was what you tried to grab if you wanted to usurp.

Under this historically familiar condition, the internal organization of a building-its subdivision into parts, the interrelation of those parts by the circulation system, and the evident hierarchies of privacy and control reflected the structure of the institution and physically diagrammed its pattern of activities. There was a complementarity of life and bricks and mortar, like that of snail and shell.

Today, institutions generally are supported not only by buildings and their furnishings, but also by telecommunication systems and computer software. And the digital, electronic, virtual side is increasingly taking over from the physical. In many contexts, storage of bits is displacing storage of physical artifacts such as books, so that the need for built space is reduced. Electronic linkage is substituting for physical accessibility and for convenient connection by the internal circulation systems of buildings, so that access imperatives no longer play such powerful roles in clustering and organizing architectural spaces. And as when an ATM screen rather than a door in a neoclassical edifice on Main Street provides access to a bank-computer-generated graphic displays are replacing built facades as the public faces of institutions.

HOW DOES CONTEMPORARY ARCHITECTURE INTEGRATE WITH THE DIGITAL WORLD?

It may be worthwhile to take a step back from electronic space to look at the state of contemporary architecture. Even before the advent of digital places, contemporary "solid" architecture clearly showed signs of confusion and a search for identity.

The language of modernism and international style was quite elementary, focusing on the integration between form, function, and structure, which were expressed in a harmonious synthesis. Conversely, examples of contemporary architecture, such as postmodern buildings, exhibit aesthetic characteristics which are completely divorced from the structure and function of the building. The architectural features are expressed solely in the facade, often detached completely from the structure of the building. A superficial reproposition of motifs of classical architecture in a stucco facade superimposed over a steel structure create a deceptive appearance compared to the original classical elements where a certain form was identifiable with the structure.

Now more than ever in the history of the man-made environment, other forces, beyond the reach of architects and planners, control the image of our urban and architectural spaces. In the past, the visual perception of urban spaces was characterized by buildings and streets, establishing very clear figure-ground and solid-void relations. This century has already seen a gross transformation of the urban landscape and territory brought by the automobile. Modern developments are often nothing more that an accommodation to automobile transportation; shopping malls and towns which cluster around major highways are a demonstration of how urban settings follow circulation patterns. In contemporary cities, electric lights, billboards, liquid-crystal displays, and neon signs as well as transportation elements, become predominant over solid elements. Often it is not a wall or a facade which attracts our attentions, but the message it conveys in the form of advertising or signage: Architecture becomes the medium of information.

What Material Is Digital Architecture Made Of?

From the industrial revolution onward, buildings have become increasingly complex entities. Walls, floors, and roofs are not just the concrete and steel which we visually perceive, but enclose mechanical and electrical systems which make a building comfortable and functional. In recent years, a new element has been added: the multitude of conduits and wires which bring us the images and information of cyberspace. The Pompidou Center in Paris, designed by the architectural studio Piano-Roger, was one of the first examples of architecture which expressed the "life" of the building. The mechanical system was emphasized in large colorful pipes, superimposed on the building facade. From the glass facade you could see the life inside the building and vice versa, creating a dynamic pulsing heart in the urban texture.

A visualization of elements comprising the immaterial life of cyberspace could bring a completely different image to our cities and landscapes. The information matrix of Neuromancer (William Gibson 1984) can find visual expression in our architecture. Architects Bernard Tschumi and Jean Nouvel, among others, already allude to the materials of an architecture for the electronic communication age; glass walls providing transparent physical support to video images and electronic billboards integrated in the facade. These are some of the first steps in the development of a vocabulary that expresses the presence of electronic space in the built environment.

Change of Typologies

The evergrowing establishment of electronic communications has begun a process which is likely to transpose the functions of our social life onto the computer screen. Our living rooms have the potential to become workplace, school, library, entertainment center, bank, or shopping mall. A redefinition of domestic architecture is needed in order to incorporate all of these functions once performed outside the home.

Parallel to the transformation of domestic architecture, is the transformation of public spaces. As the integration of video with voice communication allows face-to-face meetings, public and commercial buildings confront a limited future. Video projection screens, satellite dishes, communications towers, and LCD billboards will become the new building materials for the information age. Architecture will go beyond the static nature of stone, wood, and concrete and will become a pulsating organism providing vibrating images for our urban spaces.

HOW DOES DIGITAL ARCHITECTURE RELATE TO ECOLOGY?

Information and electronic technologies have a great effect on ecological sustainability issues. The economy of the industrialized nations is based increasingly on information technology, which controls industrial and financial processes and provides education, management, and entertainment. We are what is defined as a post-industrial information society, using production media which are different from those of the pre-industrial and industrial world.

Solutions for waste control could be addressed by the delivery of services and products through non-material media. The notion of sustainability derived from the change of material resources and waste in information technologies can consequently have a great impact on built architecture. The decreasing need for buildings as containers of functions could bring attention to the materials used; research could be developed to find new structural systems as well as studying and prototyping construction materials more suitable to accommodate the functions performed in an information-based environment.

Telecommuting, the term used to describe the growing phenomenom of people who perform traditional work tasks on a networked terminal in the home, is having a great impact on energy usage and the pollution associated with daily commuting. The quality of life in general could take great advantage in this shift of economic resources if addressed in an attentive way. On the other side of the coin, the concentration of so many human activities on the computer workstation could be physically and psychologically detrimental if the time saved in commuting would result in additional time spent in front of the computer terminal.

IS DIGITAL ARCHITECTURE CREATING A DIFFERENT ERGONOMICS?

Health problems have been associated with the typical computer worksta-tion. The main problem is in the static posture assumed when working at a computer terminal. We sit in the same chair, at the same distance from the monitor, using the same hands and finger movements in typing or using the mouse. On the issue of posture, Michele Arsenault, educator and teacher of the Alexander Technique comments (Arsenault 1996):

> In my work with young children in the school environemnt, I have come to believe that one the greatest obstacles to human physical well-being and sense of internal ease and comfort comes from the ever so humble chair and the static slumped posture which its use invariably promotes. Throughout history, this ten thousand year old human artifact has survived countless intellectual, artistic, and technological revolutions with surpris-ingly little reinvention despite substantial critical evaluation. This is a remarkable accomplishment for a human tool which, at least in the present moment, hurts us so much. We are clearly a chair dependent society and we have paid a stiff price for our conservatism as the millions of office workers who have suffered from back pain, chronic muscular tension, and carpal tunnel syndrome would testify.
>
> Up till now the alternatives on a mass scale have been few and far between for the technology itself is overwhelmingly dependent and per-haps even predicated upon this common fixture of the contemporary workplace. Try to envision the modern office drone accomplishing any-thing without his or her chair which, while often torturing the subject who sits upon it, does at least ensure that the sitter remains fixed and stationary in front of a computer monitor. Advanced human work has come to be synonymous with isolated and repetitive finger activity, activity which can, although it is not in the best interest of the body, flourish in the immobi-lizing environment provided by the chair. Few species in the animal world would survive such self-imposed disfunctional use. It's a little like cutting off the nose to spite the face.
>
> But the revolutionizing of human technology continues and one can only hope that current developments in virtual reality and related fields will free us of our dependency and lead us out of our present quagmire. Imagine for a moment the near environments of the 21st century, open flexible workstations which move and sway in response to the needs and desires of physically liberated employees forever freed from the fixed mon-

itors and keyboards of the past. And the chair? This anachronism of the early computer age, thankfully removed and relegated to the museums of ancient history.

VR systems could provide a working environment where sitting and repetitive hand gestures are reduced by the use of data gloves and other interactive devices as alternatives to the keyboard and mouse, and ultimately to the sitting position, which is so often responsible for our body pain. One could stand, walk, or lie down, in the position most appropriate for comfort and correct body use without being bound to a chair, finding the optimal synergy between mind and body, between intellectual work and physical activity.

REFERENCES

Arsenault, Michele. 1996. *Moving to Learn.*

Gibson, William. 1984. *Neuromancer.* New York: Ace Books.

Mitchell, William. 1995. *City of Bits.* Cambridge, MA: MIT Press.

A Few Hypotheses for
Reconstructed Architecture

As a conclusion to this book, this chapter contains a few thoughts about how virtual environments will transform *solid* architecture.

An effective way of understanding and actively participating in the transformation of our built environment can be provided if architecture is thought of as an integration of electronic media and physical (construction) materials. The former is provided by the synthetic world made of displayed images, simulations, and representations. The latter is comprised of traditional architectural elements, such as walls, floors, and ceilings. The relation between these different kinds of materials and media can give life to a dynamic organism, when their integration is achieved by thoughtful design.

A shift has occurred in the semantics of built architecture. Before the transformation brought on by the computer age, the perception of architecture was drawn from the space it occupied and sculpted. This is no longer true: Architecture assumes a representational and referential nature when a building represents something other than its own built space. Following in the historical tradition of trompe l'oeil, the integration of computer imaging with architecture expands the physical boundaries of the built space. Added to this static visual image are the attributes of animation and audio. Virtual reality takes this integration one step further by offering a process which is interactive, negating the real-world environment.

Regardless of the direction that VR technologies may take, the architect must rethink the tectonic nature of architecture, expanding it beyond solid materials to the fluidity of digital representations. The reconstruction occurs where the obsolete static and fixed construction of concrete, wood, and bricks finds cohesion with the representational materials. A new architectural vocabulary is needed to define this intersection between the built and the representational material.

A FEW HYPOTHESES FOR REDESIGNED ARCHITECTURE

A look at present VR systems reveals what the most needed developments are for its use for representation and design aid. The most effective use of VR will be in the integration of both. The interactively generated simulation of a three-dimensional space, achieved beyond the visual level, awaits the architect as the ultimate design means.

Presently, the use of VR in architectural applications focuses mainly on the geometric definition of the project; very few of the present VR architectural projects use the technology beyond its representational potential. The design process will undoubtedly be affected by the introduction of an immersive workstation into a studio full of paper and CAD monitors. The designer will be able to erect full-size walls and roofs using the three-dimensional medium of a VR environment. The most effective use of VR will be in the integration of interactive design and representation.

A good example of the potential that VR holds as a tool of exploration is the study of physical attributes and behaviors; static properties, including tension and compression, density and friction, deformations due to acting forces, the simulation of gravity, and other forces which act as design constraints. The immersive interaction will not be limited to the visual experience but could be expanded to the verification of the static equilibrium of the structure erected. Design could become an extremely dynamic process where "form as diagram of force" (D'Arcy Thompson 1961) could be truly explored using an environment and exploration tool much more intuitive than the differentiational calculations used by engineers. Not only materials but also energy could be simulated. Heat and ventilation could be visualized and interacted with by using fluid dynamics computational systems. Systems already in use by aeromechanical engineers to study the optimal form of an aircraft, space shuttle, or a simple automobile could be extended to architecture, providing a perfect integration between all elements contributing to the functioning of a design.

BEYOND THE SOLID-VOID DICHOTOMY

As discussed in Chapter 4, the main perceptual characteristic of solid architecture is the solid-void articulation which generates enclosures and boundaries, separating the inside from the outside. This distinction becomes obsolete for the architecture of the information age where ephemeral digital elements replace the solid materials of the real world.

Planes and Solids

Architectural elements can be characterized by a given geometry. For instance, classical architecture can be seen as a composition of masses which are sculpted to form an interior space. Walls, domes, vaults, and columns are geometric solids composed together to make a building, a piazza, or a court, defining an architectural or urban space. In modernist architecture we witness a major change in the geometry of built forms: The emphasis shifts from solids to planes. Many modernist constructions can be seen as an interplay between planes. Works of Mies van der Rohe and the Constructivist and Bauhaus schools are examples of how the composition is articulated by intersection and superimposition of planes in three-dimensional space.

The interest in planes coincides with the characterization of a virtual environment whose perception is based on representations shown on one or more planes. This is especially true in the virtual environments comprised of projections, such as CAVE-based systems (see Chapter 6), where solid elements are simulated in the planes of the representations. For this type of environment the integration of the VR system within the built architecture can greatly augment the design product.

Surface and Structure

Shifting to a different semantic context, the dichotomy between plane and solid is transformed into a dichotomy between surface and structure.

In the history of architecture, there are many examples which establish an link between the architectural elements of a building and its structure. The architectural form was often an expression of the structural equilibrium required to create a given space with certain materials; the "form as diagram of forces" can be easily recognized in the columns of a Greek temple, in the dome of a Renaissance church, or in the vertical development of a Gothic cathedral. In contemporary architecture, instead, the structure is often completely separate from the building that we perceive, hidden by walls, floors, and ceilings.

The segregation of surface and structure commonly seen in contemporary architecture can provide inspiration for the integration of virtual environments in buildings. Modern architecture can become a neutral container, similar to a barren, white art gallery, ready to be filled with works of color and light which will give a final character to the space. The surfaces we perceive, free from structural requirements, can become media for large-scale projections; the surface gains a significance beyond materiality, showing narrative, information, and entertainment. The media becomes one with the content. Architecture can be re-thought as a frame, where all the different planes of communications, knowledge, and information intersect.

SOME LESSONS FROM OUR RECENT PAST

Visionary architecture of the past holds lessons for the future. One of the most interesting examples is the work of the architecture studio, Archigram, which began investigations on the integration of architecture and technology in the early 1960s. The London-based studio was founded by a group of recent graduates: The term was created from the fusion of the two words "architecture" and "telegram." Their visionary projects emphasized the interaction between city and buildings, public and private space; the building sometimes was conceived as a " 'drive-in gallery', that is an extension of the street inside the building." (Cook 1991). The project of the greatest contemporary value is perhaps *Instant City,* from 1969, envisioned as "a network of information" utilizing audio-visual display systems, projection television, trailered units, pneumatic, lightweight structures, entertainment facilities, and electric lights." For the first time the distinction between the *hardware* (or the design of buildings and places) and *software* (or the effect of information and programmatic on the environment) is stated and pragmatically demonstrated as an architectural project. Even if the language and vocabulary used require updating, the project still holds many insights for the future of architecture in its fusion with information technologies.

Follies

Follies are architectural divertissements, constructions not constrained by any functional requirement; any wild fantasy can be expressed in this type of construction, limited only by structural requirements. Even the structures are pushed to their potential limits. These places without function exist merely for aesthetic appreciation.

A well-known folly is the Crooked House (Figure 18.1) in Bomarzo, Italy, built in 1552 for Prince Orsini. This construction, which takes the form of a small house, is unique for its precarious tilt from horizontal. The most common spatial orientations, such as those given by verticality and horizontality become ambiguous. The illusionary effects of Bomarzo create an environment which defies the laws of gravity, where our spatial perceptions are confronted and contradicted. This folly of five centuries ago provides valuable lessons to creators of virtual environments on the possibilities for perceptual distortion.

Figure 18.1 *The Crooked House, Bomarzo, Italy.*

Video Art Installations

Art and video installations can bring many insights about the possible integration of images with built architecture. Beginning in the early 1960s, the artist Nam June Paik explored the potential of television and video monitors to create a dynamic sculptural form. His use of video images as objects and his legitimization of the television set as "art" object hold lessons for the role of the computer terminal beyond its use as a visual communication device.

The 1995 exhibition Video Spaces (Figure 18.2) shown at the Museum of Modern Art in New York was built on an integration of images with the museum walls. The museum exhibit space was completely transformed by

Figure 18.2 *Installation by Teiji Furuhashi at Video Space. Courtesy of the Museum of Modern Art, New York and Canon Art Lab.*

the projected images, demonstrating the denial of its solid elements (e.g., walls, ceilings, and floors) as a result of ephemeral elements such as light and video images.

Data Places

As our society moves increasingly towards reliance on information and its manipulation, we often find that the architectural metaphor gives it a familiar face. The hierarchical composition of spaces in a city or building, through its streets, squares, lobbies, corridors, and rooms can be metaphorically used to access information. With the increasing availability of sensors and effectors, VR environments of architectural places will provide the means for accessing and visualizing information. A collaboration between architects, psychologists, and information analysts will be essential for the efficient functioning of these data places, where information space is mapped into three-dimensional space. What is already widely accessible through hypertextual two-dimensional worlds (such as the World Wide Web) will be implemented in three-dimensional architectural forms. The increasing success of VRML sites (see Chapter 5) on the WWW indicates the efficacy of the architectural metaphor; the introduction of immersive systems will further enhance the viability of this approach.

The various hierarchical levels needed to represent a certain type of information determine the kind of architectural space to be used. For instance, a colonnade with vaulted spaces (Figure 18.3) could be used to arrange databases. Floors, columns, and vaults could have links to data while the proximity between elements could identify the chronological or geographical organization. Intersecting spaces could represent relations between two different types of databases. The user could navigate this three-dimensional architectural space as a wayfinder for the selection of and access to information.

FORMAL EXPLORATIONS FOR THE ARCHITECTURE OF A VIRTUAL UNIVERSE

One of the most intriguing concepts of virtual reality is the ability to achieve a realistic simulation of worlds which are entirely the product of the imagination. One example of this sense of freedom is evident in the way that virtual worlds do not have to behave according to the laws of physics which rule over our physical world. Theories contradictory to our common spatial experience (and common sense) are easily applied to a VR environment. Buildings do not have to respond to the laws of gravity or physical material characteristics; collisions can or cannot happen; you can walk through walls; the figure-ground relations can be inverted; you can be at two or more places at the same time. New spatial sensibilities are discovered from the interactive processes used by a design in a virtual environment. The directions of left and right, in front and behind, up and down, corresponding to the Cartesian interpretation of the physical world could collapse. Two spaces related in a left-and-right relation at a certain time "t" can be in a different relation at time "t + Δt." While in our actual world we identify architecture with elements related by permanent relations, in virtual worlds space is a constant function of time. For example, if I have to ascend a stair to get from A to B, I will not necessarily have to descend to get back from B to A. Virtual spaces can hold many surprises.

Figure 18.3   *Architecture as metaphor for data places. Copyright © Daniela Bertol.*

Bodily movements can create new forms and architectures; even the simplest interaction becomes a construction. Several hypotheses can be imagined. Each step forward could add a new construction to the last, creating an endless series of spaces. A step to the left could add a convex curvature to the world and a step to the right could generate concavity. Moving up could twist the world and moving down could stretch it. Recursive processes could be the object of design too, where a room contains a copy of itself scaled up or down according to the participant entering or leaving. Similarly, a part can contain the whole, making recursive hierarchical levels.

In the same fashion, the topological relations of proximity, separation, succession, openness, closure, and continuity which—according to the psychologist Jean Piaget—form the first spatial perceptions of infancy, can be transformed. What was inside at time "t" can become outside at time "t + Δt." In virtual architecture we become children discovering new perception and learning new ways to orient ourselves.

Topological relations as well as the characteristics of Euclidean geometry such as size, distance, and angle, are confronted. The size of the inside of a space can be larger than its outside. Elements can be scaled up or down by command, giving insights on architectural characteristics.

The virtual worlds shown in Figures 18.4 and 18.5 follow the principle of dynamic construction. One lithography from *Le Carceri* by Gian Battista Piranesi inspired the space depicted in the sequence of Figure 18.4. A suspended bridge, a tower, and arches are the main architectural elements whose intersection generates ambiguous spaces. These elements are added and subtracted, rotated and displaced according to the participant's movements in an endless series of possibilities, undetermined and unpredictable. The sequence of Figure 18.5 shows an architectural world based on the addition and subtraction of elements related to the direction of navigation. Walking to the left creates new modular grids, made of different kinds of materials in an endless process. Turning to the right instead makes a cubic structure rotate around three different axes, and uncover planes showing text-based information. Looking down carves tunnels in the floor leading to an helicoidal stair opened to vaulted spaces.

A legitimate question can arise: Why do we call these virtual worlds architecture? Because they respond to one of the most basic tasks of architecture, the creation of a space which can be inhabited, which can surround us or which is defined by and defines boundaries creating an inside and outside. We can experience closeness or openness, enjoy proportions, and react to different scales—in a word, all the qualities which we associate with an architectural space.

Figure 18.4   *Sequence of views from a virtual world. Copyright © Daniela Bertol.*

Quantum Spaces

Not surprisingly, virtual worlds yield several analogies with the theory of quantum physics. In the 1920s the world of physics was shaken by a theory as revolutionary and mind-boggling as relativity. Quantum mechanics, which involves the investigation of the world of the extremely small, shook our more intuitive beliefs and paradigms of Newtonian physics.

The Uncertainty Principle, formulated by Heisenberg, was the foundation of the quantum construct, stating that we cannot know with certainty the position and velocity of a particle at a given time. The condition of the experiment always influences the outcome of the experiment. The observer and act of observation itself condition the experiment. In this fashion we arrive at the negation of the objectivity of the real world. Similarly, virtual worlds do not have existence by their own, but instead are generated by the interacting participant. The representations which comprise a virtual world do not exist statically, but are dynamically generated by the position and direction of the participant. Pushing this subjective interpretation further, the space of the virtual world itself could be generated by the action of the participant. The subject-object opposition is superseded; the subject is no longer only a perceiver of a world which exists objectively. The object of perception is created by the interaction with the subject: Virtual worlds evolve in endless possibilities.

Another major analogy is the probability assumption, also derived by quantum theory. According to quantum mechanics, there is no predictable certainty about the behavior of atomic particles in space and time. We can predict only probabilities. Contrary to the construct of Newtonian physics which describes the universe in a deterministic manner, the quantum world does not have any predetermined and precalculated existence. The maximum that Schroedinger's equation—the mathematical construct more expressive of quantum theory—can predict is only probability. Similarly, a virtual world does not have any predictable objective outcome. It is a product and producer of the subject's intentions, expressions, and representations.

Beyond Euclidean Space

The physical world of our daily life experiences can be correctly interpreted by Euclidean geometry. This is the geometry of our most basic spatial intuitions described by the Greek mathematician Euclid in the thirteenth century B.C. Measurements and calculation in the physical world can be correctly performed according to its axioms and theorems. Solid architecture responds to Euclidean laws. Buildings can be seen as artifacts of Euclidean geometry made of concrete materials.

Figure 18.5 *Sequence of views from a virtual world.*

The architecture of virtual worlds allows us to go beyond the Euclidean world. Starting from the last century, with the work of the mathematicians Gauss, Lobacevski, and Riemann, new geometries were created contradicting the axioms of Euclidean geometry. These alternative geometries, accordingly named non-Euclidean, create mathematical universes contrasting with our most immediate experiences but perfectly valid as intellectual constructions. In spite of the clear sequence of logical deductions in their formulation, the visualization of non-Euclidean geometry has not been an easy task to achieve.

Astonishing architectures can be constructed and experienced in virtual worlds inspired by non-Euclidean geometries. Walls, floors, and ceiling can be designed in worlds generated according to the laws of hyperbolic and elliptic constructions, the two main models of non-Euclidean geometries. We can inhabit these universes, where our spatial intuitions and habits have to expand into a new paradigm created by our intellect. The mathematician George Francis at the National Center Supercomputing Applications has created fascinating virtual environments (Figure 18.6) run in the CAVE (see Chapter 7). In *Post-Euclidean Walkabout,* the participant can walk through hyperbolic spaces, such as that defined by a rectangular dodecahedron or can

Figure 18.6   *George Francis in the CAVE visualization of "The Snail." Courtesy of NCSA/University of Illinois at Urbana-Champaign.*

"sew the edges of hyperbolic octagons together into the surface of a 2-holed donut." (SIGGRAPH '94). George Francis says: "Walkabout is what Australian aborigines, and also native whites, sometimes do when they drop out of their society for a while and wander about the waste regions of the Australian outback. The disorientation frequently experienced by CAVE visitors is alluded to here." (Access '94). Disorientation and confusion can be generated by the first navigation and interaction with these worlds generated according to geometries which contradict our most common spatial experiences and constructs.

Architectures based on four-dimensional space can be explored as well. As we have already seen with perspective, representations can be thought of as projections of one n-dimensional space into n-1 dimensional medium. For instance, in perspective the three-dimensional world is projected onto a two-dimensional plane. Similarly, the optimal medium to visualize a four-dimensional world is represented by a three-dimensional environment, such as that provided by virtual reality. Visionary architecture can be constructed in four-dimensional worlds. What was a product of science fiction or complicated mathematical elaborations can now be visualized, experienced, and directly interacted with. George Sandin at NCSA has realized a virtual environment *Getting Physical in Four Dimensions,* where three-dimensional sections of four dimensional objects are projected onto the CAVE screens (Figure 18.7). The participant can create four dimensional surfaces of revolution from three-dimensional curves. The objects can also be rotated and

Figure 18.7   Getting Physical in Four Dimensions. *Courtesy of NCSA/University of Illinois at Urbana-Champaign.*

translated; the four-dimensional projection point is also controlled by the user (SIGGRAPH '94).

Integrating Time with Space

The main characteristic of virtual worlds is in the fluidity and perceptual changes associated with the represented space. Virtual architectures defy permanency and become a function of time. The dynamic evolution of virtual environments in time can happen in different ways. The models comprising the virtual world can have associated transformation rules, with self constructions and destructions as a function of time, independent from participant movements. Conversely, a metamorphosis happens in the evolution of shapes dependent on navigation and generated by the participant's body movements. An example of this kind of world is illustrated in the sequence of Figures 18.4 and 18.5. Grids and other tectonic elements frame the initial world as the participant enters the world. A walk to the left adds new frames at the participant's horizon, each color at each of his displacements. Moving to the center makes the cubic structure rotate and change in scale, offering contrasting proportional elements. If the participant moves to the right the floor dimples, showing an helicoidal staircase. Moving down through the stair and changing direction toward the walls bounding the stair creates openings alluding to arcades and vaulted spaces. This world is only an example of the multiple spatial explorations offered by a virtual world: Virtual architecture becomes open-ended and endless, morphed only by one's fantasies and desires.

Summary

The architecture of virtual worlds can give us insights on our experience of space; concavity and convexity, closeness or openness, and a sense of scale are spatial qualities which could be effectively simulated in a virtual world. This exploration in virtual worlds can be a teaching experience for solid architecture. The architects of virtual environments design not only solid forms but also design concepts according to which forms are articulated, composed, decomposed, relate, or fight against each other.

But virtual architectures can go beyond spatial explorations. An architecture without functional requirements and without physical constraints can satisfy our purest spatial desires, sensorial needs, and intellectual challenges as well as expressing major contemporary transformations. The visionary architecture of the past has already expressed these notions. Leon Battista Alberti, Raphael, Leonardo, Bramante, Piranesi, Boullee, Ledoux, the Futurists, and Russian Constructivists expressed visions of architecture which dynamically integrated with the changes happening in their era: Leonardo's architectural works demonstrated the Renaissance ideal of perfection based on order and symmetry while Futurist architecture expressed the dynamism and velocity of the machine. The desire to defy the force of gravity inspired the form of Gothic cathedrals. Similarly, the spatial investigations portrayed by virtual worlds are not just abstract representations, but can have a leading role in performing the new task of architecture. Only in the thoughtful integration of virtual space with actual space—of cyberspace with the built environment—can architecture go beyond the role of physical container of information-based worlds, creating better places for human interaction.

REFERENCES

Cook, Peter. 1991. *Archigram*. Boston: Birkhauser.

D'Arcy Thompson. 1961. *On Growth and Form*. Cambridge, UK: Cambridge University Press.

Ryckaert, Victor. 1994. Virtually Seeing Geometry. Access Summer 1994.

SIGGRAPH '94. 1994. *Visual Proceedings*. Computer Graphics Annual Conference Series.

A

Augmented reality (*continued*):
　future trends, 198–199
　overview of, 193–194
　virtual reality, 72
Axonometric view, CAD, 48

B

Bajura, M., 194
Baldwin effect, genetic algo-
　rithms, 244
Bauhaus University-Weimer, 159
Benedikt, M., 205, 221, 244,
　245
Bertol, D., 97, 138
Best, K., 205, 219
Bevan, M., 131
Bibiena, Fernando, 26
Bibiena, Francesco Galli, 25
Binocular omni–orientation mon-
　itor (BOOM), virtual reality
　system output devices,
　106–107
Binocular vision:
　described, 36–37
　visual display systems, 104–105
Biological signals, virtual reality
　system control devices, 103
Blaser, E., 158
Blocksmith Project, 207–208
Boolean operations, CAD, 45
BOOM. *See* Binocular omni–
　orientation monitor (BOOM)
Borromini, Francesco, 34
Bramante, Donato, 20, 204
Brooks, F., 112
Brunelleschi, Filippo, 9, 14–17,
　34, 35
Buxton, W., 170

C

Calibre Institute:
　ESPEQ case study, 178–179
　Hertog van Lotharingen case
　　study, 179–181
　MIPIM '95 case study, 183
　NV Luchthaven Schiphol case
　　study, 183–187, 188
　Office of the Future case study,
　　181–183
　overview of, 177–178
　Taj Mahal case study, 187,
　　189–190
Campbell, D. A., 203, 205, 218,
　219, 221
Cathode-ray-tube device, virtual
　reality system output
　devices, 105, 107
Caudell, T., 194
Cave Automatic Virtual Environ-
　ment (CAVE):
　real buildings, 275
　virtual reality system output
　　devices, 108–109
Chats, cyberspace, 61–64
Chiaroscuro, perspective and,
　12
Ching, F. D. K., 218
Club Caribe, 219
Collins, R. J., 243
Color, perspective and, 12
Communication, community and
　environmental design, 204,
　212–217
Community and environmental
　design, 201–224
　CEDeS lab, 205–207
　communication, 212–217
　conceptualization, 207–208

Light:
  CAD, 49
  virtual reality aided design,
    126–127
Lighting, virtual reality systems, 96
Liquid crystal display, virtual real-
  ity system output devices,
  106, 109
Littman, M., 244
Locomotion, haptic systems,
  263–265

M

MacCormac, R. C., 149
MacIntyre, B., 196, 198
Mackenzie, M., 88
Magnetic resonance imaging
  (MRI), medicine, 75–76
Magnetic trackers, tracking sys-
  tems, 98–99
Mandeville, J., 214
Mapping, digital architecture,
  58–59
Maps, Geographic Information
  System, CAD, 53
Martini, Francesco di Giogio, 12
Masaccio, 19
Massie, T., 152
Materials characteristics, CAD, 49
Mathematics, redesigned architec-
  ture, 310
Matsuda, K., 264
Matsushita Tokyo Showroom,
  interactive walk-throughs,
  123–125
Maver, T., 134
Mayer, P., 118
McGreevy, M., 82

McKeown, K., 199
Mediascape, urban environment
  and, xx
Medical applications, virtual real-
  ity, 74–80
Metaphor, digital architecture,
  64–65
Mies van der Rohe, Ludwig, 299
MIPIM '95 case study, Calibre
  Institute, 183
Mitchell, M., 238, 244
Mitchell, W. J., 212
Mitchell, William, 60, 61
Mizell, D., 194
Model construction, CAD, 46–47
Models, virtual reality aided
  design, 137–140
Modernism, digital architecture
  and, 291
Molecular biology applications,
  virtual reality, 80–81
MOOS, cyberspace, 61–64
Morningstar, C., 219
Mouse, virtual reality system con-
  trol devices, 100
MUDS, cyberspace, 61–64
Multimedia, CAD, 52
Mutation, genetic algorithms, 238
Myers, J., 194, 199

N

National Aeronautics and Space
  Administration (NASA),
  81–82
Neumann, U., 194
Nouvel, J., 292
Novak, M., 88, 219, 237
Novitski, B., 193

Q

Quantum spaces, redesigned
architecture, 307
Quinn, R., 194

R

Radiology, medicine, 75–76
Radiosity, CAD, 49
Ragget, D., 89
Range, tracking systems, 98
Raphael, 13
Real buildings, 273–284
    interactive buildings, 281–282
    overview of, 273
    responsive environments,
        273–281
    responsive environs, 282–283
Reality, representation and,
    15–17
Real-time response, virtual reality,
    67
Reconstruction of sites, virtual
    reality architectural applica-
    tions, 131–137
Redesigned architecture,
    297–313
    formal explorations, 303–313
        generally, 303, 305
        quantum spaces, 307
        time-space integration, 312
    historical perspective, 300–303
    hypotheses for, 298
    overview of, 297–298
    solid-void dichotomy, 298–300
Reflectivity, CAD, 49
Representation, perception and,
    15–16

Responsive environments, real
    buildings, 273–281
Responsive environs, real build-
    ings, 282–283
Responsive Workbench, 143–153
    architectural design, 146–151
        "kit-of-parts" modeling envi-
        ronment, 148–151
        site planning, 146–148
    future trends, 151–152
    overview of, 143–146
Retinal display, virtual reality sys-
    tem output devices, 110–
    111
Richards, M., 194
Robinett, W., 194
Room of the Four Elements (Bertol
    & Foell), 35–36

S

Salisbury, K., 152
Sanders, D., 134
Sandin, D. J., 145, 275
Sandin, G., 311
Sangallo, Antonio da, 21
Sant'Ignazio (Rome, Italy), 25
Scale:
    CAD, 46
    virtual reality aided design,
        139–140
Schiphol Airport case study, Cali-
    bre Institute, 183–187, 188
Schmidt, A., 118
Schoffer, N., 282
Science, art and, 6, 8
Seattle Commons, 209, 210
Section, CAD, 48, 50
Seligmann, D., 196

Sensor, tracking systems, 98
Sensorama, described, 37, 39
Shaping, virtual reality aided
     design, 157–163
Sharir, J., 88
Shepard, Roger, 33
Signs, 44
Simulation:
    community and environmental
         design, 202–205
    virtual reality and, 67
Site planning, Responsive Work-
    bench, 146–148
Sketches:
    CAD and, 44
    virtual reality aided design,
         137–140, 158
Socio-economic analysis, virtual
    reality, 73
Solid architecture:
    defined, 55–57
    future trends, 297–313. *See also*
         Redesigned architecture
Solid modeling, CAD, 45
Solid-void dichotomy, redesigned
    architecture, 298–300
Sound, audio systems, virtual
    reality system output
    devices, 112–113
Source, tracking systems, 98
Space-time integration,
    redesigned architecture, 312
Sport applications, virtual reality,
    85, 88
Starnet, International, Inc., 196
State, A., 76
Static worlds, virtual reality sys-
    tems, 94
Stereoscope, described, 37
Sutherland, I., 69, 194

T

Tactile sensation, haptic systems,
    virtual reality system output
    devices, 111–112
Taj Mahal case study, Calibre
    Institute, 187, 189–190
Telecommunications:
    architecture and, xx–xxi
    digital architecture, 293
Telephone, videoconferencing, 74
Telepresence, virtual reality,
    73–74
Terravision, virtual reality aided
    design, 118–121
Texture-mapping, virtual reality
    systems, 96–97
Textures, CAD, 49
Thompson, D., 298
Three-dimensional glasses, virtual
    reality system output
    devices, 109–110
Three-dimensional representa-
    tion. *See also* Perspective
    CAD, 45–46, 50–51
    haptic interface applications,
         266–267
Thubron, C., 212
Time-space integration,
    redesigned architecture, 312
Tool-handling type haptic sys-
    tems, 260–262
Touch, haptic systems, virtual
    reality system output
    devices, 111–112
Tracking systems, virtual reality
    systems, 98–99
Transparency, CAD, 49
Treadmill, virtual reality system
    control devices, 102

virtual reality aided design,
160–163

W

Walk-throughs:
CAD, 52
virtual reality aided design,
121–125, 225
Wall, window-painting, perspective and, 12–14
Wands, virtual reality system control devices, 101–102
Wang, S. W., 157
Webster, A., 194
Wells, M., 203
Westin Hotels Guest Room 2000,
209, 211
Wheatstone, Charles, 37

Wheelchair navigation, 80
Williams, L., 157
Window-painting, perspective
and, 12–14
Wired glove, virtual reality system
control devices, 100–101
World Wide Web, virtual reality,
88–91
Wright, F. L., 149

Y

Yano, H., 265, 267

Z

Zevi, B., 20, 56
Zuccari, Taddeo, 21